IRAQ AND

William Lowther was born, educated and trained as a journalist in Britain. He worked for the *Toronto Star* and *Daily Mail*, was Bureau Chief in Paris and Washington and finally joined *Macleans* as Washington Bureau Chief in 1978. During this time he covered topics ranging from Northern Ireland to Watergate. In 1980 he turned freelance and now writes for British, Australian and Canadian newspapers and magazines, as well as producing a newsletter on US/South African relations. *Iraq and the Supergun* is William Lowther's first book.

WILLIAM LOWTHER

IRAQ AND THE SUPERGUN

Gerald Bull – the true story
of Saddam Hussein's Dr Doom

PAN BOOKS
LONDON, SYDNEY AND AUCKLAND

First published as *Arms and the Man* in Canada 1991 by Doubleday Canada Limited

First published in the United Kingdom 1991 by Macmillan London Limited

This edition published 1992 by
PAN BOOKS LIMITED
a division of Pan Macmillan Publishers Limited
Cavaye Place London SW10 9PG
and Basingstoke

Associated companies throughout the world

ISBN 0-330-32119-6

1 3 5 7 9 8 6 4 2

A CIP catalogue record for this book is available
from the British Library

Printed in England by Clays Ltd, St Ives plc

The epigraph for this book is taken from Virgil, *The Aeneid*;
translated into English prose by W. F. Jackson Knight, Penguin
Books Ltd, 1956. Copyright © W. F. Jackson Knight 1956.

For Joanna, who made it possible.

This is a tale of arms and of a man.
Fated to be an exile ...

Virgil, *The Aeneid*

CONTENTS

ACKNOWLEDGEMENTS

WHILE FAR from being an authorized biography, this book has greatly benefitted from close cooperation from Dr. Bull's immediate family. They are warm, loving people and whatever else might be said about Dr. Bull's actions — particularly towards the end of his life – he had reason to be very proud of his family. I would especially like to thank Michel Bull for the many hours he spent recalling his father with surprising objectivity and sometimes startling insight. Some sessions went well beyond midnight. Dr. Bull's widow, Mimi, is a woman of few illusions. She was able to see the best in Gerry and is left with memories of intense times. Better to have shared love with a brilliant light that sometimes scorched, than to have trudged through life with the cold grey security of a bureaucrat.

There are many others to thank. Gordon Bull, who wanted so much to know his brother but who through tragic circumstances didn't; Gerry's older sister Bernice who proves that indomitable spirit is bred in the bone; Donald Phillipson who did tireless research in the National Archives of Canada; Dr. Alfred G. Ratz who cared enough about the memories of an old friend to write it all down; many former employees of SRC still living around Highwater, Quebec, and North Troy, Vermont; the library staffs in North Bay and Trenton, Ontario; Sara Eglin who did sterling research in Britain; a Chinese gentleman in London; Dr. Christopher Cowley, who worked closely with Dr. Bull on the supergun; and Monique Jaminé, Dr. Bull's personal assistant in Belgium. In addition there were half a dozen former SRC employees in Belgium who asked not to be named for security reasons, and at least as many intelligence contacts who spoke on the same understanding. And to many others not named above: again, thank you.

On the personal side this book could not have been completed without the understanding and unstinting support of my wife Joanna. Ernest and Marta Hillen provided much needed encouragement and John Pearce, editor-in-chief of Doubleday Canada, committed time, effort and ideas that stretched well beyond duty.

William Lowther
Washington, March 1991

Note:

When writing to friends, Dr. Bull signed his name "Jerry". But his given name was Gerald, and for the sake of clarity I have used the spelling "Gerry". Likewise, I have referred to Bull's company throughout as SRC (Space Research Corporation) although it passed through a bewildering array of names such as SRC-Q (Quebec) and SRC-I (International). There are various ways to spell the Arabic names involved and I have chosen spellings which seemed to most closely resemble the Arabic pronunciations. As for dollars: amounts that emanate from Canada are Canadian dollars, those from the U.S. are American dollars. In his general business dealings from Brussels, Bull dealt in American dollars.

PROLOGUE

Dreams that Cannot Die

There are things of which I may not speak;
There are dreams that cannot die ...

"My Lost Youth"
Henry Wadsworth Longfellow

PROLOGUE

GERRY BULL was scared. He was scared of his own apartment. And with good reason. Someone was entering his orderly one-bedroom home while he was away, leaving clues, wanting him to know they had been there.

It had been little things at first. Interrupted by a phone call one night, he had switched off his VCR halfway through a rented film. The call was a request to speed up work on a problem the Chinese army was having with a new artillery system, and Bull had decided to spend the rest of the night doing the much-needed calculations. When he returned from the office the next evening he had found the film out of the VCR, rewound, and placed neatly in its box on a side table.

That was odd. He went back over the exact sequence of events. He had been enjoying the film, the phone rang, he put the VCR on pause while he answered. The conversation had been long and detailed. After it, he had turned off the VCR, deliberately leaving the movie in the machine so he could later pick up where he had left off. But now, with the film rewound and in its box, he experienced a quiver of apprehension. It was such a little thing, so innocuous, but some deep instinct would not let Bull dismiss it.

He called his cleaning lady to make sure she had not been in his apartment that day. And then he called the two other women who had keys: Monique Jaminé, his "Girl Friday", and Hélène Gregoire, the woman he referred to as his "special friend." Monique, who bought his shirts and ran his private office, confirmed what he already knew: she had been working all day, and her key was secure. As he expected, there was no reply at Hélène's number, for Hélène – who broke the loneliness Bull suffered while his wife, Mimi, lived on another continent – was out of the country and had been for three days. She was not due to return until the next day.

And that had been just the start. For after the incident with the VCR, the menace gathered. Strange happenings continued at his Brussels apartment, and the evidence deliberately left behind became more blatant. These people weren't thieves, they didn't steal. Bull guessed their purpose was to send him a message: they wanted to shatter his sense of security. It was psychological warfare. And the uncertainty had driven Bull back to sleeping pills and was undermining his nerve.

Dr. Gerald Vincent Bull had an international reputation in the arms world. He had been described as the greatest gun scientist of the century. It is a ruthless trade, and he had lived with danger for years, but there had never been anything like this. He couldn't go to the police, because they would ask too many questions he didn't want to answer. He was growing fatalistic, but that didn't stop this sudden "rat in the belly" feeling.[1]

The feeling had been there when he awoke on this Monday morning in the early summer of 1989. Even though it was now three weeks since the last incident, the fear kept building. As he locked the apartment door behind him, buttoned up his raincoat and hoisted a heavy black canvas document bag onto his shoulder, Bull was glad to be leaving.

It was a rainy morning in Brussels, and Bull, a little overweight and a lot under stress, struggled to squeeze behind the wheel of the nine-year-old Volkswagen he had commandeered from the office. The Volkswagen had been used by his son Michel as a family car, and what Dr. Bull liked best about the old station wagon was that it still seemed to have the smell of his grandchildren.

Dr. Bull's driving had attained an almost mythic reputation in the offices of his loftily named Space Research Corporation, the company he had headed for twenty years, the company he had built into one of the most scientifically analytic research-and-development establishments in the world when it came to big guns. A Canadian,

Bull felt that European drivers in general, and Belgians in particular, were "dangerous nuts". But once on the road, he was a greater menace than any of them. It was common for him to coast through traffic lights, switch lanes without signalling or simply stop in the middle of a highway if he was lost, which he often seemed to be these days.

For Dr. Bull could live in his own brilliant mind and close out the rest of the world. It was a trick he had learned in childhood when he had needed to escape the pain of being unloved. Fear and disappointment, longing and need could be boxed away for hours while he set his brain to analyse a problem. Just so long as the problem was mathematical and scientific, Dr. Bull could use it as a wall to keep out the emotional realities he couldn't cope with. And when he was behind that wall, he certainly should not have been behind the wheel of a car.

Bull had never grown to enjoy living in Brussels. Set roughly in the middle of Belgium, it can be heavy with pollution, and Bull blamed that for his frequent headaches. Some days the sky seemed to be falling in on the city. And there was a sinister look to the massive structures that housed the European Economic Community and NATO headquarters, the bureaucratic monsters that gave Belgium a claim to international influence. But it was no coincidence that Bull had located himself in Brussels.

Belgium was a world centre for the arms trade and has been notorious as such since the Middle Ages. It had a tradition for making, selling and exporting munitions with the same enthusiasm that Detroit made, sold and exported cars. When it came to clientele, there were few restrictions that couldn't be overcome. Politely put, the Belgian government was generous with "end user" certificates. Belgium exported more than 90 per cent of its total arms production. Belgian rifles were the first to reach Cuba after Castro came to power, and Belgian weapons from revolvers to rockets had been on both sides of most regional and civil wars since the 1960s.

Bull's business found an easy fit.

In the words of John Pike, a ballistics and missile expert with the Federation of American Scientists, Bull was "the greatest artillery genius of his generation ... the Wernher von Braun of big gun technology. But he was a gun genius born into a generation that had discovered the missile and lost interest in artillery."[2] It was Bull's mission to restore artillery to the prominence he believed it deserved in the annals of war.

Over the past three decades, Bull had revolutionized artillery by designing guns and shells that fired farther, with more killing power and with greater accuracy, than anything in the NATO or Soviet arsenals. His guns had halted Communist advances in southern Angola, where they had saved the forces of American-backed Jonas Savimbi in the mid-1980s. They had broken and scattered the human waves of fanatical Iranian soldiers who charged Iraq in 1987. China used his guns to guard its troubled northern border with the Soviet Union. And in the 1960s Bull had built the biggest gun in the world and fired from it a shell that had soared 180 kilometres into the sky, twice as high as any shell had gone before.

But now Dr. Bull was working on a gun system he considered much more important. In fact, on this rainy day in Brussels he was on his way to the test firing of a prototype. It was his dream, and it was code-named Project Babylon.

At 61, Bull had a ruddy complexion and a ready grin. Although he travelled a great deal, he had never learned to leave enough time to make it to the airport without a rush. He often missed flights, and on this particular morning it was going to be close. His windscreen wipers were set at full speed, twice as fast as they needed to be. (Bull loved gadgets but hadn't the patience to learn how to use them properly. He had a ten-disc CD player but had to invite one of his sons over to load it for him. With the old car, his wipers were either off or on full speed – he couldn't be bothered fiddling with the controls to find a more appropriate rate for light rain.) If he was performing as usual – and he was a man of habit – he drove rather too quickly over the private gravel road, past the tubs of flowering shrubs and the landscaped gardens that surrounded the three-building complex called Cherridreau, where he lived. He threaded the car through the twisting streets and narrow squares of the stylish southern suburb of Uccle and onto the "Ring", the multi-lane highway that circles the city. It took Dr. Bull about twenty-five minutes to reach Brussels International Airport, and he pulled level with "Departures" some thirty minutes before his Sabena flight was due to leave for Frankfurt. Leaving the Volkswagen parked in the main traffic lane, with the key still in the ignition and the engine running, Bull wrestled his bulky documents bag over his shoulder, grabbed his suitcase from the back seat, and lurched into the airport.

From a pay phone at the departure gate he called Monique Jaminé. A romantic, flashing-eyed woman of about 40, Monique adored Dr. Bull, as did many of the women who knew him. She spoke excellent English, with a slight Belgian accent that added allure even to the mundane. But Bull insisted on speaking to her in French. It had taken Monique two years to understand Bull's French, which was a patchwork of high-school grammar and Quebec vocabulary spoken without a trace of European influence. (She says that once, when Bull was invited to appear on Belgian TV, he stormed away from the lunch where details were being settled, when the producer insisted that a translator would be necessary.) Now, with his flight about to leave, Bull asked Monique to drop everything, take a taxi to the airport and pick up his car. She would have no trouble finding it, he told her, because it was blocking traffic. Before she had time to agree, he was gone, running down the narrow passage to the plane, his shoulder bent low by the weight of the documents in his canvas bag. He was often the last one onto the plane.

Inside the canvas bag were the drawings, calculations and contracts for Project Babylon and for the prototype Baby Babylon. Bull now took them everywhere with him. They were secure, he reasoned, only when he had them in sight. For not only were unknown persons entering his apartment, he also suspected there were spies in the office and that he was being followed. In an ordinary businessman, these kinds of fears might be dismissed as paranoia. But Dr. Bull was dabbling in international intrigue and in arms for the most volatile region on earth. He was not imagining things.

When he reached Frankfurt, Bull switched to Iraqi Airways for the five-and-a-half-hour flight to Baghdad, travelling first class as an honoured guest of Saddam Hussein. As he later told Monique, it wasn't until he sank into the wide luxurious seat of the Iraqi plane that he began to feel safe. He rubbed his face with a hot scented towel, and was struck again by the incongruity. Iraq was supposed to be a republic of fear, ruled by a despot. But Bull didn't need pills to help him sleep in Iraq; he was secure there. It was in the West he felt threatened.

Saddam was an ambitious man with an obsessive quest to become the "Sword of the Arabs". He believed he was destined to dominate the Arab world as Gamal Abdel Nasser of Egypt had done a generation before. Saddam saw himself as the head of an Arab superpower, controlling much of the world's oil supplies. One American newsmagazine had called him "the most dangerous man in the world".[3] Some analysts in America's Central Intelligence Agency estimate that during the 1980s Saddam had spent as much as $50 billion on the international arms market, making him the world's single biggest buyer of weaponry. In particular, he was stockpiling chemical and biological agents while conducting a near-desperate effort to become a nuclear power. Indeed, his progress in buying illicit nuclear weapons technology from abroad was so startling that by the end of the decade U.S. experts had halved their estimates – from ten years to five or less – of when he would be armed with a nuclear bomb. With 10 per cent of the world's petroleum reserves to finance them, Saddam's military endeavours knew few bounds. As we now know, Saddam military advisors had already drawn up provisional plans for invasion of Kuwait.

When Gerald Bull's own devoted engineers gathered in a little English-speaking bar near the Berlaymont, as EEC headquarters are formally named, they affectionately referred to Dr. Bull as Dr. Strangelove. It was no misnomer. Consider Project Babylon. Bull was building a gun of vast proportions and staggering potential. The barrel was to be 156 metres long – about one and a half times the length of a soccer field. With the breech and recoil mechanism fitted, the entire gun would be nearly 200 metres long. The bore was to be one full metre, which means it could fire projectiles the size of industrial garbage cans. The projectiles would be rocket-assisted and would be big enough and powerful enough to put a 50-kilogram satellite into orbit. The breech was to be as big as a kitchen; four and a half metres high, it was wide enough for two people to walk around inside it. And while the supergun was not a weapon itself – it was a satellite launcher – it was meant to pave the way for a whole new era of artillery never before contemplated outside the pages of science fiction. For Bull's longer-term goal was to build batteries of cannon that would be so powerful they could shoot across continents. The rocket-assisted shells would contain miniaturized guidance systems that would make them so accurate they would be able to hit an office building at 3,200 kilometres. Bull had already proposed such a system to the United States and to the NATO high command. But these canny groups, wary of Bull's hyperbole, were waiting to see how well Project Babylon worked before ordering further study. For they all knew through their intelligence services about Project Babylon. Only the public, which might have protested, was kept in the dark.

Artillery, Joseph Stalin's "god of war", has killed more people on battlefields this century than any other weapon. In a short essay that Bull admired, Aram Bakshian, Jr., a former speech writer for President Ronald Reagan, said: "No one, indeed, in laboratories and war colleges around the globe, can be sure what new directions the ancient art of gunnery may be about to take."[4] But even Bakshian would surely have been surprised.

As Bull had predicted, Monique had no trouble finding the car: it was still there, the subject of much angry horn blowing. But for Monique this was the final embarrassment. In the last two months she had been out to the airport twice on search-and-rescue missions when he had lost the vehicle entirely, forgotten where he had parked it and had no idea where to look. And the office was full of horror stories from staff who had accepted lifts. Monique was determined that the next week, while Dr. Bull was away, she would sell the car and make sure that in future there was always someone available to drive him wherever he needed to go. She would accept the responsibility. And it would be all right because Dr. Bull could never stay cross at anyone for long. Not if they smiled at him.

Dr. Bull had very little notion of fashion – his shirt was often hanging free from his waistband – but he had a touch of vanity. The curly black hair of his youth had turned mostly to silver and was thinning fast. Every morning he would comb the long strands on the left side of his head over to the right. The hope was to hide the bald spot in the middle. There was still a real sparkle to his wide blue eyes and, when he wanted to switch it on, there was considerable charisma. Even those who knew nothing about his arcane studies into artillery and cannon and howitzers and sleek aerodynamic shells had little trouble believing the popular idea that Dr. Bull was a genius. As he had grown older, the forward hunch of his shoulders, noticeable since his thirties, had become more pronounced. He was five foot eight, and he cultivated the notion that he had some of the appearance and all of the tenacity of a fighting bull. He liked the sound of "Taurus" and the imagery of his name. He was quick to argue, and always had been. As an avid hockey fan in his twenties, he had supported the Montreal Canadiens when he lived in Toronto and the Toronto Maple Leafs when he moved to Quebec.

Gerald Bull was as contradictory as a whiskey priest. A complex man, he somehow failed to see the frequent clash of his word and deed. A rabid anti-Communist, he worked for the People's Republic of China and lectured in that country's universities. His guns killed hundreds if not thousands of people, and yet he could not stand the sight of blood and was essentially a gentle person. Bull spent hours walking around Belgium's First World War graves, reading the markers and grieving at the loss of so many young lives.

Generous and compassionate with friends, he could be vicious-tongued when his scientific ideas were questioned or when he encountered incompetence. Ill-tempered and impatient when students were slow to learn, he would nonetheless sit up all night with a young engineer who needed help to develop an idea. Even though he dealt at ministerial level with governments, he was politically naive, almost childlike, in his understanding of international affairs.

Perverse and unmanageable, Bull inspired remarkable loyalty and gave it in return. Some of his staff, like SRC vice president Luis Palacio, had been with him for nearly thirty years. In 1980, when Space Research Corporation was rocked with a scandal about the transfer of gun technologies to South Africa, Palacio had offered to go to jail on Bull's behalf. He felt that incarceration would be devastating for Dr. Bull and he was more than ready, he was glad, to offer himself as a sacrifice. The offer had not been accepted, but its genuineness was never questioned, nor forgotten.

Bull was so soft-hearted that he couldn't fire anyone, even if they made the most appalling errors. When Steve Adams, a top engineer, left his company to work for the South African government in 1978, Bull was so angry that he nearly cried. He felt betrayed. Yet four years later, when Adams needed a job, Bull rehired him. And Bull treated everyone the same way, from arrogant PhDs to the cleaning ladies. Full of fun, he loved to play elaborate practical jokes and was delighted that his son Michel's daughter Sarah called him Grandpapa Clown. Every Christmas and birthday he bought her something connected with clowns, a china figure or a picture. "That was the kind of thing that gave him most pleasure in life," says Michel.

But Gerald Bull hadn't been in the mood for jokes lately, not since "they" had started "invading" his apartment.

Certainly the "invasions" were heavy on Bull's mind as he flew out of Frankfurt. He was on his way to the mountainous north of Iraq, to a heavily guarded, remote military site, about 50 kilometres from the ancient city of Nineveh, which about 2,700 years ago had been the capital of the world's mightiest empire. Bull was going there as a guest of Saddam Hussein, the Iraqi president who claimed to be not only a descendant of the Prophet Mohammed but also heir to the legend of Nebuchadnezzar, king of the ancient Babylonians. Nor was it just imaginative lineage that linked Saddam with antiquity. He had the same style as the ancients he admired so much. In a stone pillar at Nineveh, one Assyrian ruler boasted: "Three thousand captives I burned with fire. I left not one hostage alive. I cut off the hands and feet of some. I cut off the noses, ears and fingers of others. The eyes of numerous soldiers I put out. Maidens I burned as a holocaust." Saddam (the name means "One Who Confronts") could match and surpass. It was not without reason that he was known as "the butcher of Baghdad", a man "with the bloodiest hands in the Middle East", a man who had gassed the restive Kurds and left the corpses of political opponents to float in the capital's canals. More than a million Iraqis had fled his police state, his jails were full of those who dared criticize his regime, and international agencies claimed that torture, even against children, was commonplace. But Bull believed none or little of this at that time. He dismissed most of the allegations against Saddam as propaganda disseminated by the enemies of Iraq, of whom there were many. The devastating eight-year war with Iran had ended only months before, and the West had suddenly switched from supporting Iraq to awarding it pariah status. Bull didn't trust such a quick change in policy, he thought it could well be "dirty politics".

When the Iraqis had first called Gerald Bull in late 1987, he was in sore need of work. And to his amazement, they had gone for everything he suggested – two new conventional artillery systems and, most important of all to Bull, the supergun idea. Since 1967 he had been longing to find a backer for the supergun. He had tried to sell the idea to just about everyone who might conceivably be interested – NATO, the Pentagon, Canada, China and even Israel. No one, it seemed, would put up the money for a gun that could launch satellites. But Iraq loved the idea. Saddam saw it as a prestige project. His military advisers revelled in the prospect of owning the biggest gun in the world. Even if it wasn't a weapon, no enemy would feel safe within its uncertain but extensive range.

By way of return for the much-needed artillery and supergun orders, Bull had also agreed to help the Iraqis in other areas. And now he believed that maybe the enemies of Iraq had discovered his help. Surely that was why his apartment was being mysteriously entered, and why not-so-subtle clues were being left. He was being warned. Someone was telling him to drop the deal with Iraq. But even though he was frightened, he couldn't afford to pull out. He had no other major clients, there were no other big contracts to keep his company going ... and he was getting older. This might be his very last chance to build that supergun. At least for now, he was going to take the risks – and use pills when he couldn't sleep for worry.

What he didn't know as he arrived at Saddam International Airport in Baghdad was that the Iraqis were about to use his visit to draw him ever deeper into their most secret and dangerous schemes.

P A R T I

Gleams and Glooms

I remember the gleams and glooms that dart
  Across the school-boy's brain;
The song and the silence in the heart,
That in part are prophecies, and in part
  Are longings wild and vain.

"My Lost Youth"
Henry Wadsworth Longfellow

1

THE ROAD that led Gerald Bull to Iraq was long and tortuous. And it is not too fanciful to suggest that some of the emotional baggage he carried there was picked up in his earliest years. For Gerald Bull started life with all the advantages of Oliver Twist. His childhood was straight out of Dickens. Fifty years later, it was still haunting him, even in the midst of his international arms deals. "Coffins, that's what I remember of childhood, coffins," he would say. What Gerry wanted was acceptance. He needed to be needed. And Saddam Hussein needed him.

Gerry was born at North Bay, Ontario. Just over 350 kilometres north of Toronto, North Bay lies along the "Nipissing Route" of the fur traders. It was a major fur centre, whose population was largely of British origin with a strong French-Canadian presence. Bull was on both sides of that divide. He was born the same year that Roy Thomson, later Lord Thomson of Fleet, moved to North Bay to sell radios and washing machines and, with amazing optimism, refrigerators. For Thomson's first impressions were of a forty-below-zero hell where everyone went to church.[1] Nevertheless, it was in North Bay that Thomson founded his vast fortune.

Gerry was the ninth child of George L. Toussaint Bull, a bibulous solicitor, and his young Roman Catholic wife, Gertrude LaBrosse. It was a colourful if not auspicious beginning. Gertrude knew almost nothing of her father, a French-speaking gold prospector called Napoleon. Napoleon was locally famous because he was supposed to have taken a canoe through the Great Lakes in the late

1870s and followed the rivers into North Dakota, where he fought with the Cree and was shot in the leg with an arrow. Such high adventure, along with Napoleon's dreams of a thick vein of gold just waiting to be claimed in the untamed wilderness, won the heart of Isabelle Barker of Glengarry Township. Napoleon and Isabelle settled into North Bay, where Napoleon left his wife to work as a domestic while he sought his fortune in the bush and lived with the local Algonquin Indians. She tried to join him, staying for about a year at his camp on an island in a remote lake, but the combination of black flies, severe winters and life in a shack that didn't even boast an outhouse proved too much for her. Napoleon never found gold. And he became no more than an occasional visitor to Isabelle in North Bay. But by the turn of the century, she had borne four of his children. About that time Napoleon stopped even his infrequent visits. Isabelle heard that he had taken up with an Indian woman.[2]

Gertrude, born in 1893, was the oldest child, and with the family struggling for survival, she left her convent school at 15 to work in the office of George L. Toussaint Bull, a small, feckless lawyer who had moved north from Toronto. They were married in February the next year, 1909, in St. Mary's Roman Catholic Cathedral. Gertrude was 16, and George, with his heavy Edwardian moustache and high starched collar, was 35. As the *North Bay Nugget* reported, "The young couple were unattended."

A non-practising Anglican, George was boastfully proud of his Empire Loyalist heritage and believed his family had fought for the British in the American Revolution, before they trekked north to Upper Canada in the 1780s and settled near Trenton, on the northern shore of Lake Ontario. Despite pressure from the LaBrosse family, he refused to convert to Catholicism.

George had graduated from Toronto's Osgoode Hall Law School in 1898, and after six years working for Trenton law firms decided to strike out on his own as a criminal defence lawyer in North Bay, where there was the tantalizing prospect of making a name. He followed the circuit courts north, west and east, covering a territory that stretched nearly 500 kilometres in each direction, and his clients were loggers and trappers, miners and settlers who often couldn't pay their bills.

The Bulls' first child, Bernice, was born a respectable nine months after the wedding. Over the next eighteen years, Gertrude had eight more children. Henry, Esmond, Audrey, Clyde, Vivian, Ron, Frank and, on March 9, 1928, Gerald Vincent. Young Gerald entered an insecure financial world. Stockmarkets were starting to fall, and before he was two they had crashed into the Great Depression.

Over the years, George had moved up from his original rundown offices to rather smarter premises and was also making his way politically. From 1921 to 1925 he served on the school board. And in 1923 he was the Conservative candidate for the little town of Sturgeon Falls in the Ontario provincial elections. He was soundly defeated by Liberal Zotique Mageau. "It was the French who beat me", he complained. "There were too damn many of them." By way of consolation, powerful Ontario Conservatives made Bull a King's Counsel in 1928, just three months after Gerry was born.

As the 1920s came to a close, the depression had North Bay in its icy hold, and Bull's law business collapsed. In the spring of 1930, Gertrude loaded her family and furniture onto the train for Toronto, where George had the promise of a job with a rich friend. They rented a house on Rushton Road in a pleasant middle-class neighbourhood, and by late summer Gertrude was pregnant again.

"My mother seemed to be happy about having the baby, but I wasn't happy about it, I thought it was too many," says Bernice, who by then was 21 and married. Gordon was born on February 27, 1931. Almost immediately after the birth, Gertrude started running very high temperatures, and within a week she was back in hospital. Her condition deteriorated, and on April 1, 1931, she died. George meant to put a marker on her grave, but never did. Gerry was three years old. Says Bernice: "It was septicaemia. The doctor had two patients right near each other, my mother and another lady. And they both died. My father always said the doctor hadn't sterilized his instruments." George, then 57, was left with ten children, five of them under the age of 12. Never a forceful or assertive man, he simply couldn't cope.

The family was temporarily saved by George's maiden sister Laura, a nurse who knew how to take control. She insisted that

George and his children move in with her; she was living in the Bull family homestead, an old red-brick house on Dundas Street West in Trenton.

Gerry remembered Aunt Laura as his "second mother". She held the family together at a very hard time. George gave up his Toronto job but couldn't make a living in Trenton and began to sit home all day, drinking. In August 1932, Aunt Laura fell sick, and on Christmas Day that year she died of cancer. "I buried two mothers before I was five," said Gerald Bull.

There was no way that George Toussaint Bull could hold the centre. An educated man himself, he does not seem to have encouraged his children to stay at school. With Bernice married, the three next eldest were sent out to work and to care for themselves. The six youngest were eventually shuffled among a series of relatives stretching from Winnipeg to Montreal.

In December 1934, George married Rose Jean Bleecker, a 57-year-old widow; they'd known each other since high school. The ceremony took place in Simcoe, near the shores of Lake Erie. None of George's ten were at the ceremony, nor were they mentioned in the published marriage announcement. They had, in effect, become orphans. Even the youngest ones, Gordon and Gerry, never received a card or a present from their father at Christmas or on birthdays. "Apparently Rose didn't want to be encumbered with anybody else's kids, and my dad went along with that," says Gordon.

Gerald Bull never mentioned his father in later life, but he often talked about his mother. He tried to find a photograph of her to carry in his wallet, and he could talk himself into tears just thinking of her fate.

"Every April 1, he would talk about his mother's death," Gerald's son Michel remembers. Fully fifty-three years after Gertrude's death, Michel and his father were flying to China on an arms deal. It was a nineteen-hour flight, and Dr. Bull had been drinking. There had been a long silence, and the older man seemed to be dozing when suddenly he turned to his son and said: "Today. Do you know what the date is?" Michel knew very well what his father was talking about, but decided not to humour him. He replied that yes, he knew, it was April 1. His father persisted. "Yes, but do you know what day this is, what is April 1?" Said Michel: "Well, it's April Fool's

Day, but...." Dr. Bull, now getting agitated, interrupted: "Look, I've told you many times. It's the day your grandmother died. And she lies in an unmarked grave in Toronto." There were tears in Dr. Bull's eyes. But still Michel did not want to let his father get away with the emotionalism in which he had started to wallow: "I decided to be a bit hard on my father. And so I said that it was very sad, her being buried without a stone or anything to mark the spot, and I asked him why he didn't go back there and find the grave and put a stone on it." At that, Bull fell silent again. "He didn't want to hear that practical idea, because he was too much of a romantic fellow. He enjoyed holding the nostalgia in his mind."

On other occasions, after long exhausting days of field-testing artillery, Gerry would relax over drinks with another ballistics expert and close friend, Dr. Charles Murphy. In the small hours of the morning Bull would ramble on about his childhood. Remembers Murphy: "He thought that he might be somehow responsible for his mother's death."

Says Michel: "When I was very young and asked about my grandfather, I was told that he couldn't keep his children together because he was so old. He was supposed to be nearly seventy when his wife died, and so distraught and depressed that he couldn't do it." Thus Gerald Bull softened the story when he told it to his own children, four decades later.

Soon after Aunt Laura's death, Bernice, who by now had two children of her own, moved to the little town of Sharbot Lake, 60 kilometres north of Kingston, where her husband was working a small mica mine. Responsible in a way that her father never had been, Bernice took in three of her young brothers, Ron, Frank and Gerry.

Having lived like gypsies, in homes where they generally weren't wanted, the boys had missed a lot of school. But Bernice got them into class for September 1935. There was very little money, and Bernice could barely afford to feed her brothers through that winter, as Gerry turned eight.

Meanwhile, Gertrude's younger brother, Philip LaBrosse, was rising fast through the Canadian office of the Brunswick Company, an American firm that outfitted bowling alleys and billiard saloons.

He was moved by the company to Winnipeg, and it was there that soft-spoken, gentle Philip met Edith Keele, a woman with a knack for taking over everything that came her way. Edith married Phil in the late 1920s. They had two children. Both were born with severe defects, and both were to die as babies. Following the birth of her second child, Edith was told she would never be able to bear children again. By now Phil and Edith had been moved by his company to Montreal. The depression was still raging when Edith bought a ticket in the Irish Sweepstakes – and won about $175,000. In 1935, it was a fortune. Invested wisely, it was enough to ensure that Phil and Edith could live in comfort for the rest of their lives.

They bought the 16-hectare Glen St. Lawrence Apple Orchard, overlooking the point where the St. Lawrence River meets Lake Ontario about six miles east of Kingston.

That first summer at the orchard, with the apples needing to be harvested, Edith and Phil LaBrosse drove north to Sharbot Lake and brought Ron, Frank and Gerry back with them. The three boys were to work for their keep during July and August. Ron and Frank disliked it immensely. While Uncle Phil would go out of his way to be considerate, Aunt Edith never seemed to miss a chance to criticize and to tell them in detail about their "disgraceful" father. She told them he was a drunkard who had mistreated their mother and that if they misbehaved she would throw them out and make them walk back to Sharbot Lake. Ron and Frank turned resentful and surly. But Gerry, being younger and more vulnerable, responded by trying harder and harder to please.

At summer's end the three boys were driven back to Sharbot Lake, and Edith told Bernice that she would be glad to take Gerry off her hands. He could return with her and Phil to live at the orchard. Bernice didn't like the idea because she didn't like Edith. She felt that Edith wanted a child because she didn't have any of her own. But Edith didn't really care for children; what she enjoyed was the idea of children. "Edith wanted a child who would never be any trouble," says Bernice. "She didn't want any complications and she didn't want any commitment." Conditions in Sharbot Lake were deteriorating, though, and Bernice was forced to consider Edith's offer. Nevertheless, she took Gerry aside and asked him if he really wanted to live with Aunt Edith. Anxious for the attention, love and warmth that had been so sparing since his mother died, and also wanting to please, Gerry said that if Aunt Edith wanted him to live with her, it was fine by him.

And so Bernice gave her reluctant consent, and Gerry drove away with the LaBrosses. He was never to be close to the Bull family again. Aunt Edith would see to that.

Years later, when asked to recall how Gerry came to live with her, Edith said that when she took him back to Sharbot Lake after a summer at the orchard she found his suitcase empty. He so much wanted to live with her that he had left his clothes behind. After that, how could she do anything but take him in?[3]

Gerry didn't know it, but the year he went to live with meek Phil and domineering Edith, he lost his grandfather. That winter Napoleon LaBrosse froze to death in his island camp. Like his daughter, Napoleon was buried in an unmarked grave.

2

PHIL AND EDITH LaBrosse enrolled eight-year-old Gerry in a two-room red-brick country school not too far from the orchard. Uncle Phil had been close to his sister Gertrude and now he did what he could to make her boy happy. He took Gerry's hand on walks through the orchard, and the two would sit together in the same armchair after dinner. Aunt Edith warmed too, but not to the extent that she ever gave him a hug. And Gerry was to remember that she conditioned her affection. If he did well at school, she would praise him. But if his marks weren't good, there would be long hours of silence.

On one subject Aunt Edith never softened, and that was Gerry's relatives in the Bull family. She disliked them, as they disliked her. Gerry's father was Edith's major villain. It was having all of those kids that killed poor Gertrude, Edith would declare. What had a man of his age been doing marrying a girl of 16 anyway? Getting into her stride, Edith could conjure up such detail that Phil would break down and cry. At that, Edith would turn on him. "Just you stop snivelling," she would say. Gerry was witness to it all. His nerves must have been stretched taut. Reflects Michel Bull: "I think Aunt Edith planted some horrible stories. And maybe the horrible stories worked too well. Not only did he not want anything to do with his father, but he made no effort to contact his brothers and sisters either. And that attitude carried right on through his life."

Aunt Edith didn't let Gerry forget how lucky he was to be at the orchard. She said his father didn't want him, and Bernice couldn't afford him, and that if it wasn't for her generosity he might be in an orphanage. Years later Gerry was to remember that if he disobeyed Aunt Edith she would threaten to send him "away".

The feud between the Bulls and the LaBrosses was not helped by Aunt Edith's tendency to be tight with her fortune. She had used "Little Bright Eyes", the pet name of Bernice's little daughter, as her *nom de plume* on her sweepstakes ticket, but, according to Bernice, she never gave the girl "so much as a pair of socks". As the Bull children suffered badly through the dark 1930s, Edith did little to help. Gordon, who was then living with Phil's brother in Winnipeg, remembers, with some bitterness lingering after half a century: "Edith would send some of Gerry's old clothes for me, but there was often no wear left in them." Edith was a careful spender. In a diary she recorded every expense, right down to a five-cent tip to a waitress in a café.

Uncle Phil was understanding and warm, but he would never contradict his wife. Like Gerry's own father, Phil was not a man to make a stand. Gerry grew up among strong women and weak men.

Aunt Edith may have been a poor substitute for a mother, but she had an enormous influence. She was an autocrat with a conversational style that centred on strong views stated as fact rather than argued as opinion. And she had two pet theories, both of them to have substantial influence on her young charge.

The first was that all Communists were evil personified and were out to take over the world, at which time they would send to the salt mines anyone who dared speak their mind. Some of the worst of Stalin's purges were underway, and the newspapers gave her plenty of ammunition. Edith was so decisive and commanding that Gerry seems to have soaked it all in without question.

The second of Edith's hard-line theories concerned the rewards of work. Those who work hard prosper, she would say, while layabouts and loafers end up in poverty. To illustrate the obvious, Edith would point out to Gerry that she and Phil lived in a beautiful old orchard while the worthless Bulls shuffled from pillar to post. It would have been more than Gerry's supper was worth to remind her that she had won her money in a lottery.

Gerry discovered early that the one sure way to please Aunt Edith was to be top of the class, and so, striving for affection, he became a star pupil. But, living in the shadow of his powerful aunt, Gerry also became introverted and quiet and spoke only when he was asked a question. There were no children living close, and Gerry would spend hours on his own, in his room, reading, doing homework and staring out at the apple orchard. Says Gerry's oldest son, Philippe, "My father felt very lonely. This solitude marked deeply his character."

The brightest spot in Gerry's week was Saturday, when the family went to Kingston to shop in the morning and spend afternoons with Edith's brother Bob Keele, his wife and their teenaged children, Jesse, 19, Gordon, 18, and Bob, 16. Among the Keeles, Gerry found three older cousins ready to welcome him into their warm and secure world.

Jesse saw Gerry as a poor orphan and made sure he was pampered for at least half a day a week. Gordon and Bob wouldn't ordinarily have had much to do with an eight-year-old, but with Jesse's pushing, they kept Saturday afternoons free. And what they did was talk. In the snug kitchen in Kingston that winter of 1936 Gerry did a lot of listening, often curled up and cosy beside Jesse on an old sofa jammed in beside the stove. With the snow piled high outside, he felt warm and wanted with his older cousins.

Gerry did not see any members of the Bull family until the next summer, when his brothers Ron and Frank came to visit for a day with Bernice's husband. Gerry was behind the house talking with Gordon Keele. Aunt Edith showed the Bull boys out back and called to Gerry, "Here's your country cousins." The remark cut the Bull boys deeply, and they expected Gerry to somehow come to their rescue. But he was so shy in greeting his brothers and seemed so little concerned with the way Aunt Edith talked that they left with the impression he was on her side. He was one of them now, a LaBrosse. It was ten years before they saw him again.

The Keeles felt sorry for Gerry. Yet he surprised them. Bob was working as a counsellor and swimming instructor at a summer camp north of Kingston, on Eagle Lake. Gerry was there for a month. At the end of the first week, when Gerry had just learnt to dog paddle, Bob put a floating coloured marker 25 yards out in the lake. He tried to persuade the more experienced swimmers to jump from the dock and swim around the buoy. But they were all frightened of the deep water and wouldn't go in. As Bob was about to give up, Gerry volunteered.

"Before I could stop him, he jumped in," remembers Bob. Gerry had learned to swim only that week, and Bob didn't think he would make it even to the buoy. So he went in after Gerry but kept well back, to let him try on his own. Exhausted, Gerry got around the buoy and started back. About five yards from the dock, he was finished. Bob helped him for the last few strokes. "I hadn't realized until then – none of us had – that Gerry had that kind of spirit. He was such a quiet boy that you could underestimate him."

In the fall of 1938, as gas masks were being handed out in London and Neville Chamberlain was trying to appease Hitler, Phil and Edith made plans to spend the winter in Florida. Gerry, of course, was something of an inconvenience. The answer, Edith decided, was boarding school. And right on their doorstep in Kingston was Regiopolis College, a Jesuit high school with facilities for boarders, a reputation for strict discipline, and high academic standards. Phil was pleased with the idea because he had always felt guilty that his nephew, a baptized Catholic, was not being raised in the faith. (Although Edith had converted to Catholicism when she married Phil, she soon abandoned the faith, and under her guidance, Phil lapsed.) Gerry was told that going to Regiopolis would please his mother in heaven, because she had been a strict Catholic.

Gerry was accepted over the phone. Only when they turned up to enrol him, the day before Phil and Edith were due to leave for Florida, did the headmaster realize there had been a mistake. For the school didn't accept anyone under 12, and Gerry was just 10, and small for his age. Philip LaBrosse pleaded, and the headmaster gave in, but on the strict understanding that Gerry enrol for one term only.

Gerry was left to sink or swim in a class two grades above his standing and age. Yet it was the sort of challenge he seemed made for. As Saddam Hussein was to learn more than fifty years later, Gerry Bull responded best when the odds against him were highest.

At night the boys in the dorm would listen to American radio stations, and on October 30, 1938, they heard Orson Welles reading H.G. Wells's *The War of the Worlds*. It was the broadcast that caused panic in New York; thousands of listeners believed Earth had been invaded by Martians. The boys at Regiopolis weren't fooled, but the experience introduced Gerry to science fiction and led him to Jules Verne, an author who was to be influential much later when Gerry began to experiment with big guns. It was science fiction too that taught Gerry not to limit his imagination and to look outside the range of conventional thinking.

It is perhaps surprising, but the older boys seem to have taken the little orphan to heart. Life at the orchard had been so lonely that being surrounded by other boys, even if they were older, was exciting.

Again, Gerry strove to please. As other boys groaned at the huge amount of study to be completed after classes, Gerry took it in stride. Aunt Edith's discipline had him well prepared. When Uncle Phil and Aunt Edith returned from Florida for Christmas, the headmaster had changed his mind about Gerry. He told Philip: "He's a fine boy, that. An excellent student. It's very bad, changing schools in mid-term."[1] And so Gerry stayed, for the next five years.

Canadian prime minister Mackenzie King had publicly thanked Mr. Chamberlain for his policy of appeasement and the sacrifice of Czechoslovakia. North America had been in an isolationist mood, but gradually, as the march of Nazism continued, opinion in Canada was changing. The dorms were filled with talk of war and the possibility that senior boys might soon be in uniform. The Air Force was the most glamorous service. The Keele brothers were already talking about joining the Royal Canadian Air Force, and the boys at Regiopolis were forming a branch of the Air Cadets, with a model-aircraft club attached.

Gerry was too young for the cadets, but that Christmas Phil and Edith bought their 10-year-old nephew two balsa-wood model airplanes. The planes sent Gerry's imagination soaring. He spent hours adjusting the wings and the balance for special effects in flight. By the spring of 1939 he was a leading member of the model-aircraft club. But the models made from store-bought plans were too limited in flight, he told Wilfred Pruard, his physics and chemistry master. It was Pruard who suggested that Gerry try designing his own aircraft, keeping careful records of the effects of any changes on the model in flight.[2]

At this most impressionable age, Gerry was withdrawn and still spoke little. A sensitive child living under the shadow of a highly insensitive woman, he buried his emotions. That summer he spent many evenings alone sitting under the apple trees. He began to write poetry, but he was embarrassed by it and burned the note-books. There was a lot of romance in the soul of Gerry Bull, and little opportunity for release.

During the first week of September 1939, as Gerry returned to Regiopolis, Germany attacked Poland. Britain and France declared war. Canada remained neutral for a week, but on September 10 followed suit. There was no immediate conscription, but before the end of the year both Gordon and Bob Keele had joined the Air Force.

With the collapse of France in the summer of 1940, the Keele boys were sent overseas. Before he went, Gordon took Gerry for a long walk through the orchard to the banks of the St. Lawrence River. Gordon was 22 and Gerry was 12, but they were more like brothers than cousins. Gordon explained the dangers of war and how different actually flying in Lancaster and Halifax bombers was from playing with models. Gerry was frightened. Every morning at Regiopolis the school prayed for the soldiers, sailors and airmen on the front lines, and the priests would regularly take small groups aside to talk about war deaths. Gerry made Gordon promise that he would write. And he did.

Father Joe Driscoll, S.J., arrived to teach English, history, and religion at Regiopolis in September 1940. He recalls: "There was an intense interest in the war. Some of the older boys started to ask why they should bother to study when they were going to be shot at shortly."

That autumn Gerry had a visitor. It was after class and Gerry was in study hall. He was told that his father was waiting for him in the library. Gerry went with great apprehension to see the headmaster and told him that his aunt and uncle had instructed him to ensure that someone be present in any meeting with his father. The headmaster assigned a teacher to the role of chaperone. Gerry and the teacher made their way to the library, where they found George Bull sitting at one of the long wooden tables.

In touch with Bernice, the only one of his ten children he had stayed close to, George was in Kingston on business and knew where to find his second youngest son. He had expected the boy to be overwhelmed by the visit. But Gerry fidgeted and hardly said a word. With the teacher present there was no opportunity for intimate conversation, even if George had been capable of it. The meeting lasted for less than fifteen minutes. It ended when Gerry said he had to get back to study. There was nothing that father and son had to say to each other.

George left in a black mood. He couldn't understand why the boy had been so difficult. "It was hurtful," he told Bernice. Gerry wrote to Aunt Edith with news of the visit, and he informed her that he had followed her advice and made sure that a teacher was present. She was undoubtedly pleased to hear the meeting had been short. Gerry never met his father again.

The confusion of life, as fellow students left for the war, must sometimes have been overwhelming. One of the few things Gerry knew about his mother was that she had had a rock-like faith in the Church. At school he attended Mass several times a week, and Uncle Phil often told him how much that would please Gertrude. Gerry's religious commitment was wrapped up in remembering and pleasing his mother. He asked few questions of the priests.

After one Regiopolis graduate was shot down over Europe, Gerry built a replica of the Halifax involved and worked out its airspeed and altitude at the time it was hit by anti-aircraft fire. Carefully scaling down the event, Gerry and Mr. Truard set the model ablaze and launched it from a high window at the school. Solemnly they recorded the effects of the fire on the plane's flight path. Gerry was fascinated.

Says Father Driscoll: "Pruard was a genius of a teacher, and Gerry was especially responsive. With that experiment, it was Pruard who taught Gerry how to calculate the speeds and the effects of the fire. It was Pruard who taught him to be scientific. Now remember, I'm talking about a twelve- or thirteen-year-old boy who would sit down and work out on paper how the flight path of a bomber would be affected if one of its wings was on fire. A teacher only finds a student like that once in a lifetime."

No wonder the teachers at Regiopolis were delighted with him. When he started at the school he had been pushed forward two years, but he responded not just by living up to his older classmates but by surpassing them. Neil McCarney, Sr., who was a boarder with Gerry, remembers: "He was always top of the class or at least number two. And it was a tough school."

Along with the science and math for which he had such an obvious talent, Gerry began taking a deeper interest in poetry. He liked to recite poems and had no trouble learning long pieces by heart. The lines he enjoyed the most were those charged with emotion and loneliness, longing and the inevitability of death. They were lines he repeated often through life. Dr. Irvine Glass, a physicist Gerry worked with later, recalls: "He would quote Tennyson a lot, especially that line, 'Man comes and tills the field and lies beneath.'[3] And he often quoted from Gray's *Elegy*, '... And leaves the world to darkness and to me.' The Jesuits taught him a lot of poetry, and I think it was a comfort to him." Near the end of his life, under great pressure and fear in Belgium, he copied poems he had learned at Regiopolis on company project sheets that were meant to detail weapons systems. They were mainly poems about God.

Father Driscoll had Gerry in his study hall. He says: "I have a clear picture of him in my mind right now. He is standing there in knickerbockers with woollen stockings and a red sweater. He had curly, curly hair and beautiful white teeth. Always smiling. Gerry always had a smile."

By late 1940 the Canadian Army needed to expand a base near the orchard, and the LaBrosse land came under a compulsory purchase order. Edith negotiated a price, and she and Phil moved to Toronto, where they could be near their other investments. Gerry stayed on at Regiopolis. It meant that he saw Aunt Edith and Uncle Phil only for Christmas, Easter, and the summer vacations. He didn't complain.

When his sister Bernice was hospitalized in Kingston one winter, she wrote to Gerry and asked if he would visit her. He did, going almost every day for more than a month. She worried because he was so quiet, and she invited him to come back to live with her. Gerry declined. Bernice pressed him to talk about the LaBrosses and said harsh things about them. Gerry insisted, "Uncle Phil is all right, there's nothing wrong with Uncle Phil. It's just her, it's just Aunt Edith." So why didn't he move to Sharbot Lake? "No," said Gerry, "she's paying for my education."

In 1941 Gerry joined the Air Cadets, was issued an RCAF uniform, and began an officers' training course at Queen's University in Kingston. Most winter weekends were spent at the Keeles', and Gordon and Bob, on their first home leave, filled him with tales of war and missions over enemy territory.

The hammer blow landed on March 13, 1942. They called Gerry out of class to tell him. And he ran from the school through the streets of Kingston. Jesse met him at the door. The house was an explosion of grief. Gordon Keele, the cousin who had made Gerry so proud and had written to him from the front lines, had been killed. He was 24.

For years Gerry kept the grief to himself. He did not talk about Gordon at school. He redoubled his work and used academic study as a balm. He ranked the loss of Gordon with the loss of his mother. He thought of them both as heroic figures, victims. Says Michel: "My father once took me to see a movie about the Battle of Britain. His eyes were full of tears. He saw me looking and he said, 'That's where I lost Gordon, in the Battle of Britain.'" Even after he married, Gerry kept a photograph of Gordon Keele by his bedside.

Gerry glorified his cousin. Gordon's death was indeed tragic. But he was never a fighter pilot, and he did not go down in the Battle of Britain. Gordon was a radio operator and an air gunner, and he was killed in a training accident.

PART II

Up and Doing

Let us, then, be up and doing,
With a heart for any fate;
Still achieving, still pursuing
Learn to labor and to wait.

"A Psalm of Life"
Henry Wadsworth Longfellow

3

GERALD BULL's final months at high school were dominated by war news. Senior boys huddled around the radio at night, whooping and yelling at reports of Allied victories. Nearly all had relatives or friends directly involved, and most expected to be in combat themselves pretty soon. It was 1944, and by April the Allies had clear air superiority over Germany. Gerry graduated from Regiopolis the week after the Normandy landings. He had just turned 16, and his B-plus average was considered exceptional in view of his age and the standards at the school.

He wanted to be a doctor. Perhaps it was the dying – his mother, Aunt Laura, Gordon Keele – who had shaped that desire. Gerry was a vulnerable boy and remained that way all his life. By healing others he may have thought, at some subconscious level, that he would heal the unspoken hurt inside himself. But he wasn't well suited for the medical profession; he became dizzy at the sight of blood.

Immediately upon graduation he took a live-in job at the old orchard, picking apples. Having bought the property, the Army had rented it out to a farmer and delayed its development. Gerry thought the apple-picking would provide spending money for at least the first semester if he could get into medical school. Also, by attending the University of Toronto, he could save money by living with his uncle and aunt. Uncle Phil called the university but was told that the only department that would admit a 16-year-old was Engineering.

No point in hanging around until he was 18, said Aunt Edith. Better get him into engineering. Phil discovered that the needs of war had led to the opening of a new course in aeronautical engineering. At first the university insisted the course would be too difficult for a 16-year-old. But Phil persisted, and they agreed to see Gerry, who suddenly became very interested in learning more about flight.

Dr. T.R. "Tommy" Loudon, the professor who was to chair the new department, was in charge of Gerry's interview, and he asked only one question: "Why do you want to be an aeronautical engineer?" Gerry had changed a lot in his last year at high school. Solid marks and respect from fellow students had built his confidence to the extent that he entered school debates. He was no longer hesitant to talk, and for his age he knew a lot about aeronautics. For the next fifteen minutes Gerry discussed the problems he had encountered designing wings to get the most "lift" for balsa-wood aircraft. He knew the problems, he said; now he wanted to find solutions. Loudon did not interrupt the young man. When Gerry finished, the professor simply cleared his throat and informed the applicant that he was accepted.

Gerry moved to Toronto and into the home of Aunt Edith and Uncle Phil when the university semester opened in September. After a decade in sleepy Kingston, bustling Toronto with its three-quarters of a million population, its massive buildings and broad streets was as exciting for Gerry as it was inspiring. The city's economic base was widely diversified and it had not been hit as hard as other industrial centres in the Great Depression. Now the war had stimulated the growth of the aircraft, precision-machine and electronic industries. Toronto was a city of growth, looking forward to a postwar boom.

With Canada filling the skies with planes for the war effort and training pilots from all over the Commonwealth, aeronautics had become a cutting-edge discipline. The war was doing wonders for Canadian science. At the same time, the University of Toronto was becoming a major international institution, attracting professors from Oxford, Cambridge, Harvard and MIT. In the past, aeronautics had been available only as an option within other programmes. In 1944, for the first time a four-year honours course was being offered under the direction of Professor Loudon, whose aeronautical qualifications stretched back to 1908 when he worked as the mechanical engineer on the Silver Dart, the first plane to fly in the British Commonwealth.

Loudon was determined to give the course international standing. It was to be the most rigorous in the Engineering Department. Only twenty-two would be enrolled, and in addition to five one-hour lectures and three hours of laboratory work every weekday there were another three hours of laboratory work on Saturday mornings. Mathematical problems were assigned five nights a week for class discussion the next day.

Gerry was the youngest member of the course and he looked it. And for the first time since his country school, there were girls in the class. Most unusually for the times, there were two of them. Gerry had no experience at all with girls; he had never been out on a date. And in that direction anyway, things didn't improve. There was very little social life for Gerry. Not only was the university workload of daunting proportions, but he also took a part-time job in a grocery store, stacking the shelves and keeping stock.

Gerry had a deep appreciation of what his uncle and aunt were doing for him. It would have been difficult to go to university without their help. Aunt Edith may have fallen short on compassion, but her sweepstakes money had opened the opportunity for education. Gerry repaid the LaBrosses with loyalty. He didn't complain about Edith, and her earlier treatment of him only came to light years later when his own family asked questions.

He was full of confidence and high spirits as he embarked on his undergraduate career. "Gerry was a sparkly-eyed kid," says Clare Eatock, who was in the aeronautics course and is now an engineer with Pratt & Whitney in Montreal. "He was full of joy and energy and the sort of pranks you might expect from a high-school student." He would launch paper airplanes from the class windows or send them sailing across the lecture hall when the professor turned his back.

The aeronautics class thought of itself as special. "Toronto was a fabulous university and we saw ourselves as being the elite," remembers Colin Wrong, who sat near Gerry during the first day of lectures.

In May 1945, as Gerry's first university year was coming to a close, the war in Europe ended when Germany surrendered unconditionally. And that summer saw the first Canadian soldiers coming home, many of them to take up their education from where it had been so violently interrupted. As the university flooded with veterans, the atmosphere changed dramatically, and Gerry began to shrink back into his shell. Men in their mid-twenties, with three or four years of combat behind them, were amazed to find themselves in the same lectures as teenagers like Gerry Bull. One such veteran, Frank Hubbard, remembers Gerry in 1945 this way: "He didn't smoke and he didn't drink and he didn't have a girlfriend. He was a real shy kid." No more paper airplanes were thrown in class. The veterans wouldn't stand for it.

The academic year had just begun in September 1945 when a cipher clerk working in the military intelligence branch of the Soviet Embassy in Ottawa defected. Igor Gouzenko took with him documentary evidence and convincing testimony that proved what Aunt Edith had been saying for years – Moscow was running spy rings that were trying to steal atom bomb secrets and plotting to influence North American policy from within. The world was moving into the Cold War. Aunt Edith followed developments with the commitment of a soap opera fan as investigations led to twelve arrests not just in Canada but in the U.S.A. and Britain as well, then to the arrest and trial of Klaus Fuchs, the flight of Donald Maclean, the hysteria of the McCarthy era and the eventual execution of Julius and Ethel Rosenberg in 1953.

Gerry Bull was at his most impressionable during these years. Much of his information on current events would have been filtered through Aunt Edith, and he became, almost by osmosis, virulently anti-Communist. His position was reinforced as thousands of refugees from the Baltic states poured into Canada in the post-war years with tales of Soviet brutality and repression. On the other hand, Gerry and his fellow students were not political or even well informed. As Colin Wrong says, "When you have a workload like we had, the outside world passes you by. The real world for us was a huge pile of homework."

In his second and third years at the University of Toronto, Gerry was bogged down in study as the world of aircraft design was stumped by the problem of the speed of sound – the sonic barrier.

But in his fourth and final year as an undergraduate Gerry Bull's academic life changed again. Tommy Loudon was nearing retirement, and the university hired Dr. Gordon N. Patterson, a pioneer in supersonics, who taught a course in supersonic flow theory. Clare Eatock remembers: "Gerry became enamoured of the subject. He threw himself into it. His intense enthusiasm for Patterson's course was amazing. Supersonics were very little known at that time. We were on the frontier. And that's where Gerry wanted to be, I guess."

In the spring of 1948, Gerry graduated with a Bachelor of Applied Science degree in aeronautical engineering and signed on with A.V. Roe aircraft company near Toronto. His job was on the low end of the aircraft design division, and he found it dull; by early summer he wanted out. And his luck was in.

Patterson had been lobbying the Canadian government to finance supersonic research. If they didn't, he argued, the nation's defence and aviation industries would be left behind and the country would suffer a scientific brain drain. Canada should not wait for the United States or Britain to pass on technology, it should make its own breakthroughs. The Americans were experimenting with rocketry and missiles. Space exploration was being talked about seriously. And in the aftermath of war Canada was winding down what had been a prosperous and profitable defence industry. There was a need to generate new jobs.

After wavering for months, the government's Defence Research Board came up with a modest $350,000 grant to establish the Institute of Aerophysics, under Patterson, at the University of Toronto. The goal was to investigate supersonic aerodynamics. Patterson decided that the way to run his institute was to take on four new graduate students a year, pay them $40 a week, and set them free to work on major research projects. In effect, they would teach themselves along the way, doing pioneering work. And the institute was to operate year-round, with no long summer break. Gerry applied.

The Defence Research Board was careful with its money and controlled the selection committee, which judged Gerry to be too young, too immature, and too much of a risk. At 20 he still looked 16. But Patterson insisted. He wanted Bull, and years later he said why: "As an undergraduate he was a better than average student, not outstanding. But he had shown tremendous energy. He had terrific ability to stick with a tough job and get things done."[1] Bull was accepted.

He started his PhD programme in September 1948. His assignment was to investigate the aerodynamic characteristics of supersonic wind tunnels. But first, he had to build one.

The rather grandly named Institute of Aerophysics was tucked away in the university's civil engineering building. Patterson had a corner office, while Bull and another student, Douglas H. Henshaw, were given Room 36, next door. It was in this room that they started building a small wind tunnel as a prototype for the big one to come. That autumn was spent labouring over the mathematics, and by December they knew what was needed and began ordering the hardware. Some of it had to be specially made. The pieces came in gradually, over a period of weeks. At last Bull and Henshaw began to fit them all together. They worked all day, and it was almost midnight when they realized that the tunnel was going to be about two and a half metres long, at least 30 centimetres longer than they had estimated. Normally, that wouldn't have mattered. But Room 36 was so narrow that the tunnel wouldn't fit. A redesign would take another week. Bull was in a hurry. By twisting the tunnel around in one section of the room it could be made to fit if a 25-centimetre hole was knocked through the wall of Patterson's office. Bull picked up a large hammer.

When Patterson arrived for work later that morning he found a wind-tunnel valve sticking through the wall where his desk had been. Says the professor: "That was just the start. I was only beginning to get acquainted with Gerry Bull."

While the first small tunnel was a success, it was too limited to use as a true prototype, and Bull and Henshaw immediately started work on a larger version. This time they ordered a metal tank about two metres high and one metre in diameter to act as an air storage chamber. When it arrived, it took the two students only minutes to discover that the metal shop had made it a fraction too wide. The difference in size didn't affect its scientific value, but it wouldn't fit through the door of Room 36. Bull wouldn't consider waiting for another tank. He left it in the hall for the rest of the day and returned that night with a hammer and chisel to tear down the door frame. The building manager was furious, but Patterson made no comment on the incident.

A few days later Bull and Henshaw asked the professor if they could make a few more adjustments to his office wall. By now things had gone so far that Patterson just nodded. He arrived next day to find that Bull had been back in the night with his hammer and had knocked down the entire wall. Patterson no longer had an office. It would have taken more than a professor's private sanctuary to stop Bull. When faced with adversity he would improvise; when up against walls, he knocked them down. That's what later made Bull so valuable to Saddam Hussein. He had a "stop at nothing" quality that was eventually refined to the point that it proved fatal. But that was years ahead. As a student, his attitude served only to make him a star. Stories soon began to circulate about his wind tunnel, which was becoming so big that the professor had to climb over the structure to reach his desk in the far corner of what had once been his office.

And then the testing started. Patterson was almost deafened several times a day by the screech of air shooting through the wind tunnel at twice the speed of sound. One morning he climbed over the wind tunnel as usual, found his desk, sat down – and jumped up with a start. His chair was covered in splintered glass. During the night Bull and Henshaw had pushed the tunnel up to three times the speed of sound and exploded the observation windows in the side. Patterson found glass chips among his books and papers for months afterwards.

But the prototype worked, and in the summer of 1949 Gerry presented a thesis and was awarded a Master of Science degree for his efforts.

In August 1949, George Toussaint Bull died in Trenton at the age of 75. Gordon Bull called Gerry and asked him to attend the funeral. All ten children were there. It was the first time Gerry had seen most of them since the family had been broken up sixteen years before. "He was very quiet," remembers Gordon.

After the funeral, when the family gathered, Bernice stalked up to Gerry and in a loud voice asked him what it was like to be a LaBrosse. The LaBrosses, she said, had always been down on the Bulls, and now he was one of them – a traitor. She asked how could he stay in Aunt Edith's house after all she had said about the Bulls – just because she was able to pay for his education. Gordon recalls: "It was terrible. Bernice tore right into him. We were all trying to stop her, but it did no good. Gerry didn't respond. He just stood there and took it all. But he must have been hurt."

Gerry never got in touch with or saw his brothers and sisters again.

Back in Toronto, Patterson presented a glowing progress report to the Defence Research Board, and they persuaded the Royal Canadian Air Force to give the Institute of Aerophysics much larger quarters at Downsview Airport, north of Toronto. Office space would no longer be a problem.

Undergraduate studies had been demanding, but graduate work at the break-neck pace that Gerry Bull was setting was unhealthy. He became nervous and jumpy as he drove himself even harder. Patterson frowned on girlfriends as an unnecessary distraction, and the all-male institute had a priestly tone. Friends can remember Gerry going out on only one date. And she remembers quite well where he took her – to see the wind tunnel he was working on.

In fall 1949, the institute began building a huge $200,000 tunnel capable of producing air speeds up to seven times the velocity of sound (8,320 kilometres an hour). It was to be one of the biggest and most advanced of its kind. Bull was asked to design and perfect the test section where the highest air velocity had to be produced.

The tunnel's vacuum tank, which produces the supersonic air flow, was built of two-centimetre steel plate. A 12-metre sphere, it had to be built against the outside of the building. The observation windows on the sides of the wind tunnel were of three-centimetre-thick glass.

Late in the summer of 1950, the tunnel was nearing completion, and plans were made for a formal opening of the Institute of Aerophysics to be highlighted by a wind-tunnel demonstration on September 26. In addition to Canadian aeronautical and defence experts, officials were also to be present from Britain, the U.S.A., Australia, New Zealand and South Africa. Air Marshal W.A. Curtis of the RCAF would push the button and give the wind tunnel its first official test.

Patterson and his team worked night and day to complete the tunnel. At the same time, Bull was toiling on his PhD thesis, working around the clock either at the institute or at home.

It was about this time that Clare Eatock ran into Gerry Bull by chance in the university's student centre. "I hadn't seen him for about three years. There was a dramatic change. He had become quite driven. All of the fun that I remembered from our undergraduate days was gone. He was thin and drawn. But what I recall specifically is that his jacket was loaded down with pens and pencils and slide rules and paper, and the whole time we were talking his hands were moving over this jacket feeling the tools of the trade. He was quite nervous and quite distracted."

Three days before the scheduled opening of the institute, the wind tunnel was complete and ready for its first full-scale test. What happened next is illustrative of the pioneering nature of the venture. With the air screeching through, everyone eyed the observation windows. But no shock wave happened. The tunnel was falling short of even the speed of sound. Could their work, and the expenditure of close to $200,000, have been ruined by miscalculations?

Their best hope was that the packing that kept the wind-tunnel section airtight was leaking. Patterson, Bull and the rest of the team frantically began dismantling the tunnel. They had to remove more than four hundred nuts and bolts. And to their great relief they discovered a leak. It was nearly midnight by the time they had fixed the leak and put the apparatus back together. To pump out the vacuum sphere for another test would take an hour. Gerry Bull volunteered to stay and give the tunnel another test while the others went home to sleep. About 1 a.m., Gerry pushed the button for a second test. There was an ear-splitting shriek, a shock wave formed, and then there was an explosive crash and a couple of echoing thuds. The wind tunnel shook, and fell silent. Bull knew what had happened: two wooden supports inside the tunnel had been pulled loose. To repair the damage meant once again removing and replacing those four hundred nuts and bolts. And now Gerry was alone except for two machinists. The dignitaries would be arriving for the grand opening in another twelve hours.

They had just begun dismantling the tunnel when Kenneth F. Tupper, dean of the Engineering Department, walked in, dressed in a business suit. He had been driving home very late and had seen the institute lights on. Bull and the machinists were in overalls. The dean threw off his jacket, put on a smock and, when someone had to crawl into the tunnel to loosen bolts from the inside, insisted on doing it himself. By 5:30 a.m. the wooden blocks were securely replaced and the apparatus was back together. This time the tunnel worked perfectly.

That afternoon Air Marshall Curtis pushed the button for the tunnel's first official run. Nothing happened. Down near the front of the audience Gerry Bull started trembling. Patterson reached over and gave the button a harder poke. The switch had merely failed to make contact. This time the wind tunnel started up with a piercing whine.

Bull went back to work on his PhD thesis.

The institute was never told why the government was prepared to put so much cash into a wind tunnel. But Patterson knew. It had to do with weapons. For under a fog of secrecy, Canada was launching its own programme, code-named Velvet Glove, to manufacture an air-to-air guided missile meant to down Soviet bombers should they ever attack Canada. It was a hugely ambitious and expensive venture and would put Canadian science in direct competition with its allies in Britain and the U.S. In the grip of Cold War politics, Ottawa had decided that it needed its own deterrent against the threat of Soviet aggression.

With work going well, Patterson spent two weeks in July and August of 1950 at the top-secret headquarters of the Canadian Armament and Research Development Establishment (CARDE) at Valcartier, half an hour's drive north of Quebec City. He delivered a series of nine lectures on the problems of missiles travelling at supersonic speeds. And he received a lecture himself. Patterson was told that the Canadian government was sick of paying for the education of students who promptly left the country to work in the U.S.A. He was told that if even one of his new graduates from the institute did not enter government service, future grants to the institute might suffer. Patterson was familiar with the problem. The Canadian government at that time was paying less than half of the money being offered by American industry. Still, the message this time was grim.

On his return to Toronto, Patterson wrote a confidential report to J.J. Green, deputy director general at the Defence Research Board. Patterson's aim was to "formulate a sound basis for direct cooperation between CARDE and the Institute of Aerophysics". Quite clearly, Patterson was ready to tie his Institute very closely to the Canadian military establishment, the best source of research funds. Saying it was "very desirable that some of the students trained at the Institute should join the Defence Research Board staff", he recommended a starting salary for them of $4,500, instead of the usually $3,000.

Patterson ended by specifically recommending Gerry Bull, who was to receive his PhD in the spring: "He has done a large part of the design of our supersonic tunnel and has done research in non-stationary flow with the shock tube. In other words he knows both wind tunnels and ballistic ranges. He is an extremely able experimentalist and has an excellent knowledge of theory." Patterson also made clear just what project he thought Bull should be working on. He wrote: "We must obtain comparisons between wind-tunnel and free-flight tests in order to accurately assess the results from the tunnels." Further, he recommended that Bull start work at once on a part-time basis.[2] (Bull later recorded in his private papers that it was put to him that if he refused to work on the government's new weapons system, the institute would suffer. Anxious to please, Bull agreed.)

In his response, Green dismissed the idea of paying high starting salaries. But he agreed wholeheartedly to a close working relationship.[3] And that is why Bull's work on the aerodynamic characteristics of an intermittent supersonic wind tunnel was interrupted that December. The Defence Research Board decided to act. Dr. Gordon Watson, the board's top electronics scientist, was Velvet Glove's chief project engineer, and he needed an aerodynamicist experienced in supersonics to design the shape of the missile's body, wings and control fins. Watson was worried that Bull was too young to direct a team of scientists much older than himself. But, after a series of long interviews, Bull had the job.

Still working on his thesis, and still officially a full-time student, he began to devote what was left of his energy to Velvet Glove, spending weeks at a time at CARDE headquarters. He completed the thesis in March and formally joined the CARDE staff on April 1, the twentieth anniversary of his mother's death. On May 3, 1951, the University of Toronto awarded him a PhD. He had just turned 23 and was the youngest student ever to be granted a doctorate by the university. Bull lost a lot of weight during his last year at the Institute of Aerophysics and by his own reckoning was close to a nervous breakdown.

4

NOTHING in his life had prepared Gerry for the hard-drinking scientists of war he encountered at the Canadian Armament and Research Development Establishment. He was shy and nervous, thin, almost frail, and socially gauche. The immense effort he had put into his PhD work had left him jittery. His smile was unsure, and an engineer who worked with him at the time remembers that he "blinked a lot". At 22, he looked 18, and it was a constant source of embarrassment to him that every time he went for a beer the barman asked him for proof of age.

As Bull was initiated into the mysteries of weapons design he was also briefed on the secret history of North American military development. The Canadian version he heard had a thinly disguised anti-American slant. He was told that, starting in the late 1930s, Britain had systematically transferred its wartime technology to Canada. Laboratories specializing in propellents, artillery, radar and aircraft design had been established to work closely with similar laboratories in Britain. Even though Canadian defence scientists were recruited, there just weren't enough of them sufficiently trained to run the new establishments. Thus, on a technical and scientific level the labs were at first staffed almost entirely from Britain. The idea was for the Canadian-based labs to continue the war effort should the British Isles fall to the Nazis. This massive technology transfer meant that for a time Canada housed a more advanced weapons structure than the United States – at least until the end of 1941, when Washington entered the war and was given access.

With the end of the war in Europe in 1945, Bull was told, the Americans had taken advantage of a ruined Germany and a bankrupt Britain by pillaging technology and scientists from both. Over the next five years, leading up to Bull's arrival at CARDE, the Americans had marched ahead in almost every field, refusing to share their new technology while playing down developments in allied countries. By now most of the British scientists had left Canada for home, and the weapons laboratories were struggling to keep going with domestically trained personnel. Still, there was some surprising progress, including work on the Avro Arrow jet fighter, a plane that promised to be the finest interceptor in the world.

Canada, with what Bull later called its "ingrained national inferiority complex", was undergoing a spurt of national pride, which almost inevitably involved anti-Americanism. The role of country cousin is always hard to live with.

Valcartier in 1950, before urban sprawl reached Quebec City, was discreetly situated away from the rush of commerce and traffic. Canada's largest province, Quebec is seven times the size of Great Britain. And most of the province was empty of population, making it an ideal place for classified military research. The boom of the big guns at Valcartier disturbed more moose and wolves than people. In some ways it was almost idyllic. The rolling Quebec countryside with its high pine and hardwood forests held a constantly changing beauty. And Quebec City, with its old stone churches and squares, its narrow winding streets and superb restaurants, offered a romance and European flavour unmatched in North America. In Kingston and Toronto, Bull had heard no more French than if he'd been living in England. But in Quebec City, where he found a room on the third floor of a boarding house, little English was spoken. That is, beyond the Top Secret signs, the walls and the high wire fences that surrounded CARDE. For CARDE was an almost exclusively English-speaking enclave. "Only the janitors spoke French," says a regular visitor from that time.

Among the young engineers at Valcartier was an exciting and exacting spirit of competition and experiment. First, they wanted to show the Americans that despite their shoestring budget they were just as good. Second, they wanted to prove to the older British scientists still in charge of many divisions that they were ready to take over.

At the same time, Bull and his friends were isolated in a tiny technological ghetto. Their French was of the "*la plume de ma tante*" variety, and this created bonds that would not normally have been there. They were a hard-working, hard-driving crew who, given the least excuse, were ready to throw all-night parties. Bull soon learned to down alcohol with the best of them.

Bull's boarding house was within mortar range of the Plains of Abraham, where General Wolfe died in 1759, and in the early days, while he was still clinging to some of his solitary ways, he used to wander across the battlefield on weekends replaying the strategy that led to a British victory. Late at night, over the Manhattans he had taken to drinking, Bull told friends how much he admired Wolfe, not so much for the general's military prowess, but more for the way he chose to lead his army flotilla upstream while reciting Gray's *Elegy*. "He was a good judge of poetry," said Bull, who himself took to reciting poetry as he worked. He would amuse his fellow engineers when it was time to go home with lines from Longfellow's "The Day Is Done".

> And the night shall be filled with music,
> And the cares, that infest the day,
> Shall fold their tents, like the Arabs,
> And as silently steal away.

Through that first winter at Valcartier, Bull worked long hours on the supersonic stability calculations that would lead to a missile airframe for Velvet Glove. Working with Frank Pruden, formerly of the Royal Aircraft Establishment at Farnborough, Bull perfected a set of theoretical equations that indicated Velvet Glove could hold its body angle of attack while meeting guidance requirements. Suddenly, CARDE had a credible project. At least on paper they had the physics and the figures to bridge the shock waves of explosive force that bar the transition from subsonic to supersonic speeds.

The wings and the control fins that provide stability and precise manoeuvrability were perfected.

Velvet Glove was two metres long, 20 centimetres in diameter, weighed 158 kilograms, and its four rectangular wings each had an 82-centimetre span. The range was an impressive 4,500 metres. It was propelled by a rocket motor that burned solid fuel and was guided by radar.[1]

During 1952, his first full year on staff at CARDE, Bull won three promotions, an almost unheard-of personal climb. At university he had been a loner. At CARDE he was leading a team, and he discovered another natural talent: he could inspire people to do the highest-quality work, beyond what they would ordinarily achieve. There was almost something religious about it.

Away from the personal strictures of Aunt Edith, the Jesuits and Dr. Patterson, Gerry Bull suddenly realized that he was free. When it came to science, the only person he had to please was himself. Operating within small technical groups, he could evangelize like a latter-day Elmer Gantry. And his genius lay in using his scalpel-sharp intellect to dissect a problem of physics, point at the solution and then inspire others to do the detailed work that would achieve what he wanted. He did not have the patience for detail. The minutiae always fell to someone else.

He had extraordinary mental energy. His scientific thinking was highly imaginative and unrestricted by conventions or rules. Gerry Bull rarely failed. It was, after all, by success that he won the acceptance and the praise that he craved. He lived through his work and his ego soared.

In its earliest days, CARDE had concentrated on artillery research, and there was a major stock of field weapons on hand. By the time Bull arrived, interest in conventional ordnance had dropped dramatically, and it was generally believed that rockets and guided missiles were making field pieces redundant. There was, however, a 120-metre-long tunnel, or range as it was called, from which the air could be pumped to provide a simulation of the atmosphere at nearly any point. Artillery shells had been shot through this tunnel so that instruments and cameras could record their behaviour in flight and it could be determined just how the shock waves produced by their speed were affecting their stability at varied altitudes.

Bull was asked to provide a quick check on Velvet Glove's aerodynamic stability and drag before it moved into expensive prototype production. Normally testing would have been done with models in a supersonic wind tunnel. Not only did CARDE not have such a tunnel, there wasn't the budget or the time to buy one, and the tunnel at the institute in Toronto wasn't suitable. Still, there was growing pressure to start free-flight full-scale launches of Velvet Glove. The Cold War was ever more bitter. And in the U.S., Wernher von Braun was urging Washington to send spaceships to the moon and Mars. Ottawa wanted to show that it hadn't been left entirely in the dust.

Under enormous pressure, the scientists were nonetheless reluctant to launch Velvet Glove without the aerodynamic testing of models. CARDE turned to Bull. And for the first time in his life, Bull began to examine the potential of big guns. He decided that it might be possible to turn the wind-tunnel idea on its head. Instead of having a stationary model with air being blown past it at supersonic speeds, he would use a gun to shoot a model through the range. The actual model would move, instead of the air. Bull was familiar with the old artillery trick of using a sabot. A sabot is a wood or metal band placed around a narrow projectile to make that projectile fit a gun barrel whose bore is too wide. The band drops off when the projectile leaves the barrel. There are, of course, technical problems, not the least of which is finding a way to discard the sabot as it leaves the barrel while ensuring that it does not interfere with the projectile's flight.

Bull built a scale model of Velvet Glove, fitted it with a sabot and fired it from a smooth-bore artillery piece. The sabot was designed to fall away just before the free-flying model entered the 120-metre-long test range. The experiment allowed the model to be photographed as it travelled at supersonic speeds through the range, and it gave CARDE all the information needed to go ahead with a full-scale launch.

Bull described the development in a lecture delivered at the University of Toronto: "The scheme was pursued on a try-and-see basis and in view of the great success achieved, it was developed to the status of a major data-gathering facility."[2] In other words, Bull's method of testing the aerodynamic characteristics of models by firing them from guns became an experimental standard. Over the next few years he had two more ranges built and began developing hypervelocity gas guns so that he could shoot models through them at ever-greater speeds.

In the summer of 1952, Charles Pope, the Defence Research Board's public relations officer in Ottawa, called Bull to say that *Maclean's*, Canada's major monthly magazine, wanted to do a full-length feature on Velvet Glove using Bull as a human interest angle. Gordon Watson, Velvet Glove's chief project engineer, urged Bull to cooperate and, though unsure, he agreed. The piece appeared in March 1953, and it came as a shock. The story of Velvet Glove was secondary. What emerged was a flattering portrait of Bull under the headline, "GERRY BULL BOY ROCKET SCIENTIST." It pictured Bull as a comic-book hero out to save the Western world from the Communists. Baby-faced Bull, the nation's chief aerodynamicist at 24, was a good story. But for Gerry the article was, as he said later, "an unmitigated disaster," for it won him a reputation within the Canadian civil service as a self-serving publicity seeker.

Bull had cooperated with *Maclean's* at the request of his boss, and he'd had no idea how the story would come out. Nevertheless, the publicity-hound charges stuck. And later, reporters wanting a science quote knew to call Gerry, who talked in colourful, often exaggerated terms. At scientific conventions, Bull's papers were more likely than those of his colleagues to be used by the press because his name was known and readers were interested in him. All of this served to increase antagonism in Ottawa that eventually spread to Valcartier. But it didn't stop his promotion. In July 1953 he was made a section head within the overall Aeroballistics Section at CARDE and appointed associate professor in charge of aerodynamics at Laval University.

While Bull was enormously confident in science, he was still shy when it came to the opposite sex, and he left himself little time for dating, even though, as he told a friend back in Toronto, "The Quebec girls are so good looking they knock you over." But in August 1953, a young engineer at Valcartier asked Gerry to go on a double date with two French-Canadian sisters, Noemie and Suzanne Gilbert, who not only were beauties but also spoke English. The girls' father, Dr. Paul Gilbert, a wealthy physician, wouldn't let them go out alone – they had to chaperone each other. They lived in a magnificent house just across the bridge from Quebec City in Charny.

Gerry claimed later that it was love at first sight, and he dated Noemie through the winter.

Mimi, as she was known, was from a warm, close family. They were cultured and strictly Catholic, and although Mimi was a talented painter, her father refused to allow her to take art courses because he feared artists were not suitable company for a young lady. Dr. Gilbert kept horses, and she was an excellent rider. A slim and pretty brunette, she had grace and style. She had a ready smile and laugh and a sense of adventure. Although she had led a sheltered life, she was full of fun. Everything about her appealed to the romantic side of Gerry that had known so little expression. She was the perfect complement to his life.

Dr. Gilbert was not pleased. He wanted his daughter to marry a French-Canadian, someone from the same background.

"My English wasn't too good and he had no French at all, but we laughed a lot and that seemed to be more important than words," says Mimi. "His childhood memories were so painful that he couldn't talk about them. He was wounded in that way, and I didn't press him with questions. He read a lot of poetry to me. I liked that a lot."

They were engaged before Valentine's Day and married in July 1954. Aunt Edith and Uncle Phil were guests of honour. Along with Jesse and Bob Keele from Kingston, they were the only "family" that Gerry invited. He couldn't invite his brothers and sisters, he told Mimi, because they were strangers. The gap had grown too great. But not inviting the Bull family only made matters worse. When they heard about the wedding they wondered if Gerry had become "too good" for them – he being a scientist while they remained "ordinary working people". But although Gerry Bull had many faults – arrogance, impatience and vanity among them – he was never a snob.

Gerry's loyalty to the LaBrosses was demonstrated in the *Maclean's* article, where he said: "I have no recollection of my real mother, but no boy ever had finer parents than I had in Aunt Edith and Uncle Phil."

The young couple honeymooned in Bermuda. Back in Quebec City, they rented a ranch-style home, a converted stone barn, on Dr. Gilbert's estate, and started to throw regular parties. Mimi decorated the house with flair and fashion. She dressed in similar spirit. And Gerry Bull became not just a scientific but also a social force at Valcartier.

Acceptance into the Gilbert family did not come quickly. Dr. Gilbert spoke no English, and his communication with Gerry was always through translation and was generally cool and stilted. Painfully, slowly, Gerry learned French. In his way he became fluent, although his accent and usage were often bizarre. He believed his French was near perfect. It was a forgivable misapprehension. Gerry and Mimi always spoke English together but French when the Gilbert family was present.

As the months passed, Dr. Gilbert began to enjoy Gerry, and his affection grew into love and understanding. He saw the vulnerabilities and played to Gerry's strengths. The two became very close, not as father and son but rather as friends and equals.

Meanwhile, the team working on Velvet Glove grew from about five scientists including Bull, to some six hundred specialists spread throughout the Royal Canadian Air Force and industry. The government had spent about $24 million on the programme, including $7 million on Bull's aerodynamic test ranges and laboratory facilities. Three hundred of the missiles had been made and fired, most of them over a new test site at Cold Lake, Alberta.[3]

Dr. Alfred Ratz, a computer scientist who worked on Velvet Glove, remembers that Bull was in advance of the rest of the team. Says Ratz: "He was not someone who could just sit back and wait. He continuously bubbled with ideas." And so in his spare time, Gerry designed his own missile, a next-generation missile to follow Velvet Glove. Ratz says Bull did not stop at just the paper design. He began to get missile bodies built and taken out to the test range and fired. "Of course he could not get this done officially. He had to work surreptitiously." First, Bull put together his own manufacturing facility consisting of an old steel shed with a dirt floor behind the office building. Ratz says it was staffed by soldiers from a nearby Canadian Army infantry training establishment. The Army rewarded soldiers for jobs well done by lending them to Gerry for two weeks at a time. Says Ratz: "These were only infantry soldiers, not skilled craftsmen." Their tools and materials were limited to those that could be bought at any hardware store, yet, according to Ratz, they produced missile test bodies that performed as well as or better than the official missile.

These new missiles had a configuration that was radically different from that of Velvet Glove, or indeed of any missiles anywhere. Says Ratz: "The work is still classified, but I can reveal that his method of construction led to a final product that cost only a small fraction of the dollars needed to build a missile body in the American style. Bull felt he had demonstrated the evil of development via a large incompetent bureaucracy and that the only sensible way to managing weapons development was via a small aggressive and flexible team of technically competent and technically involved individuals."

The end to Bull's missile came in typically dramatic fashion, when the Duke of Edinburgh was invited to visit Canada and tour CARDE. The Canadian government asked Bull to prepare a Velvet Glove display. Says Ratz: "Gerry decided to reveal his new missile at this display and push Velvet Glove into the background." He prepared charts showing missile performance and comparing his missile with other air-to-air missiles in the U.S.A. Other charts showed the cost advantages and the superior development schedule of his type of management.

Ratz believes that the preparation of the display revealed several characteristics of Gerry Bull: his love of weaponry design and development; his belief in the primacy of the technical side of a project; his unmitigated courage to press on when he felt he was right; and his belief in human nature – he felt that the big shots were as interested in weapons development and as patriotic as he was, and would be moved to react in a positive way. "He really believed that such a stunt would actually break through the fog of politics and bureaucracy and reach the conscience and consciousness of the powers that be."

During the Duke's tour, one cabinet minister turned to the head of the Defence Research Board and said: "I didn't know we were developing another missile." Gerry found that really amusing.

To the amazement of the older scientists at CARDE, Bull was not fired. "But," says Ratz, "word went out from Ottawa to all of us to stay away from him."

In mid-1954 the Soviets scuttled Velvet Glove without firing a shot. They did it by introducing supersonic bombers that flew so fast the Canadian missile probably couldn't catch them. In addition, the defence mavens in Ottawa were coming to the conclusion that the Soviets no longer needed to send bombers to attack North America, for they would soon have intercontinental ballistic missiles.

Velvet Glove was abandoned.

5

UNDER BULL, CARDE'S Aerophysics Wing was developing an international reputation, and in the absence of a major project Bull continued his own private experiments with guns. The U.S. Advanced Research and Planning Agency negotiated with Ottawa to post American scientists to Valcartier, in part because they wanted to keep abreast of what Bull was doing. The Americans brought with them their own budget, and Bull quickly discovered that whereas it was nearly impossible to get funds from Ottawa for weapons experiments that had not been approved by a civil service committee, the Americans would finance almost anything. He developed a system of bypassing Ottawa and going directly to the U.S. for research money.[1]

His ties to the U.S. grew stronger still in the spring of 1956, when Bull was invited to an ammunition symposium at Picatinny Arsenal, near Dover, New Jersey. Dr. Charles Murphy, a rising military scientist with the U.S. Army, delivered a paper on ballistics, and the two scientists met that night at the bar. Canadian military officers gathered around Bull while their American equivalents flocked about Murphy. They had a lot in common; as well, both were Catholics and both had attended Jesuit high schools. But that night they were set up as rivals, not least in the drinking of Manhattans.

The drinking session was significant for two reasons. First, Bull saw for the first time that he was a force in his own right on the Canadian military front. The senior officers had made him their champion at the bar, and they had openly boasted about his accomplishments. Tucked away in Valcartier, Bull hadn't realized that his reputation had spread. Second, he had made a valuable friend and contact in Murphy. Here was someone who could link him to Pentagon contracts. "We resonated immediately," says Murphy of that first meeting. "We were two young Turks out to do great things in ballistics."

In October and November 1956, Soviet tanks rolled into Hungary to crush the popular revolt. The Canadian government of Louis St. Laurent admitted 32,000 Hungarian refugees in 1957. Many were young and well educated and their arrival reinforced the anti-Communist feelings of Canada in general and of Gerry Bull in particular. But when Bull talked about being anti-Communist – and he talked about it a lot – he did not just mean that he was against the Soviet empire. For he associated communism with self-serving bureaucracies everywhere. Gerry couldn't abide big government, which he saw as scandalously wasteful and guilty of scuttling most good ideas by taking so long to approve them. He also believed that politicians appointed their unqualified friends and supporters to important top jobs. He referred to many of the Ottawa officials in charge of research grants as "cocktail party scientists". And Gerry Bull did not keep these thoughts to himself. He voiced them loudly and clearly and often.

The friendship with Murphy grew rapidly, and the two scientists began sharing their research. Murphy was frequently at Valcartier and Bull travelled south to the Aberdeen Proving Ground, just north of Baltimore, Maryland, almost as often. "I was amazed when I first started going up to Valcartier," says Murphy. "Bull's bosses were incompetent – there was an inversion of abilities. That's not unusual in government service. What *was* unusual, however, was that Gerry was so outspoken about it. He had no patience with incompetence."

The Bull's first child, Philippe, to be known as Pilpot, was born in June 1955, and Michel, nicknamed Bako, followed in November 1956. Stephen, who became Tepi, arrived in April 1959. Bull doted on his children. "He was very good and open at showing affection," says Mimi. "With his background and everything, he might not have been like that. But he hugged them and cuddled them and he always seemed to have his arms around them. He was not restrained at all. And he was the same with all children, just very warm.'' She adds: "He had such a great need to express this warmth. And his own childhood was so cold. It must have been torture.''

As the babies grew, Gerry and Mimi continued to speak English together but decided French would be the first language at home. Gerry spoke nothing but French to his children in private. Even in his most intimate conversations with them, he spoke his fractured French, though it does not seem to have been a barrier. (In later life his children's English was better than his French.)

The Bull household was closely tuned to scientific advances, and it was thrown into a great state of excitement on October 4, 1957, when the U.S.S.R. launched *Sputnik I* and opened the space age. Bull was one of the first to see that Moscow's ability to launch a satellite also meant it could fire intercontinental ballistic missiles. Quickly he switched his energies to finding ways first to detect an incoming missile and then to destroy it before it could detonate over North America. Now he had the big project he had been looking for since the death of Velvet Glove.

He was sure that as a missile re-entered the earth's atmosphere it would create some kind of "signature", a shock wave that it might be possible to detect and track. That would be easier, said Bull, than trying to find the missile itself, which would be rather like trying to see a dime in the sky over Montreal with a telescope in Toronto. And so he set out to discover the kind of shock wave a missile would produce.

What he needed was a gun that would shoot a replica Soviet warhead through a range at about 5,500 metres per second, the approximate speed of an incoming ballistic missile. Once this allowed him to find the "signature", he reasoned, he would need an even bigger, more powerful gun to destroy the missile. He developed a plan for that too. His idea was to use the biggest artillery piece he could find as a sort of super shotgun that would fire huge amounts of shrapnel into space, right into the path of the incoming missile. The velocity would be so great that contact with even one scrap of shrapnel would destroy the missile.

Bull argued that the system could be perfected so that specific centres such as large cities could be "rendered immune against enemy attack". He added: "The whole country cannot be defended but specific centres can be – to such an extent that all attacking missiles can be destroyed before they can reach their target."[2] When Murphy visited Bull in late 1957, he found that "Gerry had developed some very fast light gas guns to get velocities like 20,000 feet a second. Other laboratories were doing it too, he wasn't unique, but he was further along than most."

The Pentagon was fascinated by Bull's research and gave him all the encouragement he needed. By now he had far more fans south of the border than he had in Canada.

But all of this was overshadowed in Canada on March 25, 1958, when the first and only Canadian-built supersonic fighter-interceptor, the Avro Arrow, lifted off on its maiden flight from Malton Airport, just outside Toronto. It would be difficult to overstate the pride and dignity this event gave to Canadian military science. John Edwin Evans, an engineer who worked on the engine, recalled thirty years later, "The employees all went out to watch the take-off. Our eyes were so darn full of tears we could hardly see the plane. We were so proud." Over the next few months the Arrow was flown at nearly twice the speed of sound.

On April 22, 1958, nearly a month after the Arrow's first flight, Bull told the *Montreal Star* that he was about to start testing instrument-bearing projectiles that could be the forerunners of a Canadian satellite. He said that such a satellite would have two objectives: a study of the infrared radiation emitted by the sun and by air molecules on the fringe of outer space, and a study of the heating a missile warhead undergoes when it re-enters the earth's atmosphere. Both projects, he said, were linked to a major study underway at Valcartier aimed at developing a reliable defence against intercontinental ballistic missiles. Bull said that Canada's satellite would be about 15 centimetres in diameter and would use a unique launching system involving a gun. He stressed that a satellite programme was not actually underway, but that the hardware for launching one either existed or was in the planning stage. Bull explained that he already had at Valcartier a hydrogen-fuelled gun that could fire small projectiles at 11,000 kilometres an hour; and he was building another hydrogen gun that would fire instrument-carrying projectiles at speeds of up to 27,000 kilometres an hour. Although Canada had never announced plans to launch a satellite, Bull was sure that tests conducted at Valcartier were intended to be backed up by full-scale firings. All of the tests, and indeed the overall Valcartier programme, were aimed at developing a defence against intercontinental ballistic missiles. Thus, Bull argued, it would make sense to launch a satellite for a single orbit around the world, say from a 160-kilometre altitude, so that its re-entry into the earth's atmosphere could be studied. For only then could the burning of the satellite, to be thought of as a simulated missile, be understood.

Bull's interview caused an uproar. For one thing, he was leaking top-secret information. For another, the classified calculations he had made to show that the gun launching of a satellite might be possible were highly speculative. Most of the other scientists at CARDE didn't believe the idea would work. Prime Minister John Diefenbaker stated that his government had no intention of undertaking a satellite project, and Defence Minister George Pearkes said it was the first he had ever heard of Bull's satellite plans. He added that neither a programme nor any money for a satellite programme would be considered that year. As head of Defence Research, Pearkes said he would launch an investigation. He was embarrassed and, more to the point, Diefenbaker was embarrassed. Bull was telephoned that afternoon and ordered to be in Ottawa the next day to "explain himself". The last plane had already left, however, and Bull had to drive most of the night to be in place on the carpet next morning.[3]

At the balling-out session, conducted by senior mandarins, Bull said that his contacts in the U.S. had personally promised him that they would make available one of their 21-metre-high Redstone ballistic missiles. Bull said that he could quickly build a 4.5-metre oxygen-hydrogen gun specially designed to be carried in the rocket's nose. The rocket would carry the gun to an altitude of about 250 kilometres, where the gun would be fired, propelling a small Canadian satellite into space at an acceleration of about a million Gs (a million times the pull of gravity). This, he said, would easily give the satellite orbital speed of 29,000 kilometres an hour.

The mandarins were furious that Bull would have the audacity to make deals with the U.S. without first consulting Ottawa. They told Bull that Diefenbaker had no intention of investing in a satellite, that the whole idea was ridiculous and that he should return to Valcartier never to mention satellites again without first getting clearance.

Bull was more angry than disappointed. Here he was offering Canada a way to launch a satellite at very little cost and the prime minister wouldn't even listen. The niceties of protocol didn't interest Bull, and he failed to see why anyone was upset by lack of consultation.

By now Frank Hubbard, the Second World War veteran Bull had met in his undergraduate days, was also working at CARDE, as an engineer. Says Hubbard: "Bull had changed a lot. He was no longer the timid little mouse. He had put on weight and filled out and he was married to a beautiful woman. He drank quite a bit, he loved parties and he was really outspoken." Yet Gerry was also developing a darker side. Hubbard remembers: "You would go into his office right after someone else and you would be told what sort of an SOB that guy was. You sort of got the feeling that you were his confidant, but then you wondered what he said to the guy who came in after you." Still, Hubbard joined Bull's wing and became his chief engineer. He recalls: "Gerry was the sort of scientist who wanted to make things go faster and better. He wasn't really interested in where the things were going."

On February 20, 1959, Diefenbaker abandonned the Avro Arrow. The government couldn't afford to continue with research and development on the project, which was still four years away from deployment. An estimated $300 million had already been spent, and it would have cost some $871 million more to complete it. Including development expenses, the Arrows would have cost $12 million each, about six times as much as contemporary U.S. aircraft. Diefenbaker had made the right economic decision, but it devastated the morale of the Canadian defence industry. For the next thirty years, Bull would lose his temper at the mere mention of

Diefenbaker's name. Bull built the Arrow up in his imagination and rhetoric to rank with the wonders of the world. Nearly 14,000 Canadians, many of them highly skilled engineers, were thrown out of work by the Arrow collapse. Among them was Bull's old university pal Colin Wrong, and Hubbard. Hubbard offered Wrong a job on Bull's staff, and Wrong started the next month. Bull assigned him to design guns.

Says Wrong: "Bull wanted a gun that would shoot a projectile at 12,000 metres a second. That's what meteorites are going at when they hit the atmosphere. The pseudo-scientific reason was to find out what would happen if a meteorite hit a spaceship some time in the future. The real reason was military. He was looking for ways to shoot down intercontinental ballistic missiles."

The party life continued. Florence Guy was a teenager whose father headed another wing at CARDE. She remembers: "You had this little group of English speakers who had formed strong social bonds. The place was full of eccentric, brilliant scientists who tended to be kind of awkward. But not Dr. Bull. He was very smooth. He had so much more charm than everybody else. As a young girl I thought he was handsome and there was an air of mystery about him. He had a very attractive wife and there was always a twinkle in his eye."

Says Wrong: "Gerry had this wonderful house with maids and fabulous furniture and everything. We thought his father-in-law was paying for it all. Gerry gave great parties, but he could be childish. I once saw him fix my wife a drink. He took an eight-ounce tumbler and put six ounces of rye in it and a couple of ice cubes then topped it off with ginger ale. Soon after, I had to take her home, sick. She didn't know what had hit her. Gerry thought it was a great joke. None of the women would touch anything that he poured for them."

On April 1, 1959, Bull was promoted again, to superintendent of the Aerophysics Wing, supervising nineteen professionals and twenty-four technicians and with complete responsibility for directing the aerophysics and aeromechanics research at CARDE. By this time he was being picked up for work each day in a chauffeured car. A note from his personnel record says: "To date Dr. Bull has recruited highly capable scientists and set up facilities which are unique in the Western World. As a result of the above, he has attracted international attention and CARDE has now a cooperative programme with the U.S. Army Rocket and Guided Missile Agency on the characteristics of re-entry nose cones. The progress to date has been most spectacular."

Still, opposition to the course Bull was taking began to heighten in Ottawa. To attain greater velocities and make his models travel as fast as spaceships, Bull was building bigger and bigger guns. By now he had a light gas gun, mounted on ten railway-carriage wheels, able to fire projectiles faster than 16,000 kilometres an hour.

But many in the science community felt that big guns were finished and that missiles and rockets were the only way to go. Bull, they said, was wasting time and money. Under attack, Bull was as petty as his detractors. He told anyone who would listen that officials at Valcartier spent 40 per cent of their time worrying about who had the largest desk.

Says Wrong: "It got so that everybody working for Gerry was hated at CARDE. If you just mentioned his name to people outside our group they would pretend to vomit. There were two reasons. First, they were full of envy. Second, he broke all the rules and got away with it."

While things were going seriously wrong with his bosses in Canada, Bull was becoming more and more the darling of the United States. His close friend Murphy made sure that all the right people knew every development. And there was strong interest in the range experiments showing the effects of re-entry on missile nose cones, the carbon-fibre caps that cover the nose or tip of missiles to protect them from excessive heat. Indeed, that interest grew so much that in March 1960 Lieutenant-General Arthur Trudeau, research and development chief of the U.S. Army, asked for an invitation to visit Valcartier. Trudeau's parents were from Quebec, and the general was entranced by French-Canadian culture. Gerry Bull turned on all of the charm, took the general home to meet Mimi and entertained him in style. Bull joked that Mimi spoke French with a Brooklyn accent, and that set Trudeau chortling.

Bull took Trudeau to Valcartier and demonstrated another breakthrough. Using his light gas gun, he fired a scientific "shell" at 9,000 metres a second through a 150-metre range in which air pressure was less than one-millionth of that at sea level. He was able to prove that throughout the flight the instruments inside the shell not only were working but were transmitting data, or telemetry as it is known, on speed and conditions. He had been able to design a shell that could cushion these delicate instruments and allow them to survive the vast forces involved in gun propulsion. The great advantage of using a gun rather than a rocket to send scientific instruments into the near atmosphere is one of cost; the potential savings were enormous. Trudeau was impressed by these extraordinary gun ideas and said that they seemed to come right out of a Jules Verne novel. That was hardly surprising, said Bull, because some of them did. Bull boasted that he had been inspired by Verne's idea of shooting a man from a cannon and sending him all the way to the moon. "That's not possible," said Bull, "but a great deal else is possible."

Trudeau still had difficulty believing Bull's figures and projections for a supergun. He returned to Washington and asked Murphy to check them out at the laboratories at the Aberdeen Proving Ground. Murphy soon reported that as far as he could tell, the figures were solid. Trudeau then told Murphy to "indicate" to Bull that should he ever leave CARDE, and should he want support for his supergun idea, Washington would be interested.

Meanwhile, Bull's situation at CARDE was becoming bitter. He was accused of being a self-promoter, the missile and satellite incidents had not been forgotten, and now he was said to be too close to the Americans.

Gerry Bull resigned from CARDE on February 15, 1961, giving three months' notice. His original letter of resignation took the form of a fierce attack on Canadian government policy, but Chief Superintendent J.J. Green persuaded him that the letter could only do him personal harm and that at least for the files he should be diplomatic. In the end Bull agreed and wrote that he was leaving "to broaden [his] experience and contacts in the non-defence scientific fields". It was his boast at the time that he was the highest-paid civil servant for his age in Canadian history: he was 33 and making nearly $17,000 a year.

Bull had arrived at CARDE as a wisp of a boy, politically and socially naive. He went there with a sense of duty, determined to help his country in the face of what he believed to be a Communist threat and to ensure that grants continued to flow to the Institute of Aerophysics. During his decade of government service, Bull changed in fundamental ways. The best thing that happened to him was Mimi. She, and her family, provided him with his first tension-free and happy home, and his marriage matured and polished him. But the hard knocks he had suffered along the way could not all be buffed smooth. He couldn't handle criticism and he never learned to separate public policy from personal attack. He took as a private affront the government's decision not to launch a satellite with a gun. Those who were not with him, he decided, were against him.

But if he had arrived at CARDE somewhat callow and without focus, he left with at least a veneer of sophistication and a very definite mission. He was determined to build that supergun and use it to put a satellite into orbit. His ego demanded no less.

PART III

His Dream, His Passion, His Delight

This alchemist with hollow cheeks
And sunken, searching eyes, who seeks
*   ... to find*
Some new enamel, hard and bright,
His dream, his passion, his delight.

"Kéramos"
Henry Wadsworth Longfellow

6

THE PRESSURE on Bull all came from within. Dr. Gilbert, his father-in-law, counselled him to go slow when he left CARDE and to take time to find the right next job. Through Charles Murphy and other contacts, Bull let it be known that he was available for consulting work. There were job offers in the U.S., including one to head up a laboratory for General Motors, but he didn't want to leave Quebec; his family ties had grown too strong. Also, the idea of launching a satellite with a gun was taking on great importance. He began to see it not just as a project but as a mission. The more Bull concentrated on his calculations, the more convinced he became that it would work. Moreover, the prospect was ideal for a country such as Canada, a nation with great technological sophistication but limited budget. For a fraction of the money the United States was spending on rocket launches, Bull was certain he could put satellites into orbit with a gun. The way Bull saw it, he was so obviously right that all he had to do was properly explain his idea to the right people in Ottawa and the finances would be forthcoming.

In April 1961, Mimi gave birth to the Bull's fourth son, Richard, to be known as Pooh.

That spring also brought with it a minor domestic crisis in the Bull household that made Gerry Bull realize the immensity of the chasm that separated his childhood from that of his sons. Six-year-old Philippe had been sick a lot that year, and the nuns at the private school the children attended suggested that he should repeat the grade. Michel, a year and a half younger, would be ready to move up in September. The question was, should the brothers continue through school in the same grade, or would Philippe suffer psychological damage knowing that his younger brother had caught up with him? Dr. Gilbert suggested that it might be best to hold Michel back. Dr. Bull argued that Michel's progress should not be hindered. In the end it was decided that the boys should continue together. Gerry Bull was struck by the stark contrast between the concern expressed and felt for his sons and the neglect he experienced in his own early childhood.

Bull had expected that after he left CARDE he would have time for reflection and renewal. The ideal job, he told friends, would be one in which he could work at big gun research while consulting for the Americans to make money.

But things happened fast, and the opportunity came in the form of Donald L. Mordell, dean of Engineering at McGill University in Montreal, one of the oldest and most respected institutions in North America.

Mordell, a tall, thin Cambridge-educated Englishman with a heavy moustache, was as taken with Bull as General Trudeau had been. A research engineer in gas dynamics, Mordell believed in Bull's dream. Not only did he think it would work, he was also inspired by the glitz and the glamour of the idea. He saw it as a high-profile venture that could bring international attention to his university, maybe make a lot of money, and perhaps just as important let him work with Bull, whose company he enjoyed immensely.

Aware of Bull's shortcomings and his inability to cope with authority and red tape, Mordell made Bull an offer. He would take him onto his engineering staff at McGill, ensure that gun research opportunities were made available, but handle all grant and government contacts himself.

On June 5, 1961, just a month after Bull had left CARDE, Dr. F. Cyril James, principal and vice chancellor of McGill University, announced that Gerald Bull had been appointed professor of engineering science in the Department of Mechanical Engineering. Bull's specialty, said Dr. James, would be the aerodynamics of aircraft and space vehicles at extreme speeds and altitudes. Bull was told that, at 34, he was the youngest full professor ever appointed by McGill.

At the time, Bull made no secret that he was doing "outside" work, and the trappings of his lifestyle – he was soon to buy hundreds of hectares of property – made it obvious that he was living well beyond the limits of a professor's salary. "In the first year after he left CARDE my father made about $100,000 as a consultant," says Michel.

Gerry Bull believed he was being well paid when he received $17,000 a year from the Canadian government in 1959. For what sort of work would someone pay him six times that amount in 1961? And who might that someone be?

It is reasonable to presume that he was consulted on weapons development, and that means, without much doubt, that the money came one way or another from Washington. Although it may have been funnelled through private industry as part of a larger contract, the Pentagon must have been the ultimate customer.

Nor is there much doubt about the nature of the work. Sources close to Bull say that he was paid to continue the theoretical calculations he developed at CARDE on what would happen to space vehicles as they re-entered the earth's atmosphere. These were the early days of the development of the intercontinental ballistic missile, or ICBM for short. The Titan ICBM underwent its first 5,000-kilometre tests that April, and after a string of failures, the Atlas achieved its first 15,000 kilometre flight that May. Testing was being planned for February 1961, for the first solid-fuel Minuteman missiles.

All of these missiles, the Titan, Atlas, Minuteman and others, were designed to travel through space until they were over their target; at that point they would re-enter the atmosphere at speeds in the range of 29,000 kilometres an hour. The friction caused by re-entry was known to generate enormous heat – enough to burn up the missile and destroy it. Thus, what was needed was a missile nose cone able to absorb the heat and emerge from re-entry with only minimal damage, so it would still allow the missile to reach its target accurately. Of all the problems with ICBMs, re-entry and nose-cone design were among the most difficult to solve. Nose cones were constantly being worked on and modified.

The United States had its own scientists engaged on these problems, yet Bull's approach was considered different and valuable. For he was basing his calculations on his experimental studies of projectiles – projectiles that had been fired from guns down the tunnel, or range, at CARDE at speeds approaching 29,000 kilometres an hour. Says one person who worked with Bull at the time: "It was always very tempting to buy Gerry's studies because he would take the theories and extrapolate." Bull's studies would conclude with imaginative suggestions for future work. Where most scientists were cautious and reluctant to project beyond where hard data would take them, Bull was adventurous and ready to predict the outcome of any given hypothesis. And he had an uncanny knack of getting it right. In the tight world of science, this fostered further jealousies and led to anonymous but damaging criticisms to the effect that Bull was reckless and given to guessing. And the truth is that he was definitely prone to selling a lot of sizzle along with his steak. Whatever the ethics of that might be, it led to Bull becoming a respected pioneering authority on ballistic missile nose cones. The U.S. shared its early technology with him to help guide his work.

On another front, the U.S. Army passed a contract to Bull at McGill allowing him to continue studying the effects on incoming ICBMs of pellets fired from a supergun. Aware that the university would not want to become involved in foreign military research, the Army disguised the project to make it look like part of a space-travel programme.[1]

Bull was given offices in an old engineering building on McGill's downtown campus, and in September 1961 he opened a postgraduate research programme on hypervelocity impact, even bringing a small gas gun with him. He began using the gun on weekends, when there were the fewest people around. "He was using a hypervelocity gun to shoot pellets into tanks of liquid oxygen," recalls Professor Sannu Molder, another teacher at McGill. "One weekend his gun combusted and shook the entire building. They needed a thirty-man cleaning crew to clear up all the dust from other offices."

The experiment interrupted by the gun accident was part of Bull's work on the anti-missile device. Bull's findings and his conclusions for this device were for the most part mothballed when the U.S. signed a treaty with the Soviet Union to ban anti-missile weapons in 1972. However, his work was dusted off and reviewed in 1983 when President Ronald Reagan decided to develop a near-perfect shield against a Soviet missile attack: the Strategic Defense Initiative (SDI), or Star Wars. While these later discussions on Bull's work remain classified, it is significant that in 1991, when much of SDI has been scrapped, one of the few remaining SDI projects being worked on by the Lawrence Livermore Weapons Laboratory in the U.S. bears a striking resemblance to Bull's ideas of the late 1950s and early 1960s.

In June 1961, Bull rented a ten-room ranch-style house in the Montreal suburb of St. Bruno, and Mimi moved with the children from Quebec City, leaving quite a gap in the life of her parents. There had once been some talk about buying a country property where both families could spend vacations or even weekends together, and now Bull saw it as a better idea than ever because what he really needed was his own private firing range, a set-up not unlike CARDE, remote and free from interference.

He found the ideal place at Highwater, Quebec, a few minutes from the U.S. border with Vermont and about 100 kilometres southeast of Montreal. The land was hilly and wooded and teeming with wildlife. It was quite unsuitable for farming and in that economically depressed area it had little commercial value. Bull bought 405 hectares for $10,000. The plan was to build summer homes for the Bull and Gilbert families at Highwater, while Bull could use the area for ballistics testing; the noise was unlikely to disturb anyone.

Through the summer of 1961, Bull and Mordell drew up plans for a project that would result in the gun launch of a satellite. They code-named their project HARP, an acronym for High Altitude Research Programme. Sometime in August, Mordell took the plans to the Department of Defence Production in Ottawa and asked for financial support. He had already been turned down by Bull's old antagonists at the Defence Research Board because the project was "not of defence interest". But the Department of Defence Production was persuaded that a large variety of military hardware, including long-range shells, would spin off HARP, and the department promised half a million dollars. There was red tape involved, and it would probably take six months to deliver the money.

During the first week of September, Mordell and Bull approached the McGill board of governors to suggest an immediate start to the project. They readily admitted that few students would be involved at any one time. But, they said, there was certain to be a great deal of positive publicity, which in turn would attract high-quality students and staff to the university in general. Best of all, HARP could eventually be a big money-maker, for once it started launching low-cost satellites, companies from around the world would line up to pay for its services. But there was an urgent need for $200,000 to develop a launching site. If McGill would advance the money, Mordell and Bull promised it would be paid back within a few months when financing from the Department of Defence Production materialized. Caught up by Bull's enthusiasm, McGill made what was in effect a $200,000 bridging loan.

The university felt that a site in the wilds of northern Quebec could be found for HARP, but Bull thought the enemies he had made at CARDE would try to undermine that idea, and Mordell suggested they check out Barbados, where McGill was already developing two other laboratories – an engineering project to convert sea water to fresh water, and a marine biology centre. Poverty-stricken, the island government readily agreed to host HARP, especially when told that jobs would be created. Barbados was ideal for many reasons, not the least of them that shells could be fired over a vast stretch of empty ocean. It didn't really matter where they fell.

In October, Bull drove down to Baltimore, where he met with Murphy who was by now head of the U.S. Ballistic Research Laboratory. Following General Trudeau's visit to Valcartier, Murphy had been ordered to conduct some experiments to find out how high it might be possible to shoot a shell from a gun. Firing from a gun with a 12.5-centimetre bore, Murphy had tracked a shell by radar to a height of 40,000 metres. This was much higher than expected, and the prospects excited General Trudeau.

Trudeau and the U.S. Army had hidden reasons for their special interest in HARP. At that time, the U.S. Air Force was launching a power play, seeking to take over full control of all U.S. military work in space. The Army wanted to stay involved in space defence but knew it was losing the battle. Trudeau and the Army saw in HARP a precursor to a possible anti-satellite and anti-ballistic missile weapon. They were thinking of the huge shotgun that Bull had suggested the year before when he was at CARDE, and they were thinking of Bull's current research at McGill, research they were financing. To the U.S. Army, HARP was a back-door method of staying in space defence. It allowed them to argue in policy sessions that they were not really financing space military research but rather providing minor assistance to a university programme. The programme, they said, would produce new information on how artillery shells were affected by winds and air currents as they travelled through high trajectories over a battlefield.

For a start, the Army did not want to allocate much money to HARP because it did not want to draw attention to its participation. Murphy explained that if McGill would accept a $2,000 grant, that grant would tie the Army to the project, and the Army would then be free to support HARP logistically by supplying guns and radars. Bull agreed on behalf of McGill and said that what he really wanted was a 40-centimetre gun – the biggest of all modern artillery weapons and used only by the U.S. Navy.

It is some reflection of how keen Murphy was to help that he found such a gun within days. It was 21 metres long, weighed 125 metric tonnes, and the Navy had been keeping it in storage for the last twenty years. As it turned out, the gun had never been used in battle, although it was designed, in 1921, to hit moving targets over the horizon. Murphy also found a second 40-centimetre gun barrel to be used as a spare, as well as a 10-centimetre gun for preliminary experiments. To complete the package, he threw in a $750,000 radar tracking system, a giant travelling crane and a truck. He said the Army could probably arrange for delivery as soon as McGill approved the Barbados site.

McGill approved Barbados, but on the financial front things were going badly. In Ottawa the Department of Defence Production discovered that before it could make good on its promise to back HARP with half a million dollars, it needed to get permission from the Defence Research Board – the lair of Gerry Bull's enemies. And the board said no. A.H. Zimmerman, chairman of the board, said later that the grant would have been made if it had been applied for by "an industrial concern". However, HARP was the product of a university and as such it didn't qualify for money from an industrial research fund. Whatever the real reason, the spoken promise was broken and the half-million dollars were never delivered. McGill was stuck with the $200,000 advance it had made, and Bull was more convinced than ever that Ottawa was being run by incompetents.

During his time at CARDE, Bull had made many enemies in Ottawa as a result of his free-wheeling work style and his immoderate language; his remarks about "cocktail party scientists" had scored some searing hits. And now there were plenty who were not prepared to give him the benefit of the doubt on a risky venture. K.F. Tupper, the National Research Council vice president for industry, wrote in a confidential memo that "the HARP Project consists merely of large and expensive gadgets". The memo, addressed to Dr. B.G. Ballard, the NRC president, added: "The HARP project does not open up any new possibilities whatsoever."[2]

Other scientists agreed that in *theory* a small satellite could be launched from a gun at comparatively low cost. But they said that in *practice* it wouldn't work. It had never been proven that the delicate instruments needed to make a satellite worthwhile could withstand the force of a high-velocity gun launch. Further, the satellite Bull had in mind was too small to be of much use. Bull's satellite plan, they said, was no more than a publicity stunt. Launching a satellite from a gun would cause a public sensation, but there would be no practical application afterwards. J.L. Orr, the industrial research adviser to the Ministry of Industry, emerged as Bull's chief critic in the committees that met behind closed doors. In a secret memo he wrote to Simon Reisman, a senior official who later became head of Canada's team for the free-trade negotiations with the U.S. in 1985, Orr said: "The effective management of a major engineering project of this magnitude is well beyond the capability of the university faculty and inevitably conflicts with their academic responsibilities." He concluded that the project was "a scientific extravagance".[3]

Bull responded by calling the Ottawa officials shortsighted and stupid. HARP, he said, would stage a series of preliminary experiments in which instrument-carrying shells would be shot a few hundred thousand metres high to test wind conditions. The information gathered would be of great use in predicting weather conditions and understanding atmospheric change. The original small satellites, he said, could be used for meteorological purposes, and eventually the system would grow to launch satellites large enough for all kinds of communications systems. Along the way, said Bull, there were sure to be military spinoffs, which could be sold to underwrite the entire programme. Just as important, he argued, HARP would give Canada an exciting and unique space programme that would encourage national pride, help to stop the ongoing brain drain into the United States and provide business for the country's struggling high-tech industry.

For its part, the university found itself swept along as HARP developed a life of its own. McGill couldn't afford to back a project of this dimension, but there wasn't much it could do to stop it.

Towards the end of March 1962, the university called a press conference in Montreal. The affair was managed by Bull and Mordell. With amazing chutzpah, they announced that for the first time in history a private institution would provide its scientists with facilities for continual and comprehensive space research projects. Bull felt compelled to add that HARP would mark the end of space domination by the great powers, for he would soon be firing missiles from his big gun in Barbados to probe altitudes as yet reached only by powerful military rockets.

Bull and Mordell stood on a small stage, in front of them three "space probes", miniature missiles with fins and bullet-shaped noses. They made wonderful photographs, and someone later called them Bull's "three bears". They represented the three stages of the space programme, jumping in size as they progressed in sophistication. The first was just short of half a metre tall, the second just over half a metre, and the third was nearly two metres high. And Bull had given them names. They weren't plain old rockets or shells or missiles. No, they were Martlets. The martlet is a footless heraldic bird, which appears on the McGill coat of arms. This naming was a master-stroke, for it gave the project a solid McGill identity and pulled the student body behind it. The impression given was that the Martlets were ready to fly and that the whole project was well advanced. Although in fact the Martlets were no more than empty shells, the press conference had thus succeeded in one of its hidden agendas: it committed McGill. The university could not now back out without losing a lot of face.

Dr. Bull made a quick chalk drawing on the blackboard behind him. He showed Earth with its 12-kilometre-high troposphere, surrounded by a 100-kilometre-high stratosphere and a 320-kilometre-high ionosphere. Beyond that, in large white letters he wrote, "SPACE".

Bull, looking the confident boffin in total control, said the project would open the next month with the first round of shots being fired from the 10-centimetre gun to altitudes of up to 50 kilometres. During this first stage, he said, the instrument-bearing shells would probe the stratosphere. Scientists needed to know much more about the stratosphere because it was being used increasingly by high-flying aircraft.

By the fall of 1963, he promised, the 40-centimetre gun would go into action, sending probes into the ionosphere. In the final stage, to be reached by Canada's centennial in 1967, the gun would fire shells containing solid-fuel rockets. Once the shells boosted the rockets to about 200 kilometres, they would be ignited by signals from the ground. A McGill statement read: "The rockets can boost the instrumentation or payload to a much greater altitude, and in due course to such a velocity that it can escape earth altogether." In other words, put a satellite in orbit.

Later, Bull saw reporters in his cluttered office. Stacks of letters, memos, magazines and engineering texts covered not just his desk but every surface, even the floor; there were tottering towers of technical journals; the wastepaper basket was overflowing with balled-up sheets of mathematical formulae. If Hollywood had ordered up a set for the office of a madcap professor, this would be it. In the centre of it sat Bull, leaning back in his chair, his feet on the desk, his thumbs in his belt. And in this setting he blasted Ottawa yet again. He said: "The general attitude toward the research scientist in this country is that he's some sort of parasite. Canadian scientists are appreciated outside of Canada far more than they are in Canada. The States are full of Canadians, many of them in senior research positions." He added: "Canadians won't gamble on research unless it's aimed at earning a dollar." Bull said he didn't expect Canada to engage in massive research programmes. "But I do see us operating in highly imaginative fringe areas, coming out with novel ideas and revolutionary-type thoughts."

The great advantage of HARP, explained Bull, was cost. Indeed, the savings from using the rocket cannon or supergun instead of rockets would be so great that HARP had the potential for providing basic space research "for peanuts". No one was suggesting that gun-launched missiles were a threat to rockets, Bull stressed, but they could save a fortune. For while rockets would always be needed for manned orbital flights such as the ones that had recently put Yuri Gagarin and John Glenn into space, they could be replaced for routine research. Bull said that for every orbital shot, about a thousand high-altitude probes were needed to measure the speed and direction of winds, the temperature, ion densities and all of the other chemical, physical and meteorological elements needed to build a scientific picture of space. Further, Bull claimed that the U.S. government was spending about $20,000 to launch each of these probes by rocket. He said that with a big gun he could launch the same instruments to the same heights for about 15 per cent of the cost.

Earlier Dr. James, McGill's vice chancellor, had explained that HARP would not draw "a single cent from the general operating revenues" of the university. He said: "It will be financed through donations and through contracts from governments and institutions desiring to utilize this unique research facility." And that was as close as McGill came to revealing that in fact HARP was a child of the U.S. Army. Indeed, so careful were they to hide the Army's backing that it was nowhere mentioned in the press conference coverage that dominated the front page of the *Montreal Star* the next day.

In the summer of 1962, three months after the press conference, the U.S. Army staged the largest "over the beach" landing ever performed. The 40-centimetre gun, together with its spare barrel, was mounted on railway flat cars and lashed to the deck of the shallow-draft USS *John D. Page*, the Army's largest and newest landing craft, for the 3,200-kilometre trip from Virginia to Barbados. Earlier, Bull's old colleagues at the University of Toronto had agreed to divert research funds from another project to have the rifling (spiralling grooves that make projectiles spin) taken out of both barrels, leaving them smooth-bored. After a nine-day journey, the landing craft pulled up onto the beach in Foul Bay, Barbados, while engineers laid 450 metres of railway track across the sand towards fields of sugarbeet. The flat cars were rolled onto the temporary track, and the giant gun was hauled by tractors towards the McGill site on a lonely stretch of the rocky south coast about five kilometres away. Track sections were pulled up and relaid at the front as soon as the weapon had passed over them. Barbadian prime minister E.W. Barrow watched the operation from the top of a sand dune, with Bull by his side. The two men laughed a lot as the giant gun was inched forward, and by the end of the first day they had become firm friends.

At the HARP base, located between Seawell Airport and the coast, McGill engineers had built a concrete gun emplacement at the foot of some cliffs at the east end of the airport runway. The radars and telemetry receivers provided by the U.S. Army were placed near the airport control tower, making Seawell the best-equipped airport in the Caribbean at that time. And McGill rented a Victorian pink stucco plantation house called Paragon House to serve as general headquarters. Set in formal gardens, the house reminded the scientists of a Somerset Maugham setting. But it quickly took on a touch of Ian Fleming when about twenty local people were hired for odd jobs, including security. As the installation grew, and as large quantities of explosives were shipped in, the security force was increased and some guards were armed, giving rise to stories that Bull now had his own private army.

7

THE PROSPECT of escaping to warm, peaceful Barbados during a Montreal winter was as tempting as summer romance. Almost every engineering student at McGill, and a good many staff, volunteered for work on HARP. But what the project offered in excitement and location, it lacked in funds. Indeed, with no government participation it was broke from the start, and Bull, though an instant celebrity, assembled just a skeleton staff.

The big navy gun, which Bull had christened Betsy, developed problems with its recoil system and hydraulics. As engineers worked on the technicalities, the gun was painted in the red and white colours of McGill, giving it something of a carnival touch.

Between July and September 1962, Bull designed his first HARP projectile – Martlet I. Basically an experimental missile, it was a 168-centimetre, 212-kilogram finned shell (about one-fifth the weight of the conventional 40-centimetre naval shell) that could carry scientific instruments and radio equipment in its nose. The 20-centimetre-diameter body was to be filled with a coloured chemical for release above the earth. Ground observers could then watch to see how the trails of chemical were blown around and so observe atmospheric winds. Most important, Martlet I was meant to test the new gun techniques, including the wood-and-aluminium sabot Bull had designed.

As Bull and his team gathered around the big gun on Barbados that fall, the world was thrown into confusion by the Cuban missile crisis. In late October, President John F. Kennedy announced that the Soviet Union had broken its promises and was building offensive missile and bomber bases in Cuba. The president imposed an immediate "quarantine" on Cuba to stop the Soviets shipping missiles to the island. Fidel Castro mobilized his forces, and as the HARP team waited for Premier Khrushchev to blink, they began to worry about their plight. If fighting broke out, Bull reasoned, Castro might decide that HARP was a new weapon system installed on his doorstep as a threat, and the project might come under attack from the Cuban Air Force.

It was late November before the tension dropped as the Soviets removed their missiles from Havana and Kennedy lifted his blockade. The crisis had delayed progress on HARP work, and now rainy weather and the coming Christmas season led to a postponement of the first firing until January. In the first week of the new year, Bull arranged for an assistant to take over his teaching duties at McGill and flew south again. This time a team of Canadian journalists went with him; the first HARP shots were to get lots of publicity. But the final preparations, working out the exact amount of propellent powder to use and problems that developed with the internal ballistics of the gun kept Bull hunched over mathematical calculations for a series of eighteen-hour days. At least once, he worked all night.

January 20 was full of slip-ups. The recoil mechanism of the gun began leaking, the speaker system to be used for the countdown, "Cape Canaveral style", didn't work, and in the late afternoon Lloyd's of London called to say that the insurance policy didn't cover public liability. At last, about six hours behind schedule, a dummy slug was fired from Betsy. It was the first time ever that a 40-centimetre gun had been fired at an angle of 80 degrees – nearly pointing straight up.

On hand for this scientific endeavour, which Bull, McGill and the U.S. Army all claimed had only fringe military significance and interest, was Major-General Chester Clark, head of the U.S. Army Research Office. A special brick observation shelter had been built about 180 metres from the gun, but Major-General Clark insisted on watching the performance in the open. He lay in the sand about 120 metres from the gun, risking being hit by falling splinters from the wooden test slug and by stones that the thunderous concussion jarred loose from the nearby cliff face. Yet the general wanted to miss nothing. Flames roared nine metres from the muzzle of the gun, followed by a small cloud of smoke from the burned cordite propellant. The 315-kilogram wooden slug left the barrel at about 1,000 metres per second (close to 4,000 kilometres an hour) and went about three kilometres into the sky, leaving a thin trail of smoke behind it. It was 58 seconds in the air, coming down into the ocean about a kilometre offshore. In the tropical dusk the event was spectacular. "I am a very happy man," said Mordell. And well he might have been. For with the university still waiting for its money back, Mordell's job could have been on the line if the experiment had failed.

The next day Bull charged the gun with 330 kilograms of cordite propellant and fired the first of his Martlet I missiles. Again the gun reared back on its hydraulic pistons and this time fired its missile to a height of 26 kilometres. The Martlet I was in the air for 145 seconds and fell 11 kilometres offshore. Two days later another slug performed much the same as the first.

On February 1, Bull ended the initial series of firings by putting up a second Martlet I, this time with a one-watt radio transmitter embedded in three rings of plastic in the missile's brass nose. It was the first attempt at shooting instruments from the cannon, and performance was vital. The missile reached a height of 27 kilometres and was in the air for a total of 146 seconds. Ground receiving stations picked up signals from the tiny transmitter throughout its journey. And with that, the McGill team returned to Montreal to assess their findings, to improve methods of communications between the Martlets and ground stations and to resume badly neglected teaching assignments.

Bull now needed to raise more money, and quickly. HARP was off the ground, but it was far from a resounding success. Bull had hoped for fourteen shots during the first series of firings and had intended to break the world record for lofting a "probe" from a gun. That record was held by his old pal Charles Murphy and had been set two years before with a 12.5-centimetre gun at the Aberdeen Proving Ground. During the tests ordered by General Trudeau, Murphy's probe had reached 70 kilometres in altitude – well over twice as high as Bull's best shot in that opening series.

Two weeks after getting back to Montreal, where the snow lay deep and the temperatures were constantly below freezing, Bull announced that his second series of shots would begin in early April and that a new missile, Martlet II, would be used. Smaller and lighter than Martlet I, the second generation of missiles would go 145 kilometres high, he said. And he boasted that work was underway on the Martlet III, a rocket-powered vehicle that could reach orbital speeds and altitudes. Martlet IIIs, he said, would be ready for launch by the end of the year. On the last day of February, Bull told a symposium on satellites and spacecraft, sponsored by the Canadian Aeronautics and Space Institute, that the Martlet IIIs would travel 1,600 kilometres into space and would incorporate a one-stage rocket. Further, he revealed that Martlet IV was being planned to carry a two-stage rocket, and that it would be capable of putting a 14-kilogram payload into orbit. Later, the payload might be increased to 45 kilograms. Bull did not mention the good news he had received from the U.S. Army: they were prepared to finance HARP's operation to the tune of $250,000 a year.

While HARP was gaining a great deal of positive publicity for McGill, the university was becoming increasingly upset at the way Bull was missing classes and paying only scant attention to his teaching duties. True, he had captivated a handful of graduate students who treated him like a god, but other engineering professors were beginning to complain that he wasn't pulling his weight in the department. Bull agreed to postpone the next series of HARP shots until after the end of semester.

Only four Martlet I models were ever made. Two were fired during the initial session and the remaining two were retired when Bull switched to the sophisticated Martlet II. The Martlet II was 1.5 metres long and 12.5 centimetres in diameter. It had an alloy steel body and nose cone and aluminium alloy fins.

On June 18, Mordell announced with enormous glee that a world record for gun-fired space shots had been set. A Martlet II, weighing 170 kilograms, had reached nearly 92 kilometres. Bull calculated that his shells could easily reach Cuba. When officials of the Barbados government worried that HARP might make their island a target in a future conflict, he assured them that Betsy was useless as a weapon because it could be so easily knocked out by the enemy.

Such concerns, however, reflect how uneasy some leaders were about HARP being situated in the Caribbean. And those concerns grew when President Kennedy was assassinated that November and suspicions were raised about Castro's involvement. But Bull was persuasive, and his friend the prime minister of Barbados was soon calmed, although political opposition groups, some of them friendly to Castro, remained unhappy.

By year's end some twenty Martlet II missiles, some of them modified versions of the original, had been fired. Less had been learned about the upper atmosphere than had been hoped, but there had been considerable progress in the design of the projectiles and a lot had been learned about the dynamics of firing the 40-centimetre gun in a near-80-degree position. And this was enough to please those who mattered. To the delight of Bull and Mordell, the U.S. Army agreed to increase its financial involvement yet again and promised $1.5 million a year for the next three years. Mordell was at least able to promise the McGill board of directors that the original bridging loan would gradually be repaid.

In January 1964, Bull and his team were back in Barbados for another round of shots. This time Mimi and the children went with him for a vacation. Michel was eight, and he remembers being driven around in an open jeep and everybody wearing special badges on their shirts to gain entrance to the HARP site. But it was the night shoots that the children found most breathtaking. Says Michel: "The nights in Barbados are pitch dark. We could hear the countdown and we were prepared, but it still took us by surprise. There was this great flash that jolted us and then we would almost settle down when we would hear the bang and that jolted us again. It was fabulous. There seemed to be so much fresh air among the people, they were so excited and so happy."

With his newest version of the Martlet II, Bull was able to reach 80 kilometres with almost every ignition, and methods of protecting scientific instruments cradled in a missile's nose cone were improving dramatically. Although Bull said, "If you want to fire an egg, you've got a problem," ways had been found to fire delicate gauges and timing devices without damage. Bull explained: "We are restricted by the size of the gun. Anything larger than 16 inches [40 centimetres] in diameter won't get in the barrel. We can't put a space station in space but, once it's there, we can send up the wrench left behind."

Bull also told a reporter that once HARP had proven itself further he hoped to abandon Betsy, the Navy cast-off, and have a gun made to his own specifications. This would be a greater gun than any built before, and it would dwarf the 40-centimetre navy gun. In fact, he said, he was hoping for a gun with a 75-centimetre bore.

Mimi was staying on in Barbados for a few extra days to paint landscapes, and Gerry took the children home. It led to an incident that became part of the family folklore. Michel and Philippe had been playing on a small farm near the HARP site when they found a chicken's nest. There were two eggs in the nest, and Philippe told Michel to save one and keep it warm so they could get a chick. Says Michel: "I put the egg in the pocket of my overcoat, which was hanging in the bedroom." Of course, the boys promptly forgot all about it. And when it was time to fly home, Mimi packed the children's coats with firm instructions for Gerry to make sure the children wore them when they changed planes in New York for the flight to Montreal. Says Michel: "As we were getting off the plane, my dad saw there was something dripping from my coat. He put his hand in my pocket, and he went white. That was when I learned how to swear in English."

The Pentagon, meanwhile, was dropping hints about its real interest in HARP. Defense Secretary Robert McNamara said that the biggest defence issue facing the nation was the protection of North America from missile attack. Under consideration was the Nike-X anti-missile system, which had an estimated cost of $20 billion to perfect and install. U.S. military analysts predicted that in any missile attack from the Soviet Union as many as a hundred warheads might be aimed at one target. However, ninety-five or more of the warheads would be dummies sent to confuse defence systems. Only when the warheads re-entered the atmosphere and the lighter decoys were slowed down by resistance could radar distinguish between the dummies and the real thing. And only then, with the warhead some 80 kilometres from its target, would the Nike-X be launched. It was a simple matter of cost: the Nike-X was a million-dollar missile, and Washington couldn't afford to have thousands of them sitting around to shoot at dummies at higher altitudes. But Bull's gun was a different matter altogether, for it might be able to fire rocket-assisted projectiles into the path of incoming missiles. The projectiles would explode at an altitude of 400 or 500 kilometres, scattering thousands of pieces of shrapnel towards the ICBMs. As Bull well knew from his ongoing research into the effects of tiny meteorites hitting spacecraft, if even one sliver of shrapnel touched a warhead, the warhead would be destroyed. And this shotgun approach could be handled so cheaply that it really wouldn't matter how many decoys were involved, for a supergun would have a high chance of getting them all at a much higher altitude than the Nike-X, leaving a greater margin of safety. If necessary, a low-level interceptor missile could then be used as a backup.

During the January 1964 tests, Bull began firing Martlet II projectiles fitted with high-explosive charges to fire pellets into space. He explained that the idea was a test in re-entry physics. In fact, it was an anti-ballistic missile experiment. This is how the *U.S. Air Force Magazine* put it at the time: "Through its relatively low cost and ability to intercept at comparatively long range, a gun-boosted system has promise of providing an area defense for a nation the size of the United States. There are positive reasons for believing that a gun-boosted system could stop a very large percentage of attacking warheads."

By that spring the rather dignified and splendid Paragon House had been equipped with a modern control panel, closed-circuit television and a communications system linking every corner of the project. Murphy from the Ballistic Research Laboratory was appointed technical supervisor, and American scientists from NASA, the U.S. Air Force and the U.S. Navy were assigned to HARP for every firing. Pith helmets were officially issued to all technical personnel, and countdowns were run with the same precision NASA was using to launch its space rockets.

But if NASA was aiming for the moon, Bull had defined his own technical goal. The 40-centimetre gun was able to launch a 180-kilogram projectile at a velocity of 1,800 metres per second. Bull knew that if the gas pressure reached at the breech when the powder was first burned could be maintained for the full length of the barrel – rather than dropping off dramatically along the way – the same 180-kilogram projectile would leave the muzzle at 3,600 metres per second. In other words, if the internal barrel ballistics could be mastered, the range might be doubled. To work on this and other highly technical problems, Bull decided that HARP needed its own research and development laboratory, including a gun-firing range. And he knew the perfect spot.

By now Bull and his father-in-law had bought between them a further 800 hectares of scenic wooded land around the site Bull had chosen for a country home near Highwater, Quebec. Dr. Gilbert considered the property a good investment, but more important it kept the family close. Bull, using his engineering talents, didn't hesitate to design his own house and built a large triple A-frame structure, with swimming pool and tennis courts, on a hillside terrace overlooking the rolling hills of eastern Quebec. Dr. Gilbert loved it, and Bull designed and built a second house for the Gilberts about 50 metres away on the same terrace. The two families had their own private compound, stretching more than a kilometre through the woods to the unmarked Vermont border. The property was ideal for gun ranges and a private laboratory.

Meanwhile, with the war in Vietnam gathering momentum, other political problems were bubbling in the U.S. The U.S. Air Force had won the Pentagon battles and been exclusively assigned the military mission in space. The U.S. Army was restricted to working with rockets and shells travelling to a maximum of 100 kilometres high. Most specifically, the Army was warned not to finance HARP attempts to orbit a satellite. This worrying development was just beginning to make itself felt when in March 1964 the Canadian Department of Defence Production quite suddenly decided that it would finance the HARP programme after all. In part, they had been pushed into it by favourable press publicity, but they had also learned in classified briefings from the U.S. Army that HARP was likely to develop gun-launched guided and controlled projectiles that could be sold to other NATO forces. And Canada was most interested in developing an arms-export industry. The U.S. Army was worried it would lose control of HARP once Ottawa became involved, but there was at least one positive gain. Ottawa's participation would allow HARP to continue with its satellite plans.

Canadian officials met with the U.S. Army Research Office in Arlington, Virginia, in late March 1964 and agreed to re-launch the HARP programme with a $3-million annual budget to be split equally between the U.S. Army and Ottawa. It was further agreed, to satisfy Pentagon demands, that the U.S. Army share would pay for gun work aimed at lofting missiles no higher than 100 kilometres, while the Canadian money would pay for shots aimed at putting a satellite in orbit. That neat arrangement was to go into effect on July 1, 1964, with the U.S. Army sending its share of the funds to the Canadian Commercial Corporation in Ottawa, where they would be combined with the Canadian contribution. McGill would be given a formal contract to run the HARP project and would bill the Canadian Commercial Corporation for all costs, not to exceed the budget total. The university agreed to finance HARP from its own funds for the anticipated short period between July 1 and when the Canadian government money was due to become available, sometime before the end of August. Ottawa also insisted that McGill establish a separate organization, away from the Department of Engineering, for financial audit and control purposes and to handle the overall contract. On April 28, 1964, the McGill board of governors agreed to establish the Space Research Institute of McGill University to handle the contract. Dr. Bull was appointed institute director, and a McGill-owned building at 892 Sherbrooke Street West was made available to house an expanded HARP team.

Bull and Mordell were convinced that HARP was entering a triumphal phase. The Space Research Institute began cooperating with major U.S. arms manufacturers to design one- and two-stage rockets for the Martlet missiles. Funds to cover the period of July 1, 1964, to June 30, 1965, were slow in coming from the Canadian government, and the university nervously advanced another $500,000 so that test firings could continue at the Barbados range that July.

By winter the Canadian money still hadn't come. It can't be proved, but it seems obvious that Bull's enemies in government were finding red tape to hold up funding. McGill advanced a few thousand dollars more, but development of Martlet III and IV came to a halt and plans to orbit a satellite were shelved. A contract to design a guidance and control system that might ultimately project HARP missiles into orbit was continued, as was a contract to build telemetry devices able to withstand 10,000 Gs. The Canadian cash for the fiscal year ending June 30, 1965, was eventually released, ten months after it had been promised.

In the middle of this most tense period, Gerry Bull's fifth son, Bobby, was born in August 1964. Bull was in Barbados a lot that summer, and though he fretted about not being with the new baby, HARP mattered so much to him that the sacrifice was made. That November, South Vietnamese forces made their largest attack of the war in southeast Asia, and U.S. military experts began to seriously consider the advantages of super-long-range artillery. Bull assured them that HARP could pave the way to systems that would revolutionize anything in Western arsenals; all he needed was time for development. No commitments were made, though General Trudeau indicated that at least for now, HARP funding was safe.

By early 1965, Bull had decided that the 40-centimetre gun in its present form would never lift the Martlet missiles much over the 92-kilometre record set the year before. His calculations did show that if the barrel was lengthened it would do better. He told Anthony Patterson, a writer with the *Financial Times of Canada*, that with the barrel extended to 30 metres, the gun should be able to put a 225-kilogram payload 1,600 kilometres into space, using several rocket stages after the initial gun boost. Within a week of making this statement, Bull had designed and ordered a 16-metre smooth-bored steel tube from Davie Shipbuilding, of Lauzon, Quebec. It cost $41,000 and was designed to fit onto the end of the existing barrel, with tonnes of extra steel being used to seal the joint. Once the tube was fitted, the 40-centimetre gun had a total barrel length of 36 metres, making it the longest operational gun in the world. That July the new gun was tested in a twenty-shot series and succeeded in sending one Martlet II to a height of nearly 150 kilometres, a clear world record.

The resulting publicity did not go unnoticed in the Canadian Parliament, and C.M. Drury, the minister of industry, was asked in the House if the "ultimate implications of the HARP project in terms of defence" had been adequately considered. In a written reply, Drury explained that from the government's point of view, HARP was an "exploratory" project. He added: "Potentially military users have indicated specific interest. HARP management is aware that such potential users are monitoring project accomplishments." Indeed they were. By this time military experts from Canada, the U.S., Britain and Israel were present for every firing. It was Bull's first contact with the Israelis, and he admired their drive and push. The attraction was to develop.

The atmosphere of the era was significant for the development of HARP. In late June 1965, American troops were authorized to fight in a combat role in Vietnam, and in July President Lyndon Johnson sent fifty thousand more troops to South Vietnam. As draft dodgers began skipping north to Canada, the U.S. military was particularly pleased to find at least one Canadian who supported the anti-Communist agenda of the Pentagon.

By now, Bull's private firing range and laboratory at Highwater were in constant use by the Space Research Institute, and it was decided to put the arrangement on a formal footing. Bull and his father-in-law formed a company to handle all of the Highwater property. Combining the first parts of Dr. Gilbert's name and the Latin root for Bull, they called their business Giltaur Corporation Ltd. Giltaur then leased the 800 hectares to McGill for use as a HARP development site to be known as the McGill Aeroballistics Laboratory at Highwater. A 15-centimetre horizontal testing gun was installed, and a sophisticated metal-working shop was built for the production of Martlet missiles. In all, McGill was paying Giltaur about $180,000 a year to rent the property. The money came from the budget provided by the U.S. Army and the Canadian government.

Again, with the start of the fiscal year on July 1, 1965, Ottawa was late with its promised research money, and there were rumours around the McGill campus that the government was ready to pull out of the project, for it had become obvious to insiders that HARP and Bull shared enemies in Ottawa. High on this list was John Orr, at the Department of Industry, who was circulating reports that suggested HARP had no commercial future. At the Space Research Institute no one felt sure of his job, and with research money promised by Ottawa but not available, the development of rocket-assisted missiles was further delayed. Into this uncertain atmosphere Bull's first daughter and sixth child, Kathy, arrived in July 1965.

In November 1965, the institute installed at Highwater a 40-centimetre naval gun with a 16.5-metre-long barrel. This gun was meant for horizontal shots to test the Martlet missiles. The missiles travelled 150-metres from the gun to an impact-point in a tunnel dug in the hillside. The idea was to experiment with propulsion charges and methods of increasing muzzle velocity. The Martlets were filmed on their short flight so the performance of sabots could be examined.

Like Topsy, the institute had grown, and by the end of 1965 forty researchers and technical assistants were assigned to Highwater. Their presence had a huge effect on the local area, as did the enormous bangs every time the 40-centimetre gun was fired. But here, Bull devised a master-stroke in public relations. He had loud-speakers installed at the bars in Highwater and the village of Mansonville, and also across the border in North Troy, Vermont. Before every firing the countdown was broadcast. The tactic won over the locals on both sides of the border, who welcomed the project as a link to the space age.

There was no such warmth in Ottawa. On February 8, 1966, Orr sent a severe criticism of HARP to Simon Reisman, then deputy minister of industry. So sensitive was the issue that Orr had the criticism classified "secret". The two-page memo ripped into the project. Orr said flatly that the much-vaunted scientific research side of HARP was "only incidental to the development of gun-launch hardware". He said: "To date a limited amount of rudimentary data on the simple properties of the lower atmosphere (e.g. wind shear and temperature) have been produced." He questioned Bull's argument that a gun could launch a satellite for a fraction of the costs involved with rockets, highly recommended further investment in rocket development and concluded that he could not recommend continued support of HARP after June 30, 1966. Reisman scrawled, "From the point of view of industrial development or productive saving, there is no case for continued support,"[1] and sent Orr's memo to Drury, his minister. When news of the Canadian disillusionment filtered back to the U.S. Army, they decided to protect their interests by opening a HARP experimental centre at the Yuma, Arizona, proving grounds. Another 40-centimetre gun was prepared for use under U.S. staffing and funding. This move made American participation in the programme completely independent of Ottawa.

But it did not sway the Canadian civil service. On February 9, 1966, a senior member of Orr's staff, R.K. Brown, wrote in a memo to his boss: "Although personalities should not affect the decision, they cannot be ignored, and one of the reasons that no Canadian government scientists have been closely involved in the control or direction of the project, nor an assessment of its relationship to other space activities, lies in the personality of Dr. Bull, and it need hardly be said that there will continue to be difficulties in this area."[2]

Bull seemed to have at least two distinct personalities. He was rude and abrasive with his critics, especially those in government. Yet he demonstrated great charm and humour with his colleagues, especially those who supported his work. One government critic described him as acting like "a spoiled child", throwing temper tantrums every time he couldn't get his own way, unable to deal with people who questioned his ideas.

Sannu Molder, an engineering professor who worked alongside Bull at McGill, recalls: "Gerry was full of ideas and vigour and he challenged everyone around him." He still loved to play little jokes. Once he saw a university groundsman smash into Professor Molder's car. Later that day Bull had one of his students call Molder pretending to be a police officer and saying that Molder was to be charged with careless driving. Bull enjoyed such schoolboy pranks, and they served to cut tensions. Says Molder: "He created an atmosphere that you don't often have in a university. He was infectious. The people working with Bull were jovial and competitive at the same time. He had a tremendous amount of intuition. He could see solutions to problems at a glance. That was really his strong point. No one ever made guns and projectiles work the way that Gerry made them work."

In mid-February, to the great annoyance of Orr, Drury recommended one more year of finance for HARP. He outlined his reasons in a confidential cabinet document. First, he wanted a Science Secretariat report on HARP, and second, he pointed out "certain political implications" of discontinuing support for the project. Drury knew that the Canadian press was firmly behind HARP and that the government would encounter enormous criticism if it cancelled the project suddenly. He preferred to play for time and give HARP another $2.5 million. The next month, Orr sent another secret memo to Reisman stressing again that in his opinion HARP was "redundant" and that all Canadian space research funds should go towards developing a rocket system known as Black Brant. Orr made it clear that HARP and Black Brant were in competition and that while Black Brant was a purely Canadian venture, HARP "is almost entirely directed to U.S. military interests". Black Brant, which was basically a research rocket for taking scientific instruments into the upper atmosphere, was being developed by Bristol Aerospace, and it had the solid backing not only of CARDE but also of the Defence Research Board. Unlike HARP, it had friends in all the right places.

Bull struck back through the press. Mordell, on Bull's urging, gave a series of interviews in which he said that because Ottawa could not make up its mind about funding, the HARP programme had come to a halt. The HARP sites in Barbados and Highwater were "in a state of near inactivity". Mordell added: "We cannot plan any shots. The whole situation is bad for the programme's development and for the staff's morale." He went on to say that while there would be an inevitable and damaging delay, the U.S. would take over total funding if Ottawa backed out and the programme and its scientists would move south of the border. Thus, once again, "and as with the Avro Arrow", Canada would lose a valuable scientific resource as a result of inept political manoeuvring.

In Ottawa, Bull met with Drury and pleaded for another year of funding because, he said, by the end of that period HARP would be able to get enough commercial contracts to support itself.

Drury, ever fearful of a hostile press, wanted to please Bull. But nothing happened very quickly. In mid-March, Reisman and Orr told Drury that whatever HARP did, it would never make money by putting a satellite in orbit because such a satellite, restricted in size by the barrel of the 40-centimetre gun, would be too small for commercial use. "In no event," they said should assistance be used for purposes of achieving orbital capability." In May it was decided to finance HARP for one more year with a total of $1.5-million. Drury went out of his way to stress that the money was being made available only because Dr. Bull had promised that HARP would be self-sustaining by 1967 and because there would be a risk of losing valuable scientific brains to the U.S. if funds were cut off immediately.

Meanwhile, the American Army was increasing the number of shots it was firing from the 40-centimetre gun at Yuma. On the night of November 18, 1966, one of Bull's Martlet missiles was fired to a height of 180 kilometres, a world record that was to stand for more than twenty-five years.

Bull announced that the funding delays had set the HARP project back at least two years. He said the government was "hopelessly incompetent", that there had been active opposition from civil servants "who know nothing at all" and that a "smear campaign" was underway by scientists working on the Black Brant rocket project. Journalists, whose imaginations had always been fired by the HARP project, accused the government of "selling out" the nation's top scientists. By way of response, Orr sent a confidential memo to Drury with a copy to Dr. H. Rocke Robertson, principal and vice chancellor of McGill. He wrote: "HARP is basically a U.S. Army project directed toward U.S. military objectives. The bulk of the effort is centred in the Ballistic Research Laboratory at Aberdeen, Maryland, and the HARP-McGill effort is only a minor part of the total programme. To suggest that the government should be committed to support every glamorous scheme that ingenious enthusiasts can concoct is sheer nonsense." He concluded: "If Dr. Bull chooses to direct the efforts of his Space Research Institute into serving the special research demands of the U.S. Army rather than any Canadian interest, then he should look to the U.S. Army for full financial support and should not castigate the Canadian government for allocating public funds to more worthwhile pursuits."

It was never actually said, but as a result of U.S. Army funding for HARP, Bull had become firmly linked with the Pentagon in the minds of many Ottawa civil servants. And because of the Vietnam War, a venture that was largely scorned and despised in Canada, the Pentagon had a bad name. The situation provided another reason for those who were ill-disposed towards Bull to sabotage his efforts.

Later in the year, Drury confirmed that Ottawa would not spend another cent on HARP after June 30, 1967, by which time it would have sunk a total of $4.3 million into the project. Responded Bull: "The treatment we've received from Ottawa has been unscrupulous and unreasonable. Clobbering the project now makes Canadians look like a bunch of morons."[3]

Washington's advice was to move the Space Research Institute from McGill to an American university and for that university to find grants from the private sector. In the meantime, between December 1966 and March 1967, the U.S. Army, acting on instructions from Murphy and General Trudeau, transferred $3 million worth of equipment to the HARP ballistics laboratory at Highwater. The move ensured that Bull could at least continue experimental work on rocket-assisted advanced Martlet missiles.

In March, the Canadian government's Science Secretariat issued a long-awaited report on HARP. The Chapman Report, named after J.H. Chapman, who had chaired the study group, damned HARP with faint praise. It said there were three advantages to the system and two disadvantages. The advantages were that guns could loft missiles to a height of about 160 kilometres with more efficiency than rockets; that guns were cheaper than rockets; and that they were more accurate than rockets. The disadvantages were that the accelerations from a gun barrel were so great – as much as 10,000 times the force of gravity – that the vehicle being lofted and all of its components had to be capable of withstanding such a force; and that the size of gun-launched vehicles was obviously limited by the diameter of the barrel. But the report did nothing to persuade the Canadian government to change its mind about discontinuing its funding.

Bull opened negotiations first with the University of Vermont and later with Norwich University in Vermont to take over the Space Research Institute. Both schools were interested and both tried to help, but they simply couldn't raise the money. In June 1967, the U.S. Army dropped out – closing the Yuma project – because increasing costs of the war in Vietnam were tightening budgets. Bull used what was left in his own research budget to pay all outstanding loans from McGill, and resigned. In the end, HARP had cost the university nothing and gained it some wonderful publicity.

HARP had developed into a terrible burden for Mordell, but he never regretted his support. He later said that it provided him with "the best fun of my life". Mordell said: "I am not sure if I was the midwife or the paediatrician for HARP. Whatever, as a result of HARP I became a friend of Gerry Bull, and that was the major thing for me. He was a man of immense courage and determination. Nothing could deter him. Difficulties were a spur to him. As others gave up, he would plough on and win."

The HARP situation could hardly have been worse when the Bulls' second daughter, their seventh and last child, Jane, was born in July, 1967.

At least for the present, HARP was dead. But it had served to prove to the satisfaction of Gerry Bull that big guns had a scientific and military future. Looking back on HARP's achievements, General Trudeau wrote in late 1990 that the project had mapped and measured the ionospheric winds that affect weather patterns. He added: "Fully half of all such wind measurements recorded to the present time were made by HARP in its relatively short, active life span."

Early in September 1967, officials from McGill, the Canadian government and the U.S. Army met in Montreal to decide what to do with assets of the HARP programme. Bull had been told in advance that Ottawa wanted to destroy the HARP guns by cutting them into pieces and also wanted to break up the laboratories. But he had a legal ace to play and was determined to carry on the programme, although he had no idea where the money might come from. As the Montreal meeting got under way, Bull sent a bailiff to serve notice on the university that all clauses in the McGill lease with

Giltaur Corporation for the lands at Highwater must be fully met. The lease ran out in a few weeks, and as there had been no moves to renew it, Giltaur asked – in accordance with the lease – that the Highwater property be restored to its original condition within thirty days. To meet that demand, the university would have had to reforest hundreds of hectares that Space Research Institute had cleared for ballistics experiments. The meeting was adjourned for legal consultations. In the meantime, Bull presented a solution. He said that Giltaur would waive the legal clause if McGill, acting on behalf of the Canadian government and the U.S. Army, transferred all HARP facilities at Highwater and in Barbados, including the guns and the laboratories and all the equipment they contained, intact, to a non-profit organization "for a nominal sum". Bull had previously incorporated Space Research Institute as a private, non-profit scientific organization with offices in Highwater and in North Troy. He now further offered that Giltaur would assume all financial obligations for maintenance and protection of the facilities as of the date of transfer, and would keep the facilities staffed, operable and available to any U.S. government agency at no cost. McGill, particularly anxious to be rid of support costs, agreed, and Ottawa and the U.S. Army also went along with the proposal.

Bull's idea was to have the assets transferred to the Space Research Institute office in North Troy and then to have them managed by Norwich University, where there was still a lot of interest. By January this had happened, and McGill was totally out of the picture. Norwich University asked that a U.S. corporation, with adequate capital, be formed to manage the institute.

In May 1968, Peter and Edward Bronfman, of the Montreal liquor family (Seagrams), had taken control of Great West Saddlery, an old established Canadian company, and were using it as an investment shell to acquire new companies. Attracted by the glamour of the HARP programme, they agreed to take it over. The plan was to open a new company called Space Research Corporation (SRC) to replace Space Research Institute. They bought out the Giltaur holdings for about $2 million, most of it paid in the form of shares in Great West. Great West Saddlery also bought out the

Norwich University interest by agreeing to pay all outstanding Space Research Institute debts.

Space Research Corporation was now an independent commercial concern controlling state-of-the-art ballistics research laboratories and workshops and big guns in Barbados and Highwater. Contracts were being offered by the U.S. Army and by NASA, but because the work would be classified it was necessary that it be carried out in the U.S. Bull was appointed technical director of SRC, and using finance provided by Great West Saddlery, the company began buying land in Vermont adjoining the holdings in Quebec. By early 1969, SRC straddled the border and the International Boundary Commission gave permission for a private cross-border road to be built through the forest, connecting both sides of the company. The compound was officially considered U.S.-controlled, allowing use of the extensive Canadian facilities for U.S. classified military work.

But U.S. security clearance was slow in coming, and the Bronfmans changed their plans for Great West Saddlery. By the end of 1969, they wanted out. Meanwhile, the shares in Great West had shot up in value, and Bull sold all of those that he still held. That gave him enough cash to pay back the Bronfmans all they had invested, and to buy from them the land that had been purchased in Vermont. "The sale of their shares brought Gerry the most money he ever made in his life," says Mimi. She adds: "The money was enough to let Gerry take over the company. Suddenly we were quite wealthy."

Counting property and capital investment, Bull was a millionaire. But he still had no liquidity, and Peter Bronfman, impressed with Bull's insistence on paying all of SRC's debts to Great West Saddlery, introduced Bull to the First Pennsylvania Bank and helped arrange for the bank to loan Giltaur Corporation enough money to continue research-and-development projects.

With the dawn of the new decade, Bull found himself owning and running one of the most sophisticated ballistics laboratories in private hands anywhere in the world. He was ready to launch a new career as an independent weapons scientist.

8

GERALD BULL was in a remarkable situation. Along with his father-in-law, he owned the HARP facilities at Highwater. Here was a private citizen with enough firepower in his back yard to start a war. And he controlled the firing range in Barbados, with title over Betsy, the biggest gun in the world.

As a result of his work at CARDE and HARP, Bull had an international reputation in ballistics. In the narrow world of gun and shell design, Bull was a major figure. Defence departments from Tel Aviv to Thailand knew about Betsy and that Bull had fired missiles to record heights. Intelligence agencies had watched the demise of HARP and the rise of Bull's new company, SRC.

Bull's attraction was that he could design conventional projectiles to go farther than anyone else's. And in battle that would matter a lot. Michel Bull explains it well when he compares an artillery duel to a snowball fight. When two boys with woolly gloves face off in the snow, the one with the strongest arm can keep the other at bay. In fact, the strong arm can keep the weak arm so far back that the weak arm has no chance of scoring a hit. But sooner or later, the strong arm is sure to land one on target. All other things being equal – accuracy and payload – range is everything with snowballs and big guns. Thus Bull, holding the promise of long range, was courted by those in need of a strong arm.

During the ten years that he was to run the Highwater compound, Bull had dealings with no fewer than thirty countries. He worked for Egypt and Israel, The Netherlands and Italy, Britain and Canada, Venezuela and Chile, Thailand and Iran, South Africa and Somalia. They all flocked to Highwater to consult the great Dr. Bull, the wizard of guns.

His first significant job came from the U.S. Air Force, and it directly involved Bull once more in nose-cone technology. Scientists at the Kirtland Air Force Base, at Albuquerque, New Mexico, wanted to test a ballistic missile nose cone they had developed. The cone was a metre long and weighed 45 kilograms. Without actually sending it up on a $1-million missile, they needed to know how the cone would fly at high speed and if it was properly shaped to stay on target.

During the summer of 1969, Bull welded two extra tubes to the barrel of the 40-centimetre smooth-bore gun at Highwater, making it 52 metres long and eclipsing Betsy. That November he fired the nose cone from his new long gun, propelling it with a massive charge that risked blowing up not just the gun but part of his compound as well. The roar drowned out anything heard from the one-time McGill laboratories. But Bull's calculations proved true, and the gun withstood the charge as the nose cone left the barrel at 3,000 metres per second – it was the first time a nose cone of that size had been fired that fast. The gun was mounted horizontally, and the cone travelled for about nearly a kilometre before pounding into a huge sandbank. Special cameras filmed the short flight, and by studying the pictures the scientists at Kirtland learned all they needed to know about the flight characteristics of their cone.

Bull expected that success to lead to a steady flow of business, but it didn't, and the first years of life for the Space Research Corporation were lean. The nose cone work had gone to Bull because he was the only one equipped to do it. But the U.S. military had no intention of divesting contracts from its regular suppliers.

He was able to stay afloat because countries employed him to solve their minor artillery troubles. Iran wanted to know why their new shells were tumbling instead of spinning towards the end of flight. Taiwan was puzzled by erratic performance from its 155-mm guns. Bull became "Mr. Fix-It" for the world's artillery.

For the ballistics side of his business, Bull hired the best of the HARP team, young engineers he had trained himself. And to run the compound and test-fire guns, he employed local people and paid them extravagantly well. In both cases, he won and gave deep loyalty. That's how it was throughout Bull's life – his employees became his friends. And his friends would do almost anything to help. Which may partly explain why General Arthur Trudeau lobbied the Pentagon in the early 1970s for a contract that would allow Bull to continue studies on a space gun to counter incoming missiles and to shoot down enemy spy satellites.

The contract was meagre, but again Bull believed it might lead to a breakthrough, and for nearly two years he compiled volumes of complex calculations. The Pentagon became so intrigued and impressed with his findings that, to help him along, they afforded him access to some of the most restricted and secret weapons research in their arsenal. In mid-1972 senior officers in Washington realized that in allowing Bull access to defence secrets they had broken multiple security laws, because not only did he not have the needed clearance, he wasn't even a U.S. citizen. To cover their mistakes, they persuaded Senator Barry Goldwater, the conservative Republican from Arizona, to pass a private act of Congress in October 1972 granting Bull American citizenship. Three months later he took his citizenship oath in a private ceremony. The presiding federal judge was specially flown to Vermont from New York.

The following year, after Bull had submitted plans for his space gun, the Pentagon scrapped the idea. The reasons are classified, but sources directly involved at the time say that the very nature and size of Bull's supergun made it inflexible; its field of fire was narrow and set; and it could never cover a large enough area to stop a significant number of incoming missiles. The gunners would never be able to quickly swing its barrel through a wide arc to cover the horizon, so twenty or thirty of the guns would be needed to guard each site. And even then, they would be highly vulnerable to incoming fire.

There was another, more subtle factor. The major American weapons companies, the notorious military-industrial complex, were lobbying against Bull. They wanted to keep him on the fringe where he could never get too large a slice of the defence budget pie.

In an attempt to attract more attention in Washington, Bull appointed former government officials to his board of directors.

First there was his old friend General Trudeau, who was now retired and had a home in Vermont. Later, Bull added Sterling H. Cole, a one-time congressman who once chaired the Joint Atomic Energy Committee. Cole said publicly that the Pentagon decision not to go ahead with Bull's supergun project was "a great tragedy in national security". Cole thought he knew why the multiple Pentagon contracts that Bull had expected were not forthcoming. He guessed that it was because the Pentagon's own weapons laboratories could not admit the "superior competence" of Bull's work without acknowledging their own failure.[1]

Nevertheless, some developments did keep Bull's name at the forefront in Washington. National Security Advisor Henry Kissinger was planning secret peace talks to end the war in Vietnam when in April 1972 thousands of North Vietnamese and Viet Cong troops launched an invasion of the south. About the same time, the Soviets began providing Hanoi with 130-mm coastal guns with a range of 30 kilometres. The 12.5-centimetre guns on U.S. Navy destroyers had a range of only 20 kilometres. Thus, as the ships approached the coastline there was a 10-kilometre journey during which they were vulnerable but could not reply to incoming fire.

Bull had a reputation for working fast. Now the U.S. Navy sent a senior officer to Highwater: they wanted Bull to design a shell that would fire from the destroyers' existing guns but would travel 10 kilometres farther than a standard shell so that it could match the Soviet 130-mm weapons. And they wanted the shell quickly. Later, Bull remembered: "They were in a panic. We were given 120 days to produce a new shell. It would normally have taken a couple of years. But we put a crew together and in 120 days we had a shell for them. It was a sabotted shell and it had a range of 35 kilometres. And so we had them back kicking Communist ass with five kilometres to spare."

That was exactly the sort of "mission impossible" that Bull thrived on. But still, there was little follow-up business.

Soon after opening SRC, Bull had started work on what was to become the centre of his business life. Armies throughout the world used 155-mm gun systems with a range of under 20 kilometres. He set out to design a shell that would fire from these existing guns but with substantially increased range. He took the standard artillery shell, shaped like a big revolver bullet, and made it sleek.

So far, no one had been able to overcome the massive techno-logical problems inherent in this. As with the Martlet missiles de-signed for the HARP gun, Bull's first 155-mm shells were sub-calibre, or of lesser width than the gun barrels they were meant to be fired from. A series of ingenious sabots were invented to make the shells fit the barrel; still there were disadvantages. Bull's sabotted shell would certainly increase range because it was lighter and more aerodynamic than the standard shell. But inevitably that meant that it carried less explosive power – it had less bang for the buck. Nevertheless, the Israelis bought a shell adapted for their 175-mm guns and let it be known they could use it to threaten Damascus from the Golan Heights.

Yet NATO wasn't interested, and Bull went back to the drawing board to develop a full-bore extended-range shell. His final product had a long, tapering nose fitted with four protruding metal nubs that improved spin, balance and accuracy because they made direct contact with the rifling inside the barrel. The body of the shell was forged to exacting specifications to cut drag and air resistance.

It took Bull and his top team nearly four years to perfect the projectiles, but when they had finished, their shells, now made of extremely hard 9260 steel, fired from the same gun as standard shells, would travel one and a half times farther. Bull also re-designed the internal workings and filled his shells with high-energy explosive. In a controlled test, Bull's shell shattered into 4,756 fragments. This compared with the 1,358 fragments from a TNT-filled NATO shell. In the cold assessment of a NATO general, "Bull's shells had a very nice killing pattern".

In 1973 the large Belgian munitions company Poudreries Ré-unies de Belgique (PRB) paid Bull $75,000 for a series of demon-stration firings of the new shell at a range in West Germany. PRB had just appointed a new director general, a highly personable, driving businessman called Joseph Severin. Severin flew to Montreal, toured the Highwater compound and explained to Bull that the underlying weakness of NATO conventional artillery de-velopment was its domination by a small group of government arsenals and their close ties to "friendly" subcontracting industries. Further, he convinced Bull that while SRC might be rich in technology and good products, it would never get out of the laboratory without an international partner. Consequently, Space Research Corporation International (SRC-I) was established in Brussels, with PRB holding 38 per cent of the shares.

Severin also persuaded Bull to develop not just shells but artillery systems to fire them. He suggested a 155-mm gun-howitzer to start with, in two versions: one designed to be towed around the battlefield behind an armoured vehicle, and the other with its own built-in transportation.

Bull and his engineers developed both systems on the drawing board and code-named them GC-45. It amused Bull that the popular press thought GC stood for Gun Canadian when in fact it stood for Gun Calibre. The 45 referred to the length of the barrel. Thus, if the calibre was to be 155-mm, the barrel length would be 45 calibres, or 45 times 155-mm, which made it almost seven metres long. Bull's calculations had showed that this simple equation – barrel length equals 45 times the calibre – resulted in the optimum barrel for field artillery.

Further, his calculations showed that this weapon with its longer barrels would fire his extended-range shells for 30 or more kilometres, compared with a maximum of about 20 kilometres for standard guns, and would do so with increased accuracy and explosive power.

At least in theory, Bull had developed a gun system far superior to anything in the NATO or Warsaw Pact arsenals. But if he expected huge orders, he was sadly disappointed. For while he was working on conventional artillery, the Americans had spent millions of dollars developing rocket-assisted shells. Although these shells cost many times what Bull's shells cost to produce, they were equal in performance. And because the investment had already been made in research, and because the domestic military lobby was so strong, the Pentagon turned its back on Bull's low-cost conventional product.

Meanwhile, PRB began to develop SRC-I in Brussels. They advertised the new extended-range full-bore shells worldwide and spread word that Bull was ready to produce a new gun system to go with them. As a result, foreign delegations of generals and cabinet ministers and senior civil servants started pouring into the Highwater compound for briefings and demonstrations.

And they found a most extraordinary set-up. Bull used to call it his "Camelot". Visitors to the Space Research Corporation usually approached through the Vermont village of North Troy, which is little more than a fork where two country roads meet, a three-minute drive south of the Canadian border. Not marked on standard maps is a narrow paved road veering off to the left. The asphalt soon gives way to gravel and mud as the road rises and dips for about three kilometres through dense bush and into the gently rising slopes of the Cold Hollow Mountains. It led to a set of high chain-link gates with an armed guard on duty. Only those with passes or letters of appointment were allowed through. Just beyond the gates was a low, single-storey building. Like all of the structures at SRC it was of white-painted concrete block, and it housed not just the guard but also a U.S. Customs officer who checked all incoming and outgoing vehicles, for this 1,600-hectare compound, half of it in Canada, was also a private border crossing.

The road continued up a steep hill and then split, one branch going sharply left, the other carrying straight on towards Canada. The road to the left led into a large paved parking area kept floodlit at night. Set back from the parking lot, surrounded by thick under-brush, was the three-level administration and draughting building, equipped with giant cameras and high-tech measuring devices to analyse artillery shells in flight. There were some twenty offices here, a large kitchen, bathrooms and showers. The road led beyond the parking area and narrowed to a two-rut track that twisted through the bush for nearly a kilometre to the western limits of the compound and the electronics shop. The size of a high-school gym, this is where Bull's companies were to develop radar guidance systems and, in one effort to diversify from weapons, simulators to train air-traffic controllers.

The other road, which crossed the Canadian border, did so at a place unmarked and disregarded. The International Boundary Commission had given permission for this road to be built – the first new crossing allowed anywhere along the 6,400-kilometre border for fifty years. Permission had originally been given to allow joint U.S.-Canadian development of HARP when it was being run as a non-profit university research project. Now U.S. and Canadian Customs were uneasy about the arrangement but allowed it to continue under a state of constant review, for Bull convinced them he was working for the defence of both nations.

Just across the border were two small buildings, the powder magazines. The road dipped into a long valley that had been cleared at ground level. This was the horizontal firing range. At one end, gleaming white, was the 40-centimetre gun. At any given time there could be six or seven other artillery pieces here, ranging from 10 to 20 centimetres in barrel diameter. Behind the permanently placed big gun in its massive concrete pit was a closed-circuit TV camera to record firings.

The road wound behind the main gun pit, and on the right was another large emplacement of two 10-centimetre cannons with their barrels pointing skywards. Bull called this area his "vertical launching pad".

The road continued past the launch control building, with its computerized control board and giant TV screens, similar to a small NASA establishment. On the right were the telemetry towers, to record the signals sent back from radio and other communication devices installed in shells and rockets. Nearby was a small building to house gas guns, and behind it a radar tracking station. A little way along the road on the left was the main industrial complex containing workshops, machine shops, a photographic department and an auditorium for technical lectures. There was also a gatehouse and Customs station, this one manned by the Canadians. Past Customs the road jogged to the right, passed the Bull family home and went on to the main gates. Beyond them was a side road that led to the village of Highwater.

There was some $15 million worth of equipment (with a $30-million replacement value) in the compound, most of it donated, via HARP, by the U.S. Army. And while employment levels varied greatly through the 1970s, there were sometimes three hundred people working there full time.

Mimi had a paddock and barn near the house, and she kept horses on the property. Particularly in the spring, she would rise early and go riding through the compound before the staff arrived.

But mostly Gerry was away, travelling from country to country searching for contracts and research money. It was never his intention to manufacture either guns or shells; he wanted to sell ideas and concepts and engineering drawings. Production would be left to the customer.

As Bull entered middle-age he grew a few grey hairs, and he developed a paunch. When he wasn't travelling, he tried to keep fit playing touch football with his three oldest boys, and in winter he would ski with Mimi. But as the costs of maintaining the compound continued to rise, he found himself out of the country seeking new business more than six months a year. And the worst part about that was being away from his family. He was almost a stranger to his youngest children. In an effort to be at home more, he encouraged prospective customers to visit him.

The SRC staff was such that big-spending weekend parties had become the rule. On the American side, near North Troy, a local businessman developed, on the strength of SRC business, a thirty-bedroom lodge with a restaurant, bar and disco. Now, visiting delegations were included in the parties, and when they were important enough, there would always be plenty of good-looking French-Canadian women on hand, invited down from Montreal by the young engineers. Bull enjoyed the glamorous image.

The delegations would usually fly north from New York to a small private airport in Vermont, where they would be met by one of Bull's discreet drivers. They would be taken to register at the lodge, and from there one of the senior engineers would accompany them on a tour of the compound.

Invariably, the delegations were overwhelmed by the scale and the scope of the place. But rarely did Bull put in an appearance during that first tour. The visitors were promised a meeting, later. The build-up was as suspenseful, as dramatic and as impressive as the compound itself.

That night there would be a party at the lodge. And once the visitors, the engineers and their ladies were all in place, there would be an expectant hush and the great scientist would stroll into the bar.

With his charisma, his grin and his total command of the surroundings, he was the star. And the delegations almost always left feeling privileged to have actually met this genius, the greatest gun scientist alive. Once he arrived he was in the centre of everything, entertaining with anecdotes, laughing, joking, being endlessly generous and effortlessly international. "One night, I counted five different languages being spoken in the bar," says a former waitress.

It was in the mid-1970s that Bull's compound and company set-up began exploiting its unique advantages. Because SRC straddled the border, it could mix and meld the export laws of two countries. For example, the U.S. allowed the export of arms to allies such as Israel. Canada, on the other hand, banned all arms sales into the Middle East. The development work on the sub-calibre extended-range shell was done on the Canadian side of the compound, but Bull had the shells built by Chamberlain Manufacturing, which operated an ammunition plant in Scranton, Pennsylvania, and Washington issued an export permit for them to be sold to Israel.

At the same time, although Ottawa had stringent laws governing the export of arms, it did not require end-user certificates for "inert" items sent to friendly nations. That meant Bull could export his shell casings, or rough-cast forgings as they were known, to anywhere in Europe, just so long as they were empty and without explosive charges or fuses. In that way he could send them to PRB in Belgium. PRB in turn could arm the shells and sell them to anywhere that Belgian law would allow. And Belgian law was a good deal less strict than Canadian or U.S. law. Confident that he could sell to whichever country he wanted, Bull set up workshops on the Canadian side of the compound that could produce the most sophisticated experimental shells in small quantities.

Says a U.S. Customs officer once assigned to the south gate: "It was crazy." The compound was a no-man's-land. The border was completely ignored, and Bull had his own private and exclusive free-trade zone. The one rule was that all Canadians had to leave and enter by the north gate while all Americans had to use the south gate.

This ballistics laboratory and test range that straddled the border came complete with a huge loan from America's oldest bank, First Pennsylvania. Following the introduction by the Bronfman brothers, First Pennsylvania had been nothing but generous. The bank's faith in the company was backed by glowing reports from General Trudeau on SRC's potential. Although SRC lost $600,000 in 1971, the bank had still made a $5-million loan and revolving credit agreement the next year. Under the agreement, the bank was given veto power over SRC's major business decisions. When conditions didn't improve through the spring and summer of 1973, the bank had to loan the company $100,000 a month to make interest payments on the original loan. Without seeming to notice, the bank had dug itself so deeply into SRC that it couldn't afford to get out. In late 1973 it made another $4.5-million loan to keep the company going, and by November 1975 the debt had reached $11 million.

The pressure on Bull to make money was enormous. And it showed. He developed sagging wrinkles around his piercing eyes, his hair began to thin and the ever-hunched shoulders hunched even more.

Nor was money his only worry. The mid-decade was marred by two deaths. In September 1974, on a visit to Toronto, Gerry found that Uncle Phil, by now in his seventies, was living in pain. He wasn't complaining, but Gerry could see there was something seriously wrong. He talked it over with this father-in-law and arranged for Phil to be examined by friends of the family, doctors in Quebec City. That December the doctors performed an exploratory operation on Phil and found he had inoperable cancer. Aunt Edith said she had never noticed there was anything wrong with Phil, and it came as a terrible shock to her when he died in January. In September 1975, Dr. Gilbert, Bull's father-in-law and the president of Giltaur, also died. It was a big blow to Bull. Family members still recall him breaking into uncontrollable sobbing at the funeral. He had no other close male friendship quite like it. The men had spent hours together on winter nights playing dominoes, sometimes until after midnight, shouting and laughing at the simple fun of the game. The death left a hole that no one was ever quite able to fill.

In 1976 the Thai Marine Corps became the first customers for Bull's new full-bore shells, buying several thousand rounds. And in January 1977, Severin of PRB visited Highwater again and gave Bull nearly $5 million to help pay for the production of a prototype of the GC-45 gun.[2] Things were at last looking up.

But if all seemed to be going well at the main compound, the same could not be said for the holdings in Barbados, which were essential for long-range testing of shells. There, SRC was under attack from the left-leaning opposition party, who claimed Bull was turning the island into a military outpost. When the opposition won the September 1976 election, they made it clear that Space Research Corporation was no longer welcome. With former prime minister Barrow's help, Bull negotiated with the government of nearby Antigua to open a firing range. He agreed as part of the deal to provide training for the Antigua Defence Force and to use it as a paid guard to watch over the testing site, the guns and the ammunition. SRC sent radar systems to Antigua to help track the shells in flight and installed high-tech ballistics-monitoring equipment from Barbados. By early 1977, Antigua was prepared for long-range shell testing.

And that was when the real trouble started.

PART IV

A Care that Almost Killed

But sorrow, and a care that almost killed
Kept me from what I may accomplish yet ...

"Mezzo Cammin"
Henry Wadsworth Longfellow

9

THE NATURE of Bull's business meant that his fortunes were tied to war. Thus, although he probably never consciously made the connection, it was potentially good news for SRC when vicious guerrilla fighting continued in Angola after the Portuguese granted its independence in November 1975. The fractious liberation groups could not settle their internal political disputes and called on their allies to arm them.

Although Bull must have been aware of the situation, there was no reason for him to link southwest Africa with a call he received from Brussels in February 1975, from retired U.S. Air Force colonel John "Jack" Frost. Frost, a well-known arms dealer, said he was representing the Israelis, and he asked Bull to immediately sell Tel Aviv 15,000 extended-range full-bore (ERFB) 155-mm shells. Bull was surprised by the urgency of the order, but he was able to arrange for Chamberlain Manufacturing in Scranton, Pennsylvania, to make the rough-cast forgings (or casings) for the projectiles.

The forgings were sent to workshops on Bull's compound for high-grade milling, and under a U.S. arms export permit they were shipped to PRB in Belgium to be armed with fuses and explosives before going on to Israel.

Meanwhile, the war in Angola was intensifying. There were three major guerrilla groups, each known by the initials of its Portuguese name, and each backed by a different foreign power. In the south was Jonas Savimbi's UNITA, fighting alongside invading forces from

South Africa. In charge of the centre of the country, including the capital of Luanda, were the MPLA and its Soviet allies. In the north, the FNLA, supported by the CIA, was in charge. No wonder that as the skirmishing spread into set battlefield confrontations, this became known as the "alphabet war". Moscow decided that it couldn't lose Angola at that stage in the superpower Cold War and began sending huge amounts of weapons while encouraging the Cubans to commit twenty thousand highly trained troops as "advisers" to the MPLA.

In the hands of the experienced Cubans, the Soviet weapons were devastating, especially the Russian 122-mm rocket, which had a range of 20 kilometres. John Stockwell, head of the CIA's Angola Task Force, reported back to Washington that in one crucial battle in November 1975, two thousand rockets rained on the FNLA force "as it broke and fled in panic, scattering across the valley in aimless flight, abandoning weapons, vehicles and wounded comrades alike".[1] In effect, the FNLA was finished. Soon after, the Communist forces turned south to face UNITA and the South Africans. Says Stockwell: "The obsolete South African cannon pounded away, but their firepower was a fraction of the rocket salvoes and their range scarcely over half that of the 122." The South Africans were forced to withdraw in bitter defeat. It was the first time they had ever backed down in Africa, and the experience left Pretoria smouldering for revenge. The United Nations' arms embargo, imposed to help counter apartheid, robbed Pretoria of ready access to modern military technology. The CIA, by now backing UNITA, wanted to send new weapons that would allow the South Africans to defeat the Cubans and the Angola Communists. But the State Department overruled that idea as a gross violation of the UN embargo. Still, like Moscow, the CIA did not want to "lose" Angola.

As far as the South Africans were concerned, Bull's shells and the GC-45 gun he was working on were just what they needed. The Israelis were closely cooperating with the South Africans on military matters, and in fact it was for Pretoria that the ERFB 155-mm shells had been ordered. The shells scored well in Southern Angola and in November 1975 officers from the South African military intelligence service took Lt. Col. John Clancey, a Marine officer on assignment to the CIA in Pretoria, out for lunch. They explained again the urgent need for longer-range artillery to match Soviet rockets and pleaded once more for help – if not from the Pentagon then from the CIA. Clancey was left to fall back on his own imagination. He dediced to put the South Africans in touch with Jack Frost in Brussels. Frost had worked with the CIA on classified deals in the past and Clancey thought he might be able to help. Within days, T. Denys Zeederberg and Piet Smith, senior Armscor officials, were holding secret talks with Frost. In January, 1976, Frost introduced them to Luis Palacio, Bull's oldest and most trusted employee, who was in charge of the SRC-I office in Brussels. The South Africans told Palacio that their own domestic arms industry – known collectively as Armscor – was secretly working on a new 155-mm howitzer that would be fully motorized and mobile, and customized for use over the sort of rough bush terrain they had to fight on. Further, the South African howitzer was being developed along similar lines to the gun Bull was making. The South Africans suggested that SRC sell them the technology to make the ERFB 155-mm shell and at the same time combine forces for the development of the howitzer so that South Africa's ballistics engineers could work alongside Bull and his engineers for joint research and development. As part of the deal, South Africa would invest enough money into SRC to ensure its survival. And all of this, the South Africans said, could be done under a cloak of the strictest secrecy. In the meantime, and to consider details, Palacio was invited to visit Johannesburg.[2]

Palacio called Bull to discuss tactics. Bull certainly needed a big customer. He had great sympathy with the South African role in Angola – fighting to keep Moscow and Cuba from taking over the country. The issue of racism was never considered. In the rush and worry of his own business problems he told Palacio to go ahead and explore the possibilities of a deal.

Palacio went to South Africa in early March, and then flew to Rio de Janeiro to meet with Bull and Joseph Severin of PRB, who were considering a proposal to produce the GC-45 system in Brazil, from where it could be exported worldwide. Now the three men concentrated on the problems and the advantages of dealing with South Africa. Severin was generally in favour of letting Pretoria pay for further development of the new gun on the strict understanding that the product would be made elsewhere for worldwide sales and Pretoria would have production rights for domestic use only. PRB had dealt extensively with Pretoria, and Severin was reassuring on the obstacle of the arms embargo: "Everybody breaks it," he said. Palacio too was enthusiastic, and Bull began to breathe more easily about his financial prospects.

Some indication of the speed of development of the South African proposal can be gathered from the fact that Zeederberg and Smith arrived in Highwater for the full Bull treatment on March 28, 1976, the day after Bull returned from Rio. The men from Armscor brought with them Colonel P.M. Lombard, head of the South African artillery school at Potchefstroom and the man who had headed the artillery battle in Angola. Also on hand were J. Swart and M.J. Smith, officials from Cementation, one of the Armscor group of companies. The five South Africans toured the compound and were given a party in the lodge. On April 7, just before they left, they signed a contract to buy 35,000 ERFB 155-mm shells with an option on 15,000 more. The contract was between Paragon Holdings Ltd., a Bull "box" company named after the old plantation house in Barbados, and Colet Trading Establishment, a Liechtenstein front often used by Pretoria.

Before the end of that month, Bull met with the State Department's Office of Munitions Control in Washington. He wanted to make sure that if he had his shell casings made again by Chamberlain in Scranton, there would be no restrictions on exporting them in that rough, inert state. He was assured there would be no restrictions because rough nose forgings were not considered weapons. Just to be absolutely certain, Bull followed up the meeting with a letter, and was again reassured in a written reply. Later, the Munitions Control Office was to say it thought the shells were destined for Israel. On April 30, 1976, Bull ordered 53,000 155-mm rough-cast shell casings from Chamberlain.

Soon after, Bull flew to South Africa. He liked the South Africans. He found them direct, no-nonsense types who immediately impressed him with their knowledge of artillery and their penetrating interest in his work. Bull was impressed by South African advances on the 155-mm cannon, particularly the work they had done on mobilizing the weapon. But he was much in advance of the South Africans when it came to ballistics, and he was shocked at the aged equipment they were using on their testing ranges.

It was easy to appeal to Bull for help. He so much wanted to please that he could hardly say no to anything once he realized that he was wanted and needed. And so it was that he agreed that a team of South African engineers could work alongside his own men at the PRB offices in Brussels. In addition, he said that he would send a team to South Africa to set up a modern testing range and to teach the South Africans how to load and arm the ERFB 155-mm shells.

There was no mention of apartheid, and as far as Bull could see the black population appeared to be doing much better than blacks in the rest of Africa. The visit convinced him that there was nothing wrong in dealing with Pretoria and that the anti–South African sentiment being whipped up in North America was the work of left-wing ideologues. "He found the South Africans to be like the gentlemen of the Old South, the ones who ran the plantations," says Charles Murphy. He adds: "Bull grew up in Canada at a time when there were really no blacks there. He had no sensitivity to black problems because he had no exposure to black people." For whatever reason, Bull didn't bother to examine the veneer of South African manners. In fact, knowing the project was underway, he divorced himself from the South African deal to concentrate on finding new business and to set up the firing range in Antigua. For a while, he was no longer involved with or even aware of the deal's progress.

In Bull's absence, Rodgers Gregory, a former U.S. Army colonel and Norwich University official who had been appointed head of the U.S. operations for SRC, handled the North American end of the South African contract and visited South Africa himself. Palacio set up the cooperative work programme in Brussels, and Steve Adams, a Vermont engineer who had been serving as project manager for the development of the ERFB 155-mm shell, was in charge of SRC operations in South Africa.

During September and October, Gregory and Adams shipped a radar tracking system – to follow shells in flight – from Montreal's

Mirabel Airport to Cementation Engineering in Johannesburg. They also sent seven cutaway demonstration shells, which were used to instruct ballistics workers on how to load and fill the ERFB round.

In the meantime, Bull had revived U.S. Army interest in his GC-45 work, and they made a series of test gun barrels to his specifications at the U.S. Army Arsenal in Watervliet, New York. Bull was glad to get the barrels made so quickly because that November Gerry Ford was defeated in the presidential election, making way for Jimmy Carter, the religious former Democratic governor of Georgia. Bull's friends in the Pentagon were appalled by Carter's victory and spoke darkly of well-meaning but naive human rights policies that could upset friendly regimes from Iran to the Philippines. There was a general feeling that defence procurements would tighten and that arms deals would be made more difficult.

In December, South Africa picked up its option to buy the extra 15,000 shells and increased pressure for quick delivery.

As the year drew to a close, Bull began preparing to test ammunition and his U.S.-made barrels in Antigua. The first rough forgings had been completed in Scranton and were trucked north to the Space Research Corporation, where U.S. Customs agreed they could be exported into Canada without any special permit. At the workshops on the Quebec side they were milled to perfection, and the entire first batch of about 2,000 were shipped to Antigua along with a number of standard and experimental 155-mm howitzers for testing.

The testing started in January 1977, and as Jimmy Carter was being sworn into office in Washington, the political opposition to Prime Minister Vere Bird of Antigua went into high gear. They accused Bird of importing weapons, including tonnes of small arms, and claimed he was planning to stay in power through force and create a military dictatorship. Bull worried that the prospects would eventually grow strong enough to stop the testing. And just in case, a complete ballistics instrumentation testing system was flown from New York aboard a South African airplane to Cementation Engineering in Johannesburg. On their own, the individual parts of the system were not on the Munitions Control List and so there was no difficulty obtaining an export licence. However, the shipment certainly broke the spirit of the arms embargo, because once the components were gathered into a system, they had no other purpose but the ballistics testing of artillery.

In late May, SRC shipped 14,800 finished shell casings from Saint John, New Brunswick, to Antigua. The Canadian government issued an export licence for the inert shells, understanding that the casings were to be used for testing at the Antigua range. During the second week in June, the SS *Tugelaland*, a cargo vessel partly owned by the South African government, picked up the shell casings in Antigua and ferried them to Cape Town.

Pretoria was now satisfied that deliveries could be made discreetly, and on July 7, 1977, J.S. Coetzee, the chief manager of commercial sales for Armscor, met in London with Bull and his lawyers and officials of the First Pennsylvania Bank. The bank still controlled Bull's company and was carrying Space Research Corporation debts that hovered around $10 million. Coetzee was representing Space Capital International N.V., a finance company registered in Amsterdam. It took two days to reach agreement, but when the haggling was over, Space Capital invested $10 million in return for 19.9 per cent of Canadian Technical Industries, the holding company Bull used to control SRC. SRC forthwith paid $6.3 million off its debt to First Pennsylvania, and the bank agreed the remainder of the money could be used to continue operations.

Within weeks of the London meeting, the *Tugelaland* called at Saint John and picked up thirty-two containers, ten of them empty. Inside the other twenty-two were stacked some 10,000 shell casings. In Antigua, twelve containers were taken off the ship, including the ten empty containers. Three other containers were put on board. Two were filled with spent 155-mm shells, for study; the other contained two of the U.S.-made experimental 155-mm barrels. The ship's manifest listed Barbados as destination, yet the ship ended up in Cape Town.

As testing at the Antigua range continued through the summer, the political protests grew. By the end of August there had been a series of break-ins, shells had been stolen, stones were being thrown at SRC workers, and the range was in a state of virtual siege. Bull suspended testing until things calmed down.

That fall, Joshua Nkomo, one of the black guerrilla leaders trying to overthrow the white minority government of Ian Smith in Rhodesia, visited Fidel Castro in Cuba. Castro told him that Cuban intelligence was picking up reports from dock workers in Antigua that a Canadian-based company was shipping small arms to Rhodesia. Nkomo was on his way to make a speech in Canada, and as soon as he arrived in Ottawa he called a press conference. Without naming SRC, he made his allegations.

Canadian prime minister Pierre Trudeau, incensed, ordered an immediate investigation. It took the Royal Canadian Mounted Police less than an hour to discover that Space Research Corporation was the only Canadian arms company with links to Antigua. An hour after that they found that SRC had fifty-five containers on the docks at Saint John ready to go to Antigua. Police were on the scene before nightfall and the containers were opened. The contents were found to conform to the declared export licence – 21,624 inert shells bound for the test range on Antigua. The RCMP reported back to Ottawa that all was in order and that further checks showed that SRC and Dr. Gerald Bull had never been involved with small arms. Canadian intelligence contacted the British MI6 and was assured that the Smith regime in Rhodesia was not using – and did not even have – Bull's advanced artillery technology.

There the matter might have ended, except the RCMP intelligence service sent an agent to Antigua just to make sure that all of the shells were in fact being used in tests. The agent found it was impossible to say exactly how many shells had been fired, but a check of the inventory showed that the two American barrels were missing. He asked where they were and was told that so many shots had been fired from the two barrels that they had worn out and been dumped in the sea. That was all too neat for the RCMP. They had been inclined to believe that Nkomo was wrong and that there were no illegal arms deals passing through Antigua. Now, they felt there was a cover-up under way and began to probe deeper.

Meanwhile, Nkomo's accusations caused a furore in Antigua. Premier Bird promised an independent inquiry and Bull kept his test range closed. The shipment from New Brunswick was cancelled and the inert shells remained on the dock.

On October 20, Steve Adams, the 155-mm project manager, left Vermont with a ten-strong ballistics team. All members of the team had been with Bull for at least five years, and all were mid-level technicians and engineers – computer experts, photographic technicians, gunners and mathematicians. They told friends they were being assigned to the Brussels office for three weeks; only wives were allowed to know that the real destination was South Africa. To keep the South African connection quiet, within the compound it was referred to only by the code name Miami.

In Brussels, the team was given tickets for a flight to Johannesburg, leaving the next day. Travel expenses were paid in cash. They were briefed not to take photographs or buy souvenirs and were each given a slip of paper to fit inside their passports. In Johannesburg, Immigration officials put their landing stamp on the slip, for removal on departure. From Johannesburg the team was flown to the diamond capital of Kimberly. From Kimberly they were driven in Army vehicles 100 kilometres to the remote community of Schmidts Drift, a few small stores and a hotel. But near it, hidden in the bush behind chain-link fences, was a large Defence Force artillery range. And waiting for them at the range were all of the radar and computers and high-tech devices that had been shipped during the past year. Also waiting for them were nearly 30,000 ERFB 155-mm shell casings.

Over the next two weeks the team set up the equipment to create a complete state-of-the-art ballistics testing range, began training Armscor personnel how to use it, and set up a programme for arming the inert shells, fitting them with fuses and high-explosive materials. They worked long hard hours, and at night they slept in camouflaged tents. But to a man, they loved the place. The camaraderie, the efficiency of the South African soldiers and the beauty of the velt left them longing to stay.

The week after the team returned to Vermont, South African prime minister John Vorster announced: "There are those in the world who believe they can bring South Africa to its knees with a mandatory arms boycott. I tell them they have another guess coming."

To the delight of all concerned, Adams took the team out to Schmidts Drift for a second session of training South African technicians early the next year.

While in South Africa, Steve Adams had mightily impressed the top brass at Armscor. Not only was he fully informed on the new gun system and its ballistics but he also demonstrated enormous knowledge about weapons development and sources of supply. Cementation Engineering offered him a job at a salary he couldn't refuse, and in March 1978 he resigned from SRC to move to Johannesburg. Bull was furious. His anger spilled over to encompass not just what he saw as Adams's treachery; Bull believed he had been double-crossed.

The week after Adams moved, $1 million was paid from a Swiss account directly to First Pennsylvania Bank. The debt was going down, the financial pressure was beginning to ease. And there was another piece of good news. The Antigua government's probe into Nkomo's allegations of gun-running to Rhodesia absolved SRC of any wrongdoing. The report was largely ignored, though, because it came as Ian Smith began handing over power to the black majority, and the fight for democracy in Rhodesia appeared to be won.

Bull scarcely noticed, busy as he was with other concerns. Earlier in the year he had made two trips to Spain, and now he announced a contract with the Spanish government to buy ERFB shells through an agent in Barcelona called Barreros Hermanos International. That March a Danish ship picked up the 21,624 shells that had been stored at Saint John for the last five months and sailed them to Barcelona.

The sale to Spain triggered renewed interest within the RCMP. In April they sent another officer to Antigua. He found that SRC had 2,508 shells in stock and gathered evidence to show that no more than 2,000 shells had ever been fired in the tests. As 30,000 shells had been shipped to Antigua, that meant 25,492 were missing.

The RCMP talked to MI6, where there was considerable interest in why the shells sent to Barcelona were still sitting on the dockside. That May, two months after the shells had been unloaded in Barcelona, British agents watched as the *Breezand*, a Dutch ship, picked them up. The *Breezand* was monitored as it sailed south and unloaded the shells – in Durban, South Africa.

British intelligence did not inform the RCMP – perhaps because they were investigating larger-scale weapons deals and did not want Pretoria to be tipped off by RCMP action against Bull – and Ottawa innocently issued another export permit to allow Bull to sell more shell casings to Spain that summer. In July a West German tramp steamer picked up 12,000 shells in Montreal and took them to Barcelona. A few weeks later the shells were shuttled on, again to Durban.

Following the Nkomo allegations, Bull had become extremely nervous about exposure. But he thought the whole business had blown over, until the late summer of 1978, when he started to get pointed calls from BBC's "Panorama" and CBC's "fifth estate", which were engaged in a joint investigation of Bull's dealings with South Africa.

Their one-hour documentary, aired in early November 1978, alleged that Bull had shipped shells to South Africa. The RCMP investigation intensified, and within a month the U.S. government convened a grand jury to determine if SRC had broken U.S. export laws. Bull resigned as president of SRC, flew to Belgium to take over SRC-I and left Rodgers Gregory to sort out the mess. Gregory's first act was to order all files on "Miami" destroyed. A week or two later, on December 20, 1978, the RCMP raided SRC offices in Highwater, looking for what had already gone.

Antigua premier Bird made a radio broadcast saying that if the allegations made in the BBC-CBC film were true, he would ask Space Research to leave the island. It became a major international political issue, and opposition forces tried to use it to force Bird to resign.

Bull arrived in Belgium feeling very much alone and under attack. He knew that the allegations, by now broadcast worldwide, would make it nearly impossible for him to get any more Canadian or U.S. government contracts. And South Africa was finished: Pretoria had all of the technology to go it alone with final development. If he wanted to save SRC, he had to find new business. PRB, though, refused to take the calamity seriously. They urged Bull to move all of his operations to Belgium and in the meantime opened negotiations with Voest-Alpine, the Austrian government's nationalized arms company, for a deal in which they would manufacture and sell the GC-45 howitzer and extended-range ammunition under licence. But Bull was frightened of the judicial process in North America. He was frightened of the condemnation that would come from academia, and he was frightened of the social disgrace he faced.

The grand jury process is supposed to be secret, and Bull and SRC lawyer Kirk Karaszkiewicz, of Philadelphia, were angered by leaks, most particularly to the *Burlington Free Press*, which assigned eager young Sam Hemingway to the story. Over the next two years, the lanky Hemingway and Washington freelancer William Scott Malone devoted untold hours to digging out SRC's South Africa connection. Using the freedom of information laws and hundreds of interviews, they pieced together the story in detail and depth.

Bull argued that, strictly speaking, he had committed no crime. His letter from the Munitions Control Office allowed him to export the rough nose forgings without a permit, and Canadian law allowed him to export inert weapons systems without an end-user certificate. And that was all he had done. He insisted, even to his family, that he was not aware of all the South Africa deals.

About this time, Bull received an invitation from a Michael Chang (not his real name) in London to discuss "trade". Bull flew to Britain for a secret meeting in the businessman's elegant Belgravia home. Chang was about fifty, spoke near-perfect English and had the quiet and dignified bearing of a diplomat. He first told Bull how much he admired the work SRC had achieved on the 155-mm gun. He then explained that he had left China in 1948, when the Communists took over, and that many of his friends had suffered terribly under Mao. However, he said, since Richard Nixon's 1972 visit to Beijing, China had begun to open to the West while remaining suspicious of Moscow. The best tactic now, Chang believed, was for the West to develop strong ties with China, for such ties could serve only to pull the nation towards Western values and away from ruinous communism. It could be argued, he said, that dealing with Beijing might be considered an anti-Communist act.

The two men then discussed one of Bull's favourite topics, the Second World War. They talked about the "help China" syndrome that had been so popular in North America during the early years of the Cold War. Finally, Chang revealed that he had a "sponsor" who wanted Bull to visit Beijing to look at the munitions factories, perhaps to lecture at a university, and lastly to consider entering into competition with others, including the British government, who would soon be vying for a contract to sell ordnance.

As always, flattery went far with Gerry Bull. Still, he was undecided and uneasy when he left Belgravia. Although he found the prospect of dealing with the Communist Chinese repulsive, he was delighted to be wanted at a time when old friends were proving hard to find. He held off on making a decision, but over the next few weeks he started to talk quite a lot about the "help China" syndrome, about the opening of Beijing to the West and about the wisdom of wooing the Soviets' most belligerent neighbour.

Meanwhile, Bull's worst business fears were coming to pass. On December 9, Gregory announced that as a result of contract losses, SRC was in danger of shutting down. Forty-five workers were laid off. Ten days later Gregory said the firm was in "desperate trouble". In Antigua, Bird decided the evidence for a South African connection was building and asked SRC to leave the country.

In early 1979, the grand jury began offering immunity from prosecution, and some members of the SRC staff who had journeyed to South Africa testified in secret.

On April 28, with a bravado that sickened Bull, South Africa announced that it had developed a 155-mm howitzer and shell system all on its own and "in record time". Prime Minister P.W. Botha said suggestions that the system had been smuggled in from another country were "devoid of all truth".

With the return of summer, Bull flew home from Brussels and took over again from Gregory as boss.

A month later, Hemingway's associate, Malone, met Bull in Washington and persuaded him to talk. Bull freely admitted that an

SRC team had been to South Africa but insisted that "unscrupulous European business agents" had been responsible for diverting the shells. He said: "We set up an honest deal with the Spanish Army."[3]

That winter, the U.S. prosecutors began to pressure Bull and Gregory for confessions. Because of the letter Bull held from the Munitions Control Office, the government did not have a solid case. It could clearly prove a break in the spirit of the law, but the letter was a different business. Privately, the lawyers said pressure was coming from Washington, where President Carter wanted to show that he stood by his strict anti-Pretoria policies and needed an example. Bull argued back that the U.S. Army and the CIA always knew and approved of his dealings with South Africa. After all, it was the CIA contact Frost who had introduced the South Africans to SRC in the first place. Bull never revealed that Frost had shares in SRC's Brussels operation, but the fact that he did makes it not impossible that the CIA was fully informed of all SRC's operations.

By way of countering this defence, the prosecutors suggested a plea bargain: if Bull and Gregory and the company would plead guilty to some reduced charges, no company employees would be charged; if Bull and Gregory refused, then everyone involved in the technology transfer to South Africa would be charged. Gregory begged Bull to go along with the prosecutors and get the whole thing over with.

On March 25, 1980, Bull, Gregory and SRC all pleaded guilty before U.S. District Judge James S. Holden to joint charges that they exported at least 30,000 howitzer shell forgings, two 155-mm gun barrels and a radar tracking system to South Africa in violation of U.S. law and the UN embargo. Bull at first told the court that he could plead guilty only to the two gun barrels and the radar system, but after further discussions with his lawyer he let the full slate of charges stand. The prosecution told the judge that although only 30,000 forgings were mentioned in the charges, it could be shown that nearly 53,000 had been exported. Gregory stood stiffly with his fingertips resting on the table in front of him. "I supervised the packaging, loading and moving of the items," he said. Bull, his stoop more pronounced than ever, said: "As chief executive officer, I approved it and knowingly let it take place." Bull and Gregory were released on $35,000 bonds. As he left the court Bull was trembling. "I just feel very worn out," he said.

He arrived home that night to receive more bad news. Aunt Edith was seriously ill in Kingston. Bowed with so many other problems, he took the news hard. "She was such a cold person," says Mimi. "She couldn't show affection. She had made Gerry so insecure. He always felt that he would be sent away if he misbehaved or failed to please. But in the end he loved her."

Within days, Aunt Edith died. But with her last act, she threw Gerry a life raft. She split her fortune between Gerry and his cousins, the Keeles. Gerry received about $80,000. The money could not have come at a better time.

The American court case caught Canadian Justice officials by surprise, for they had not expected the plea bargain and were now unsure what to do about their own investigations. No decision had been made by Ottawa when Bull and Gregory returned to court for sentencing on June 16.

Judge Holden said the case was "tragic" because of Bull's reputation as a scientist and Gregory's outstanding military record, which included a Purple Heart. Said the judge: "The tragedy lies in a breech of trust that brought on this investigation." The prisoners were asked if they had anything to say. Bull replied in a whisper, but even so the words kept catching in his throat. He said: "I am deeply sorry for this mistake and for any way it has harmed the image of the country. I am very proud to be an American and I believe deeply in what it stands for."

Bull and Gregory were sentenced to one year each in jail with six months suspended. SRC was fined $105,000. Mimi and 21-year-old Stephen, sitting directly behind Bull in the ornate courtroom, both broke down in sobs. Bull and Gregory were ordered to report for jail no later than noon on July 30, 1980.

10

BULL NEVER seriously believed they would send him to jail, and the court decision came as a shock. He was convinced he had done no wrong, and he suffered the poison of injustice. As he listened to the sentence he felt, he said later, as if he was drowning.

In the following days, Mimi grew increasingly anxious as Gerry fell into depression and took to wandering around the compound at Highwater, muttering to himself. Although she tried to stay calm for him, she was livid that he had ever agreed to plead guilty. She was sure that Gerry could have beaten the charge and it had been so uncharacteristic of him not to fight.

Mimi asked Marcel Paquette, Bull's close friend and Canadian lawyer, for help, but he could not console her. Bull was "devastated", said Paquette. He added: "The sentence is almost enough to kill him. After he goes to jail he will never be the same."

Bull and Gregory were to serve their time at the minimum-security Allenwood Prison Camp in Montgomery, Pennsylvania. Allenwood had been in the news as the temporary home to the Watergate convicts and was said to be a "country club" jail, a joke. It was a penitentiary with a dormitory setting, no prison bars or jail cells or guard towers. In effect, the prisoners were their own jailers. Someone sent Bull a cartoon of a prosperous businessman in prison stripes, smoking a cigar and ordering a gin and tonic from the warden, who was serving behind the bar. It didn't cheer up Bull at all.

Bull started to drink cognac in the afternoons and on into the evenings. Instead of relaxing him, it seemed to make his problems worse. He couldn't sleep. He began taking sleeping pills. The alcohol and the pills combined to keep him in a state of perpetual haziness. He looked haggard and ate little. The booze made him talkative, and while he picked at his food he went over and over the "facts".

As he saw it, he had broken no law in ordering, in milling or in exporting the forgings to Spain and Antigua, and what happened to them after that was somebody else's business. Certainly his engineers had worked with South Africans in Brussels, but under Belgian law that was legal. The American staff had gone to South Africa on freelance contracts issued by the Brussels office, again perfectly legal. Gun barrels and radar equipment had been exported to Antigua under lawful agreement. Once on the island they had been used, they had become surplus, and they had been sold as such to a foreign customer. But at that point it had nothing to do with the U.S., and if any law had been broken it was the law of Antigua. Bull would not even admit to his own family, even when he had been drinking, that he had deliberately set about to sell arms to South Africa. And he denied that South Africa had a share of his company. PRB and Gregory had organized the sales contract, he said. As far as he was concerned, the shells were going to Spain and to Antigua. He had been so busy trying to drum up new business that he hadn't followed the details of every deal. If he was guilty of anything, it was that he hadn't been vigilant enough on the administration side. But he was a scientist, not an accountant – how could he know every jot and tittle of every contract?

Bull must have known that Space Capital International, the company that invested in SRC, had connections with Pretoria, but he would never admit it. In the same way, he must have known that his shells were going to South Africa. But again he would never admit it. He lied to himself, and he came to believe his own lies. Always emotionally fragile, he was now becoming mentally unstable.

This was the time when his children could have been a great comfort. But instead of growing closer, he drifted even further away. Philippe, his oldest son, was now married and living in Austria, where he was attending medical school. Michel was living in Quebec City, as was Stephen, who was studying at Laval University. But the other four were living at home. Richard was 19, Bobby, 16, Kathy, 15, and Jane just 13. Says Michel: "My father disconnected himself from the family. His problems were overwhelming, and they came at the very time that my youngest brothers and sisters really needed him." A gap developed that was never to be properly bridged. Kathy and Jane never got to know their father well.

Nine days after the sentencing, Space Research Corporation closed down. Two hundred employees were sacked, including the entire machine and production shop staffs. That day, Bull stayed in bed.

The next day, he forced himself to deal in some practical way with what was happening. Mimi shouted him into action. He pulled himself together enough to invite about fifteen of his key engineers and technicians to his home. He told them he hoped they would all work for him again some day.

He also told them that he hadn't wanted to see so many of the lower-level workers fired; he knew how hard it would be for them to find a job in that economically depressed area.

Bull and his family owned 80 per cent of Canadian Technical Industries, the SRC holding company. But the company debts were being carried by the owner of the other 20 per cent, Space Capital International, which had control of most assets and which was representing South African interests. The South Africans had demanded that their investment be protected. They had insisted that SRC be put into liquidation before other creditors could make claims, and they didn't care about employment problems in a tiny corner of North America.

As the company gates were closed, U.S. and Canadian Customs officials insisted that the cross-border road be blocked and that all cross-border privileges end. A small bulldozer ploughed up the road connecting the two sides of the compound.

Bull set down his thoughts in shaky handwriting in a little diary. There were a lot of profanities about South Africa. One way or another, South Africa had acquired all of his artillery technology. It was enough to save them in Angola and defeat or at least hold their own against the Cubans. And by way of return, they had closed his company. It's nothing personal, they had informed him. Just good business.

Meanwhile, Marcel Paquette was negotiating with the Canadian government a plea-bargain agreement to end the RCMP investigation. Ottawa did not want to face the costs of a long trial and agreed that any charges the RCMP might lay would be essentially the same as those already dealt with in the U.S. It came as an enormous relief to Bull to hear that Ottawa would charge only the company and not any individuals. Privately, Canadian government lawyers told Paquette they were shocked at the U.S. sentence and didn't think the evidence justified a jail term.

As Paquette haggled over what size of fine would be appropriate in Canada, Bull's mental condition slipped further. He seemed to have no hold on reality. He was often drunk, and in that condition he would sit for hours babbling to himself. Increasingly alarmed, Mimi called in a psychiatrist, and the doctor advised immediate hospital care. At first, Bull refused, but when Paquette suggested that the time he spent in hospital might be taken off his prison term, Bull saw the idea as a lifeboat. If it meant getting out of going to jail, he would do it. On July 17 he checked into the Silver Hill Foundation in New Canaan, Connecticut, a leading psychiatric treatment facility.

During the long interview for new patients, Bull said life was no longer worth living. Dr. Robert Humphries, the specialist assigned to his case, decided Bull was on the brink of black despair, and assigned a nurse to watch him twenty-four hours a day in case he attempted suicide. When his children came to visit, Bull would take them into the rose garden, and the nurse would walk a discreet five metres behind. He called her Mother San. The faithful Charles Murphy, who visited every week, concluded that the hospital was good for Gerry if only because it stopped him drinking.

Bull began a series of extensive psychotherapy sessions, and details of his loveless, insecure childhood came pouring out. Dr. Humphries wrote to Judge James Holden that Bull showed "suicidal tendencies and tendencies towards self-destruction", and he should stay in hospital for at least four weeks and maybe as long as two months. And Bull's new lawyer, J. Stanley Pottinger, former head of the Civil Rights Division in the U.S. Justice Department, also wrote to the judge asking for a reduced sentence. Holden refused to reduce the sentence but agreed that Bull need not report for jail on July 30 with Gregory. Instead, he postponed the start of Bull's jail term to August 30.

On August 13, while Bull was still in Silver Hill, Paquette reached agreement with the Canadian government, and Space Research Corporation was charged with exporting 53,000 long-range artillery shells to South Africa in violation of the UN embargo. Lawyers representing Bull pleaded guilty in a Montreal court, and on August 15 the company was fined $55,000. Within the week, it was announced that all of the assets of SRC – listed at $15.7 million – were to be sold by tender offers.

In the wake of the sale news, Pottinger presented Judge Holden with another petition from Silver Hill doctors saying that although Bull had improved he was still "in rather desperate psychological condition" and not fit for jail. This time Pottinger and the doctors asked that Bull be allowed to serve his sentence in the mental hospital. The judge postponed Bull's prison check-in time to September 30 but refused to cut the sentence or rule that it be served in the hospital.

By now Bull was twisting and squirming and ready to try anything to get out of going to jail, his hopes having been raised only to be dashed. In mid-September, he claimed that he had been pressured by lawyers into pleading guilty in the first place, and he asked to change his plea. Dr. Humphries said that Bull would not have been competent to make informed judgements when he pleaded guilty.

The doctors were saying that Bull's ego, while huge and healthy on the surface and in the field of science, was ready to disintegrate on the personal level. Bull had spent his first twenty years of his life in an emotional storm, and the pressure of simply staying afloat had left deep scars. His gratification came from impressing people with his scientific and academic achievements. His reputation was paramount. If his reputation was damaged, he was nothing. Thus, going to jail – the plight of a common criminal – would destroy him.

In his petition to the court, Pottinger said: "Dr. Bull has already suffered unusually severe reactions of dishonor and loss of dignity and self worth. The sentence has had its intended effect." The plea went on: "Dr. Bull has already suffered gravely ... He has felt a crushing sense of self-betrayal of his own deeply held values of honor and patriotic duty, values from which his professional life has been nurtured."

But the United States legal system is not geared to take fragile egos into consideration, and Judge Holden ordered that Bull report at the jail by 3:00 p.m. on October 1.

Bull had appeared in court himself for that final plea. Murphy and Paquette were there for support. As he left the court, Bull saw Hemingway of the *Burlington Free Press* in the car park. His fists raised, he ran at Hemingway, shouting, "I'm going to hit you!" But before he reached the reporter, Paquette and Murphy restrained their friend and got him into their car. As they started to drive away, Bull broke into sobs.

Murphy, Mimi and another family friend drove Bull to Silver Hill the next day for a final check-up. They carried on from there to Allenwood. At 2:30 the next afternoon, Bull turned himself in. As she left the prison gates, Mimi said that she was quite sure she could serve the sentence much better than her husband.

11

ALLENWOOD PENITENTIARY was not as bad as Bull had feared. Walking through the gates on that first day was the hardest part. Once he was processed and issued the Army fatigues he would wear for the duration, Bull found that the grounds were no more guarded than his own compound had been. He shared a cell (the door wasn't locked and there were no bars on the windows) with a Yugoslav who had fought as a partisan during the Second World War. Bull liked him immediately. By the end of the week, the pair were sitting up talking until two or three in the morning. Bull even toyed with the idea of writing the man's biography.

The hospital stay had been good for Bull. For the first time in his adult life he had been able to talk openly, soberly and at length about his childhood. He told the doctors about his sense of responsibility for his mother's death. They traced that back to a conversation he had overheard as a child. Someone, either his sister Bernice or Aunt Edith, had said that his mother should never have borne so many children, that if she hadn't been a Catholic, she would still be alive because she would never have had the last two children. Gerry's birth, it appears he told himself as a youngster, had weakened his mother in such a way that she could not survive the birth of her last child.

No matter how comforting and reassuring friends such as Murphy had tried to be, Bull couldn't get this notion out of his mind. His mother had become a tragic heroine of sorts. Bull had by this time become a Catholic more of convenience than of devotion, yet in jail he attended Mass every week and started to pray again. As he told friends later, he prayed to his mother.

When Mimi had dropped her husband off at the prison gates, he had told her he wanted no visitors. "Forget me for the next six months," he said. "Forget that I even exist." But she visited every week, as did Murphy, and Bull was obviously pleased to see them. "In a way, it was terrible," she remembers. "We were in a room with everyone else and everyone could hear what you were talking about. Space Research Corporation was in bankruptcy, and every week I would turn up with a bunch of papers for him to sign. He was signing away all that he had worked for. I would ask him what he wanted me to do, and he would say to burn everything."

One week Mimi arrived with the four youngest children. "I wanted him to know that they felt no shame and that they were as proud of him as ever," she says. The prison term had come as a substantial shock to the children. They had been aware that their father was in some legal trouble, but they had no idea it was serious. Bobby was 16, and he remembers vividly the day his father went to jail: "It hurt, it hurt a lot."

Two weeks after Gerry was incarcerated, Mimi got a call from Michael Chang in London. He was shocked to hear that Bull was in jail and was sure that there had been a miscarriage of justice. But in the meantime, he asked Mimi if she would deliver a letter to her husband.

The letter brought with it a breeze of relief. It again invited Dr. Bull to do business with the People's Republic of China. Beijing, conveyed the letter, was very interested in Bull's ideas for long-range 155-mm artillery and shells, and it didn't give a hoot about the jail sentence.

Says Mimi: "We had lost almost everything with the bankruptcy. I handled the financial details. The money Gerry made in the deal with the Bronfmans, all of the HARP assets, the land and the property, it all went to pay debts." Mimi did manage to keep the house in St. Bruno and the house at Highwater along with about two hectares of land. They also had the $80,000 inheritance from Aunt Edith, the only cash they had left. It was this money that would re-launch Gerry into business and keep his family afloat.

As fall turned to winter Gerry pulled out of his depression, his self-pity turning to anger, anger that came flooding out on December 8, when Bull agreed to see Warren Perley, a reporter from the *Montreal Gazette*. He had refused dozens of requests for interviews that year, but Perley's letter struck a special chord because it asked simply for the opportunity to present Bull's point of view. They met in Allenwood's small, comfortable lounge. At first, Bull appeared shy and soft-spoken. Perley asked him about his early life, and Bull recalled in a matter-of-fact, almost casual way that his father had been a heavy drinker and had abandoned his nine children. He said that he never saw his brothers and sisters again because of religious differences. He was a Catholic and his mother had been a Catholic. The rest of the family were Protestants. It was Us and Them – Gerry and his mother, the other eight children and their father.

As the conversation progressed Bull became animated and vibrant. His hands and arms were in constant motion as he stressed points and made his argument. "I remember him as being very forthright and very volatile," says Perley. "He spoke with passion. And he struck me as a very honest man." (Later, Perley interviewed nearly a dozen prominent Canadians whom Bull thought of as his friends. To Perley's amazement, most of them didn't want to have their names used: "They were frightened to be associated with Bull because he was too outspoken for his own good, and for their good.")

Bull said he was "bitter", that his jailing was unjust. He had understood that he had been working with the blessing of the CIA in allowing weapons technology to go to South Africa, but now felt he had been used as a scapegoat by Jimmy Carter. For when Carter came to power, suddenly South Africa was a pariah in Washington. To emphasize the new mood, said Bull, the Carter Administration had decided to make an example, to signal that all cooperation with Pretoria had ended.

Bull repeatedly emphasized that he had done no wrong and that he had no regrets or moral qualms. There was, he said, an ironic injustice in his being prosecuted for sending arms to South Africa while the U.S. government supplied weapons to dictatorships and military juntas such as those in South Vietnam, Iran and Chile.

Then he hit his stride with a stream of classic Bull rhetoric designed to insult and infuriate the Establishment. First he turned on Canada: "Canadian civil servants have sabotaged the Canadian defence industry for the last twenty-five years. The New York City police force is about as large as the Canadian Defence Department and far better equipped. I was proud of Canada during the Second World War, but not now." As for the United States: "They're a gutless, confused bunch. The U.S. has obsolete conventional weapons and no morale in their Armed Forces. They couldn't defeat Timbuktu in a fight."

And what about the future? "The North American operations are finished. I have offers from all over the world. As soon as I'm free to travel I'm out of here, gone. I see hope in a country like China. They have the moral fibre to stand against Russia."

Despite his anger and bitterness, Bull remained busy and even at times excited by challenges. He was assigned to re-engineer the prison heating plant and in his spare time he researched the origins of the prison chapel, formally surveyed the graveyard and read extensively from the prison library on the area's history.

Mimi stayed at home with the children that Christmas Day, but Charles Murphy visited Allenwood. He was delighted to find a guard dressed as Santa Claus and a big Christmas tree in the dining hall. By January the warden and Bull were on first-name terms and Bull was getting ready to face life on the outside.

Bull was released from Allenwood on February 13, 1981, having served four months and seventeen days. He got forty-three days off for good behaviour.

Mimi met him as he checked out. In her purse she had tickets for Martinique and hotel reservations for three weeks in the Caribbean sun. Bull, fit and trim, looked better than he had in two or three years.

From the beach and the bar, Mimi and Gerry surveyed the wreck of their business world. Mimi had not previously been closely involved in running SRC, but with her husband in jail, she had been forced to handle the company's collapse and bankruptcy. The North American business and the Highwater compound had folded into liquidation, with assets sold to cover debts. All staff had been paid off. Gerry and Mimi were on their own, with only Aunt Edith's inheritance money to live on.

Mimi now told Gerry something that puzzled and pleased him, yet also made him uncomfortable. While he had been in jail, several of his long-lost brothers and sisters had called Mimi, or written to her, to offer their support.

For the present, the future looked bleak. His options were strictly limited. Having just stepped out of jail, it was highly unlikely that any university would hire him. His market was restricted to government contracts, and the anti-apartheid lobby would see to it that no business was forthcoming from Washington or Ottawa. Despite what he said to Perley about having offers from "all over the world", Bull had only one business lead – China. Mimi agreed that at least for the moment he should go to Europe and rebuild from there. She hoped that eventually memories would fade and he would be able to return to work in North America.

It was agreed that Mimi would keep their home going in Montreal and Gerry would travel and find work. They expected he would be on the road almost non-stop at first, living out of a suitcase and staying in low-cost hotels, so there was no point Mimi going with him. Besides, the four youngest children still needed her to be with them.

Bull felt so disillusioned about North America that he refused to go to Montreal from the Caribbean to pick up the clothes he would need. Instead, on March 5, he flew from Guadeloupe to Paris while Mimi returned alone to Canada. From Paris he went to Brussels and moved into a room with a kitchenette in a small hotel. He still had strong contacts with PRB, and he was hoping they would help him find work. "It was a sad and lonely time," says Mimi. "He missed me and he missed the children and we missed him very, very much."

There was another controversy to worry Gerry Bull as he moved to Europe: he was now being linked to South Africa's nuclear weapons programme. The story dated back to September 22, 1979, when a U.S. surveillance satellite over the South Atlantic picked up a mysterious flash just off the coast of South Africa. In a report to the White House the CIA said technical information and analyses "suggested" the flash was caused by a nuclear explosion with a force of less than three kilotons. The agency also informed the White House that South Africa had been performing extensive research on nuclear weapons and was capable of creating an atomic blast. It added: "Israelis have not only participated in certain South African nuclear research activities over the last few years, but they have also offered and transferred various sorts of advanced non-nuclear weapons technology to South Africa."[1]

Now investigative journalists in Cape Town were reporting that South Africa had developed a "nuclear bullet" after modifying Bull's 155-mm artillery. They were simply putting a small atomic warhead on the shells in much the same way as NATO nations had done. Said one reporter: "Western observers believe that South Africa is aiming at the production of neutron missiles, having decided that these would be the answer to any concerted military attempt by black African states to invade it – especially if such an invasion was backed by Communist powers."[2]

These reports were followed by charges made on the British TV programme "World in Action" that Bull had actively helped Israel and South Africa develop nuclear weapons. The programme said the flash recorded by the American satellite came from an atomic warhead placed at the tip of one of Bull's shells and launched from one of Bull's guns. Asked about the allegations, Bull threw his hands into the air and shouted: "That's a complete, utter lie! We never worked with nuclear weapons at Space Research."

Once he calmed down, Bull explained that any shell, including his 155-mm, could be adapted to fire nuclear warheads. However, his calculations showed that the maximum weight that a 155-mm shell could carry would be about 18 kilograms, and of that only some 14 kilograms could be nuclear material. "So," he said, "the nuclear yield from a 155-shell would be a maximum of 150 tons of high explosive." (The Hiroshima bomb was a hundred times more powerful.) "Anyone spending a billion dollars on development wants a hell of a lot more out of it than a pipsqueak 155-mm nuclear shell. It's not even a credible deterrent."

Knowledgeable sources connected with the making of U.S. nuclear shells say they are certain Bull had nothing to do with nuclear weapons. "He simply didn't have that kind of knowledge," says one

U.S. scientist, and adds: "There is not a scrap of evidence to link Bull to the South African nuclear programme. Nor is there any evidence that Pretoria has nuclear shells." Nevertheless, the nuclear flash served to further blacken Bull's name and make it even more difficult for him to get new business contracts.

No wonder Bull was desperate for the South African affair to end. It seemed to have developed a life of its own. It did not stop being a daily concern until after March 30, 1982, when the U.S. House of Representatives subcommittee on Africa met for a special hearing on the case. Before the subcommittee was a staff study by Steve Weissman that confirmed that between 1976 and 1978, SRC had shipped about 50,000 155-mm extended-range artillery shells, at least four 155-mm gun barrels including three advanced prototypes, and other technology and technical assistance to South Africa.

Weissman stressed that the letter Bull had received from the Office of Munitions Control "encouraged SRC and its financier, the First Pennsylvania Bank, to proceed with their plans to ship arms to South Africa". He added: "According to the preponderance of evidence, it is probable that a U.S. defense consultant who was assisting the CIA's covert action program in Angola – and was under the supervision of the CIA officer – planned with South African Government officials shipments of U.S. origin arms to South Africa for use in Angola. At the very least, this episode suggests serious negligence on the part of the Agency. At most, there is a possibility that elements of the CIA purposefully evaded U.S. policy."

The report said that the Justice Department had accepted a plea bargain only because it feared that in a trial there would be the "appearance of possible U.S. Government authorization of SRC shipments to South Africa". Weissman said the arms deal had been worth $19 million to SRC and had allowed the company to clear its debts with First Pennsylvania Bank.

"The SRC-ARMSCOR transaction," he concluded, "resulted in a major increase in South Africa's overall military capability. At the time, South Africa had only a few older, foreign-made 155-mm gun systems with the range to neutralize the [Soviet] 122s. Through SRC, the South African military acquired the G 4 gun-howitzer and companion extended-range shells which surpassed Soviet 122-mm and 130-mm artillery in both range and lethality."

There was one other fascinating revelation in the report. Jack Frost, the CIA contact in Brussels, had grown frightened of the deal after becoming involved in 1975. Too many people knew about it for a convincing cover-up to stick. So, to protect himself in any future prosecution, he informed the Office of Munitions Control that a "shady" South African arms deal was going on. But he need not have bothered. No investigation was opened.

From an early date in the course of the South African deal, at least some officials within the CIA, the State Department and the Pentagon knew everything. They let it happen because it suited their purposes. They did not want the Marxist government in Angola, backed by Cuban troops, to succeed in squashing the pro-Western UNITA force. And if that meant arming South Africa to prevent a Communist takeover, then so be it.

While the South Africans are normally secretive about arms dealings, a glimpse at the SRC deal from the Pretoria side was afforded in late 1984, when Piet Marais, chairman of Armscor, talked with *International Defense Review* magazine. He confirmed that in 1975 the South African Defence Force was using old 14-centimetre artillery pieces in Angola with a range of about 17 kilometres. He said they were being "outgunned" by Russian weapons and that Armscor "started scouting around the world" for artillery with a range of 26 kilometres. "We came across this man Gerry Bull ... We got Bull to do the theoretical calculations." A prototype of Bull's GC-45 gun was produced and tested in Antigua. "Following the tests," said Marais, "we brought all that stuff back to South Africa in bits and pieces: the gun barrels, the mounts on which they had been tested and some of the test equipment. From then on, we started developing an artillery system. Gerry Bull's people gave us assistance with certain calculations again, but from 1976 onwards we worked in South Africa." Marais went on to say that two prototypes of Bull's design were made but that they "did not work out at all". And he insisted that it was South African ballistics experts who went on alone to modify the Bull plans and to produce a topline artillery system known as the G-5.

In early 1991, the U.S. Defense Intelligence Agency released, under the Freedom of Information Act, a study of Bull's dealings with South Africa. Said the study: "The South Africans were not without their own indigenous capabilities to design theoretically the requisite system but they lacked the sophisticated computer equipment necessary to assist in the development of extended-range artillery. Bull was in terrible financial straits ... he developed prototype gun barrels and manufactured them along with new projectiles."[3]

We will probably never know exactly who contributed what to the South African artillery system, but clearly it was a joint development, with the South Africans themselves making major contributions. What emerged first from the work was a towed 155-mm artillery piece, the South Africans' G-5. It incorporated Bull's idea of a long 45-calibre barrel. The South Africans took this basic system and developed from it a self-propelled gun they called the G-6. The 42-tonne G-6 can fire accurately at ranges up to 40 kilometres, 10 kilometres farther than NATO's 155-mm guns. A South African lieutenant has been quoted as saying that, at 30 kilometres, "you can hit a fly on the wall with a G-6 – and take out the whole house." The South Africans, more than any others, perfected Bull's work and produced from it the greatest artillery pieces of their day. It was these big guns that eventually held Communist forces back in southern Angola. That stalemate led to the withdrawal of Cuban troops from Angola and independence of Namibia.

On July 9, 1979, under subpoena from the grand jury, First Pennsylvania Bank produced the contract between Bull's front company, Paragon, and the South African front company Colet for the development of Bull's GC-45 gun, which was referred to as the G4. Under the contract both companies had the right to manufacture the guns, but clause 1.3 said: "Paragon will not sell manufacturing know-how or G4 guns or components to any Communist country or any country in Africa, south of the Equator." It was also made clear, however, that both parties could make the gun and sell it. The South Africans did not have to pay Bull any further royalties, and he received nothing for the hundreds of guns Pretoria subsequently sold around the world.

PART V

The Wind Blows East

Turn, turn, my wheel! All things must change
To something new, to something strange ...

The wind blows east, the wind blows west.

"Kéramos"
Henry Wadsworth Longfellow

12

A FEW DAYS after Bull settled into his kitchenette, an old friend from Quebec, who had moved to Brussels years before, threw a party to celebrate Bull's fifty-third birthday. Gerry arrived to find Mimi waiting for him: she had flown over as a special surprise. He was delighted.

Bull's only business lead was China, but despite all of his bravado he felt uneasy about pursuing it. He wasn't sure he could justify working for a Communist government. Nevertheless, he called Michael Chang in London, and the businessman promptly invited Gerry and Mimi to dinner in Belgravia to meet his wife and to "explore" the future. The two couples got along famously. Chang was an independent wheeler-dealer with links to European financiers doing business in the Far East. Following one particularly successful non-military deal, Beijing had asked him to investigate buying a new ordnance system. They had expressed specific interest in the work of Gerald Bull.

The Changs became the first new friends the Bulls had made in a long time. Mimi had shared Gerry's apprehension about working for Beijing, but now they both felt reassured.

Michael Chang remembers: "We found Gerry to be a very simple, gentle person, hungry for affection and approval. The prison experience had left him feeling that he could do whatever the hell he wanted." Into the contrary mix of emotion and sentiment that formed the foundation of most of his decisions, Bull also cast this time a peppering of hostility towards the West. Washington probably wouldn't want him to deal with China, and that was all the more reason to do so.

Before Mimi returned to Montreal, she and Gerry talked at length about their life together. She had never really questioned Gerry's work. He had been involved in weapons research when she had met him, and, though at heart she was something of a pacifist, Mimi hadn't given it very much thought. Gerry stressed he was in the "defence industry" and that he strongly believed all nations had a right to defend themselves. But now Mimi wondered if he shouldn't diversify. That way it would be easier for him to return to Canada. He said that he was all too anxious to diversify but that he couldn't find an opportunity.

In the meantime, Gerry said it made no sense for Mimi to move to Brussels. He would be travelling constantly and she would be left alone. But whenever he knew he would be in the same place for a month or so she would come over to join him. For the long run, he still loved Highwater and hoped that one day he would retire there.

"It made things very difficult for me," says Mimi. "The children were growing up, but they were still a handful and they needed their father. And I wanted to be with him."

The next month, April 1981, Bull and Chang flew to Beijing. They were met by a government minister, chauffeured to a small luxury hotel and treated as though they were making a state visit. Bull was invited to address teams of senior engineers and academics on ballistics in general and on project HARP in particular. The sessions were hushed and intensely polite and were followed by enthusiastic questions. Bull was impressed. He began to feel comfortable in China. He wasn't drinking and he didn't need sleeping pills. Once again, he was a celebrity surrounded by students.

"I could see that he was being renewed," says Chang. "A lot of Gerry's actions were linked in some way to the shock of being sent to jail. That whole episode with South Africa, he couldn't fathom it. He was politically naive. He was a very lovely person lost in a world that he didn't understand."

After a few days in Beijing, Bull was asked by senior Army officers to tour the Chinese arms-making facilities. He was amazed at the huge factories around Beijing and major interior cities. They had been built with Soviet guidance in the 1950s, and a Warsaw Pact production system had been imposed with stifling rigidity. For nearly thirty years the Chinese Communist Party had been running these ordnance manufacturing plants from the instruction book without change or development. Factory workers were required to follow orders right down to the minutiae of which hand was used to pick up a screw, with no allowance made for the worker being right- or left-handed. It was a backwards, slow and clumsy system, but it worked.

Back in Beijing, the Army officers told Bull that China wanted to introduce new artillery. Between 1964 and 1969 there had been nearly 5,000 clashes along the northern border with the Soviet Union, and Beijing had learned, as the South Africans learned later, that modern Soviet weapons had a far superior range to their own guns and howitzers. Beijing had spent the 1970s trying to develop a long-range system but had failed. Now it wanted to buy Bull's expertise. While the last ten years had been relatively quiet, relations with Moscow had not been normalized, the border was still closed, and troops and artillery remained in place on both sides.

The Chinese were adamant about staying independent and self-reliant. Whatever new system was purchased, they wanted all of the licensing rights to make every scrap of it in China. And under the complex Chinese decision-making system, the final determination on which gun to buy would be made not by the political leadership alone but by a consensus of the factory workers, the Army and the Party hierarchy. Bull knew he couldn't deal with bureaucracy on that scale, but he agreed to submit a written proposal to sell his GC-45 system to Beijing on the condition that Chang act as middleman to smooth the way, as Mordell had done on the HARP project.

Bull returned to Europe and completed the submission within a few weeks, suggesting the Chinese buy a full set of drawings and plans for the 155-mm gun howitzer then being manufactured by Voest-Alpine in Austria. The Austrian company had bought the technology outright from SRC in 1978 for a one-time fee of $2 million. They paid no more royalties. Again, Bull was not benefiting from sales made by Voest-Alpine. They had modified Bull's GC-45 design and were selling it under the name of GHN-45.

In fact, Bull had made some appallingly bad deals on his GC-45. He had been forced into them because not only was he desperate for money to continue research but he had also needed immediate cash to meet his monthly payroll. Had Bull been a better negotiator, it would not have been unreasonable for him to expect as much as 5 per cent of the sales price of all export orders filled by South Africa and Austria. In round figures, the artillery pieces sold for $1 million each. That would have given him $50,000 on every piece sold, or $5 million on every hundred. Between them, South Africa and Austria sold more than six hundred 155-mm guns based on Bull's design during the second half of the 1980s. Those deals alone should have made Bull a multimillionaire.

As he bargained with the Chinese, Bull suggested they buy the manufacturing rights to his long-range full-bore ammunition including a new dimension called base-bleed. The base-bleed concept did not originate with Bull, but at that time he was the only ballistics scientist able to perfect the idea. It was simple in theory but complex in practice.

As a shell travels to its target many forces work against it. One of these forces is the vacuum that forms immediately behind the shell as it moves forward. This vacuum in effect sucks at the moving shell and causes a drag, reducing the shell's range. Bull designed a tiny motor to be fitted at the base of each shell. On ignition, the motor would burn a chemical compound that would release or "bleed" a gas to fill the vacuum and stop the drag. Even Bull had been surprised by the results during experiments at Highwater and on the range in Antigua.

Bull told the Chinese that, using his full-bore extended-range base-bleed shells, the Voest-Alpine version of his 155-mm gun would have a range of about 40 kilometres and would give Beijing the most advanced system on the market. Bull would be willing to customize the system for them and act as a consultant throughout the lifetime of the contract.

Once the submission was completed, he settled into an unhappy loneliness. He called Mimi every day. Members of his old team from SRC and SRC-International called with words of encouragement. Luis Palacio, still in Brussels, where he had been running SRC-I, took a job with Mecar, an American arms company with headquar-

Below: *Gerry Bull aged ten, in the fall of 1938, about to start his first term at Regiopolis College in Kingston, Ontario (Courtesy the Bull family)*

Above: *Gerry's mother Gertrude is seated, centre, in this picture taken in North Bay in 1907. She was 14 and would be married two years later. Her younger sister Florence died the following year after suffering an appendicitis. Gertrude's brother Milton is standing and Philip (Gerry's Uncle Phil) with his lace collar and button shoes is seated at the right. (Courtesy the Bull family)*

Above, left: *Gerry and Mimi on honeymoon in Bermuda in July 1954 when at 26 years old he was Canada's chief aerodynamicist. (Courtesy the Bull family)*

Above, right: *Aunt Edith and Uncle Phil at Gerry and Mimi's wedding in Quebec City, July 1954. (Courtesy the Bull family)*

Below, left: *Gerry Bull's 1948 class photo at the University of Toronto*

Flip Schulke/PHOTOPRESS

Above: *In the largest "over the beach" landing ever attempted, the U.S. Navy rolled* Betsy, *the first of the 16-inch HARP guns, across the sands of Barbados and towards a permanent firing site. The landing, in the summer of 1963, was accomplished by inching the 21 metres-long barrel, weighing 125 tonnes, along temporary railway tracks laid specially for the job. (Flip Schulke/Photopress)*

Right: *Dr. Bull takes a break during 1965 gun tests for the HARP programme in Barbados. (McGill University Archives)*

Flip Schulke/PHOTOPRESS

Above: *Dr. Gerald Bull on the telephone in HARP's paragon house fire control headquarters. He is sitting in front of the control panel on the night before a major firing in the mid-1960s. (Flip Schulke/Photopress)*

Left: *With* Betsy *in place at the HARP firing rounds on Barbados, a team of scientists from McGill pushed one of the first wooden slugs into the breach. Pith helmets were issued as part of the HARP uniform. (Flip Schulke/ Photopress)*

Opposite: *The 40-centimetre gun* Betsy *fires a Martlet missile into the night sky over Barbados early in 1963. Later, the gun was extended to twice its original length. (McGill University Archives)*

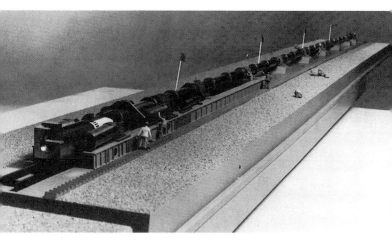

Above: *The Project Babylon model that went on display at the Baghdad International Exhibition for Military Production in May 1989. The figures were added for scale. The supergun barrel was 156 metres long. (Photo by Dr. Christopher Cowley)*

Below: *Dr. Bull's original GC–45, the gun designed and developed at Space Research Corporation's compound at Highwater, Quebec, in the late 1970s. This is the weapon that started a revolution in the world of artillery. (Photo by Christopher Foss)*

Above: *Many military experts believe that the most effective gun ever to be developed from Dr. Bull's original design ideas was the South African G–6, known as the Kalahari Ferrari. Self-propelled, it can travel at amazing speeds over rough terrain and played a major role in stopping the advance of Cuban forces in Angola. (Photo by Christopher Foss)*

Left: *Dr. Bull's 210-mm self-propelled howitzer, known as Al Fao, went on public display at the Baghdad International Exhibition for Military Production in May 1989. Visitors were not allowed a close inspection because the gun, billed as the largest mobile artillery piece in the world, was far from finished. It would not have gone into production for another five years. (Photo by Christopher Foss)*

Mimi and Gerry at a University banquet in Beijing in 1985. Gerry was not only designing a new gun system for the Chinese at the time, he was also giving a series of lectures on ballistics to graduate students. (Courtesy the Bull family)

Right: *Mimi Bull (top, centre) follows her husband's casket after the funeral in Montreal, April 1990. (Canapress)*

Left: *In one of the last photographs ever taken of Gerry Bull, he and Mimi have lunch in New Orleans during the February 1990 Mardi Gras celebrations. He was assassinated a month later. (Courtesy the Bull family)*

ters in Belgium. Monique Jaminé, the Belgian "Girl Friday" who had acted as a sort of office manager for SRC-I, signed on with PRB. Engineers and scientists from the old Highwater team took jobs from Montreal to Melbourne. And Bull sat in his rented room, and planned.

Over the summer and fall of 1981, PRB and Voest-Alpine gave Bull small consulting jobs. The major one came after an accident that had occurred during the testing of an experimental artillery piece. PRB had provided the propulsion powder and Voest-Alpine the gun barrel. On the first firing, the gun had blown, causing extensive damage. Now a fierce argument was underway about who was at fault and who should pay for the damage. Bull was employed as an arbitrator, a free agent commissioned to assign liability. It was a difficult and complex job, involving constant travel between Brussels and Vienna.

In Montreal, Mimi was concerned that Gerry was falling into a depression again. His voice sounded flat on the phone and there was no trace of humour in anything he said. The whole South African incident had aged her greatly. Michel, by now a qualified accountant working in Quebec City, saw his mother's anguish the most clearly. In June, he travelled to Brussels and found his father to be bitter and hurting. But he was also struck by Gerry Bull's unyielding spirit and drive. It was at the worst of times that Bull's unshakeable belief in himself truly shone through.

For the first time, Michel sensed that his father needed him. "He couldn't ask me to join him, because he had nothing to offer but insecurity," says Michel. But his father didn't need to ask. Michel returned to Quebec City, resigned his job, and with the nervous blessing of his wife, Danielle, took their $10,000 in savings and moved to Brussels. Danielle would join him when he found a home, and in the meantime he would return to Canada for one week each month.

Father and son began to travel together, sharing hotel rooms and hamburger lunches. Michel's role was to handle the finances once the money started to flow. But right from the start he ran into a problem: Dr. Bull would rather work for nothing than risk losing a deal.

Come autumn, Beijing replied to Bull's proposal with interest, but they wanted changes in the gun's wheel base so it could operate in deep mud, and they wanted proposals to make it more accurate. Further, they wanted plans to build factories for the gun's production, and they wanted specific cost figures. On top of all that, they wanted to see samples. Bull had proposed a series of innovative production techniques, but the Chinese rejected these. They were not interested, they stressed, in front-line technology. It was subject to too many errors, too many failures, too many difficulties that might result in workers or soldiers or Party officials failing to meet deadlines or goals – and that was just too costly in personal terms under the Beijing regime. They were too scared of new ideas to risk implementing them.

Finding samples was a major problem, but eventually Bull persuaded Voest-Alpine to sell the Chinese two guns. He also negotiated with PRB to sell propulsion charges and for a company in Switzerland to make examples of his base-bleed shells. Now things were on the move, though there was still no income and major new proposals had to be prepared.

While in London for talks with Chang, Bull was called by an old British friend who had been a manager of the Barbados range. He invited Bull to spend a few days in the Devonshire resort of Torquay, and Bull fell in love with the town and the region. It was a three-hour train ride from London, but Bull nevertheless rented a house there, and it was in Torquay that he began designing the specifics of the Chinese artillery.

At the same time, Bull and Michel continued to shuttle around Europe doing small consulting jobs for munitions companies to cover their expenses. On one of these trips they received a phone call from Sarkis Soghanalian, a Lebanese reputed to be one of the world's wealthiest arms dealers and known in the trade as the "merchant of death". Soghanalian, a barrel of a man with a permanent five-o'clock shadow, told Bull that he had close ties to Iraq and was helping to arm that country for its war with Iran. Soghanalian invited Bull to visit Baghdad, all-expenses paid, to discuss the possibility of modernizing thirty-year-old Soviet-supplied artillery.

Bull went early in 1982, but when it became clear to the Iraqis that he had nothing to offer but drawings, they lost interest. When he returned to Brussels, he called Mimi to tell her about his excursion into the Arab world, and the prospect frightened her.

Bull's nightly calls home were what kept him going during what he later called "the dark days". He tried to spend as much time as he could in Torquay, but there were constant calls from PRB. He began to dread the weeks when Michel was away and he was left alone in Brussels. On one level he simply couldn't cope. One night, late as always, he checked out of his hotel and raced for the airport, only to miss the last flight to London. It was near midnight as he stood in the terminal with a suitcase in each hand and a heavy document bag slung over one shoulder. He needed someone to look after him.

He phoned Monique Jaminé, his one-time office manager. After hearing his plaintive tones, Monique drove out to the airport. She recalls: "He was standing in the airport looking like a great big hamster. You know, he never grew up. He was always a little boy. And most of the time he was a little boy lost, looking for his mother." She took him to another hotel, booked him in and even took him up to his room to make sure he was comfortable. She arranged for him to get an early wake-up call so that he could catch the first flight to London, and then she dashed home to her "other children".

Through the early months of 1982 Bull worked sixteen-hour days on the Chinese gun proposals in his Torquay house. Michel stayed with him for weeks at a time. Torquay was ridiculously inconvenient, but Bull didn't care. By spring he had made friends with his neighbours, had started to drop by the local pub now and again, and he looked forward to going on mystery bus tours through the countryside on Sunday afternoons.

In April, Beijing sent a team of eight ballistics experts to London to open serious negotiations on Bull's proposals. The negotiations, tense and hard, lasted five weeks. One night it fell to Michel to entertain the group as his father headed back for a weekend of peace in Torquay. Michel rented a limousine and took the Chinese experts along with their interpreter to see Petula Clark in the West End production of *The Sound of Music*. On the way to the theatre Michel explained the story and added that the Von Trapp family had moved to northern Vermont, close by his father's old SRC compound. But a great deal was lost in translation, and it wasn't until the music began that the Chinese guests recognized the songs, which had only recently started to play in China.

"Suddenly, the Chinese negotiators all started to sing in that special pitch the Chinese seem to have," remembers Michel. The staid British audience turned in horror on the group, shushing them. "You can't imagine the embarrassment. It seemed to take minutes for them to quiet down."

Before the end of May the Chinese signed a contract with Dr. Bull and his new company, again named SRC. Almost immediately, Bull and Chang flew to Beijing and on to a remote test range in Manchuria, near the disputed border with the Soviet Union, where the sample guns were already waiting. Now the Chinese began to press Bull hard to do more and more for less and less. The tests were handled by veteran Chinese Army gun teams who boasted of guns that could be fired non-stop until their barrels melted. They were interested in two major areas. First, how the guns would handle under battle conditions, and second, how accurate they were. Moving through deep mud, part of one gun undercarriage broke, and the base-bleed ammunition got damp and some of it wouldn't work. But the Army was still impressed by the range of Bull's shells and with the rapid fire the guns were capable of sustaining. However, through the high winds of Manchuria, Bull's streamlined shells proved to be less stable in flight than the stubby Soviet models, and the Chinese wanted greater accuracy. Bull guaranteed he could produce it.

It was a question of spin. On leaving the barrel, Bull's shells were spinning one full revolution for every three metres travelled. Since they were moving at about 900 metres per second, the shells were spinning at a rate of 18,000 complete revolutions per minute. And the Austrian-made shells being used for testing were not properly balanced. The shell walls were a thousandth of a centimetre too thick in some places, causing them to flutter in flight. This was something Bull knew he could fix.

When it came to technical specifics, the Chinese insisted on negotiating directly with Bull, and Chang couldn't protect him.

Bull, the world's worst businessman, kept agreeing. In the end, he signed contractual clauses, without Michel's guidance, that committed SRC to do about twice the amount of work originally expected for about one-third of the price originally anticipated. Michel, by now executive vice president of SRC, almost went berserk when he saw the final documents. Officials from the Chinese government eventually realized that Bull was offering too much for too little and gave back some of the concessions they had won. They feared he would end up ruining himself and producing nothing.

Bull returned to London and a conference with Michel on future strategy. The Chinese contract was for just one year, but now cash was available to rent an office and start to gather the old team. Michel stressed that everything must be done above-board and according to law. There must be no slip-ups like the South African affair. Thus Michel flew to Washington and an appointment with the U.S. Office of Munitions Control. He briefed the office on exactly what technology was involved with the Chinese contract. It was agreed that some of the technology was American in origin, but after some weeks of consideration an export licence was issued. The The deal fitted within U.S. policy guidelines. In fact, under the Reagan Administration it had become much easier to get export permits for munitions. The office encouraged Michel to keep it informed.

"It's none of their god-damn business," his father roared when Michel got back to Brussels. Still, Michel noticed that his father seemed pleased that the deal had been cleared.

Bull toyed with the idea of buying a house in Torquay and running the operation from there, but Michel insisted that Brussels made much more sense, and in June 1982 a small office with shared facilities was rented not far from EEC headquarters. Michel rented a house close by and was joined by his wife, but Gerry continued to live in apartment hotels, saying that he would still need to travel extensively. For much of the rest of 1982 he worked alone from the house in Torquay.

One of the first members of the old team to join the new set-up was Steve Adams. Adams called Bull from South Africa. His work on the 155-mm was finished, he was looking for a job, and he wanted to mend old fences. After a few minutes on the phone, Bull agreed to forget his anger. Best of all, Adams said he had made such good money in South Africa that he could afford to work without salary for a few months. That clinched it. Before long Adams was a vice president of the new company.

When the Chinese contract was renewed for another year in 1983, Michel rented a set of private offices in Brussels and much of the old team was reassembled. Monique and Luis Palacio joined, along with half a dozen engineers and draughtsmen who had been with Bull in Highwater. Bull reluctantly gave up his Torquay house to move back to Brussels. That year he made an even more difficult journey. For the first time since leaving North America, Bull returned to Montreal for the wedding of his son Stephen.

Although Mimi had made half a dozen trips to Europe with the younger children, it was the first real family party since Michel's wedding three years before, and Mimi half hoped it would encourage her husband to consider basing himself in Canada again. But business was just beginning to pick up in Belgium and Bull wouldn't hear of it.

In the spring of 1984, the Chinese signed a three-year contract with SRC for the rest of the 155-mm system. The contract finally put Bull and his company back on their feet. "We made no money out of the Chinese deal," says Michel, "but it generated enough work and enough funds to let us re-establish." Now Michel rented a three-storey office building at 63, rue du Stalle, on the smart side of town, and the staff shot up to nearly sixty.

The three Chinese contracts, officially signed with Norinco, the government-owned North China Industries Corporation, added up to one massive deal worth about $25 million. For their money, the Chinese got a 155-mm towed artillery piece, which they later designated MF45. It fires 40 kilometres using base-bleed ammunition and about 30 kilometres with standard ammunition. Following extensive work and testing by Bull, its accuracy, though secret, is said to be "remarkable". The gun is a slightly more advanced rendering of the Voest-Alpine GHN-45, which in turn is an improved version of Bull's GC-45. Mounted on a conventional split trail carriage, the gun's 45-calibre barrel can be swung back 180 degrees and locked into position to make the entire package much shorter and more compact when being towed over rough terrain. As part of the deal, Bull had to provide Beijing with factory layouts and detailed instructions for making every part of the gun, from the smallest screw to the forged steel barrel. He also provided full production details for his extended-range full-bore base-bleed shells.

The mid-1980s found Bull spending two or three months of every year in China, often in remote locations barred to other foreigners. A research office was established for Bull and his staff at the university in Xi An, and the university in Nanjing featured him as a regular guest lecturer. Twice, Mimi flew to China to vacation with her husband, and she was taken aback by the great respect and honour that was shown towards him.

After the collapse of SRC in 1980, a dozen of the senior engineers had set up two companies on or near the old compound. Denis Lyster and C.B. Shepard formed Phoenix Engineering, of Newport, Vermont, while others started up North Troy Engineering. As the work from China began to build, Bull offered contracts to his former colleagues. Lyster and Shepard became involved in some computer research and even visited China once to advise on a production problem. All of which was carefully watched by the same U.S. Customs agents who had been responsible for instigating the South African charges.

Early in 1984, they launched an official inquiry aimed at bringing further charges against Bull for illegally selling weapons technology to China. Bull was furious. In a telephone interview with the *Boston Globe* he yelled: "Some backwoods Vermont Customs agents want me to be dead and want Space Research Corp. to be dead. Well, the government of China does not want Space Research to be dead. This is the most vindictive, sick thing I ever heard of. If Customs want to get me, let them come and find me."

Customs agent John O'Hara, in charge of the inquiry, responded: "Bull is under investigation. It is not a vendetta at all. Now, instead of shipments to South Africa, it is shipments to a Communist country." On March 29, Customs agents raided the homes of Lyster and Shepard looking for documentary evidence. Both men insisted they had done nothing wrong, but Customs passed along "evidence" to a U.S. Attorney recommending that charges be brought. The allegations went to the State Department, and after an internal investigation no further action was taken. As far as Washington was concerned, Bull's China dealings fell within the law.

Securely back in business, even if he was not making much of a profit, Bull soon reverted to his old self. The charisma returned. Again he began to enchant those around him. And best of all, for those who cared, his old sense of humour was back. Palacio noticed it when the team went out to Manchuria for a firing test. Palacio had just bought a new Mercedes and was bursting with pride over the first luxury car he had ever owned. When they returned from the tests to Beijing, Palacio found a telex waiting for him. His wife had crashed the car, it was wrecked, but, said the message, "Thank God no one is injured". Palacio was devastated – until he caught sight of Bull grinning. The boss was back to his old tricks.

13

BY THE SPRING of 1984, Gerry Bull
was re-establishing his priorities. On the strength of the Chinese
contracts, his company was up and running again. Yet he was still
living in an apartment hotel and travelling at least half the time. One
thing was clear: he didn't want to make any personal commitment to
Brussels, he didn't want a car, and he didn't want an apartment.
And he didn't want Mimi to move there. He wanted to be free to
come and go as he pleased, with no ties. Gerry told his wife that he
still couldn't reduce his travel commitments and that if she was in
Brussels he would feel guilty leaving her alone. In Montreal she was
surrounded by family and friends. He was avoiding responsibility,
sacrificing his home to satisfy ambition.

By now, Mimi was visiting Brussels three or four times a year and
staying for two or three weeks at a time. Gerry was establishing a
pattern of returning to Montreal for Christmas and for a summer
visit. But at most, he was going to be with Mimi three months a year.
The sacrifice was heavy for both of them.

That year they bought a little three-bedroom house on the southern tip of Spain, close to Gibraltar. It was to be their hideaway.
There was a swimming pool and a patio that was swept by a breeze
from the Mediterranean. When Mimi was due to arrive, Gerry
would send Monique Jamine down to make sure that the linen was
fresh and the pool was clear. He wanted Mimi to find everything
perfect.

"Gerry had never taken a vacation, he was always working and travelling," says Mimi. "Now we had a place to be alone together. Every few months we had two weeks in Spain. It was not often, but it was high quality. For the first time in a very long time, he was able to relax. We would play tennis and backgammon and he would write. We would go walking along the harbour and look at the boats."

But wherever he went, two issues were never far from his mind. First, there was the South African conviction. In North America anyway, it had robbed him of respectability. Now he began to scheme for a pardon. He convinced himself that if the case was properly reviewed in political perspective it would be seen that he had committed no crime and that he had been the victim of changing Washington policies. With the conservative Reagan Administration in power, a pardon seemed possible. Second, there was the question of his Canadian citizenship. In 1978 he had applied to have his Canadian passport renewed, only to be told that he was no longer a Canadian citizen. It transpired that under Canadian law the government could take away citizenship if a Canadian applied for the citizenship of another country while resident in that country. And someone in Ottawa – Bull was never able to discover who – had chosen to exercise that option. It was true that Bull had become an American citizen in a courthouse in Vermont, but he had returned that night to sleep at home in Canada and in fact had never lived in the U.S. Bull believed that the decision to take away his Canadian citizenship was vindictive. It meant he had to travel on an American passport, and he hated that: the Americans were the ones who had sent him to jail. He began to hire lawyers to investigate the possibility of winning back his Canadian citizenship.

On his last trip to North America, Bull had visited General Arthur Trudeau, who was living in Washington. The general agreed that Bull should push for a pardon, and he suggested that Bull put his case in writing, complete with supporting documents. And this Bull did. He prepared three volumes, with a total of 1,169 pages, about the same length as the complete works of Shakespeare. The volumes were entitled: "A Review and Study of the Case History of Dr. G.V. Bull and the Space Research Corporation and its Related Companies in North America with Supporting Relevant

Documentation". The volumes were purportedly prepared by three of Bull's oldest friends, but in fact Bull dictated much of the text directly to Donald Mordell, referring to himself throughout in the third person. As a frontispiece, Bull used a motto he had found engraved above a fireplace in a seventeenth-century Belgian chateau: "When reason sleeps, Justice is badly served". Noted Bull: "A wise saying, perhaps by someone who suffered similarly to the story told herein."

The very act of preparing the volumes in such intense detail, gathering letters and reports, contracts and court documents, engrossed Bull. By the time he had finished, in September 1985, he was obsessed with his own case. From then on, barely a day passed that he didn't talk about it at length with his staff and friends in Brussels. Every other concern paled. Copies of the three volumes were sent to friends and influential leaders in Congress and the Pentagon. But there was little or no reaction.

By now Bull had moved into an apartment hotel closer to the office. His new room was drab, and on her first visit Mimi found it so depressing that she couldn't bear to stay there, even for an afternoon. At the SRC office, one of the engineers told her about an apartment for rent in a new development close by. The next day Mimi went to see the apartment. It was on the sixth floor of the middle building in a three-building complex on avenue François Folie, in a section of Brussels called Uccle. There was one bedroom, a galley kitchen, a living room with a dining nook and a balcony. But the best thing about the apartment was that it was bright and airy, and it lifted Mimi's spirits just being there.

That night she persuaded Gerry to inspect and rent the apartment. Mimi stayed an extra week to buy furniture and decorate. She chose flowered prints and light, bright colours, aiming to keep an air of springtime in the rooms.

Gerry launched a new personal project. This time it was not an obsession but a passion. He began work on a book about Project HARP and the building of the biggest guns in history. This was his first professional love, and he was soon spending most of his time on it. He became fascinated by the "Paris Guns" used by the Germans in 1918 to bombard Paris from some 120 kilometres. Almost nothing was known of these guns, which were destroyed by the Germans right after the First World War, and Bull embarked on an extraordinary odyssey. He searched through Europe for every scrap of information about them, travelling thousands of kilometres to museums and retirement homes in West Germany where he found engineers who had worked on the concepts, and eventually hiring a full-time German-speaking researcher. When he located files and folios of long-forgotten engineering designs and drawings, he recreated the guns on paper and used detailed computer tests to analyse their performance. He wrote later: "Since the HARP guns were developed from the application of existing state-of-the-art ordnance technology and hardware, it was considered essential to attempt to relate them to their historical predecessors. Otherwise these enormous guns performing unprecedented firing programmes stand in isolation, dangling in history."

Bull brought in his old friend Charles Murphy, still with the U.S. Army, and entrusted to him some of the more difficult calculations involved. Bull would do most of the research and writing, but he wanted Murphy's name on the cover as a joint author. It was not that he needed any extra prestige, rather that he wanted to thank Murphy for his support and friendship through difficult times. Bull decided to combine the stories of the Paris Guns and Project HARP into one volume.

Over the next few years, as Bull considered Project HARP and its prospects, he became more convinced than ever that a purpose-built gun – not old converted Navy guns such as those used in HARP – would be able to launch mid-size satellites of great scientific use. Not only that, but once the gun was built it could perform such launchings for about $5,000 a shot, a fraction of the cost of a typical rocket launch. If anything, he now had greater enthusiasm for building a satellite-launching gun than ever before.

Work on the book and hopes for the pardon were running strong in late 1985 when Bull received a surprising invitation. He was asked to give a paper on Project HARP to a secret scientific conference on the military applications of a supergun. The two-day conference, to be held November 4 and 5 in Arlington, Virginia, just outside Washington, was being organized by the Strategic Technology

Office of the Pentagon's Defense Advanced Research Projects Agency (DARPA). Bull asked Luis Palacio to accompany him, and he considered the invitation an unofficial welcome back into the inner sanctum of America's scientific military establishment.

Only five papers were to be presented, and only twenty-three scientists would be present, including Bull, Palacio and Murphy. There was no mention of South Africa, and Bull was treated as a distinguished scholar.

The conference was opened by Dr. Fred Quelle, of the Office of Naval Research in Boston. Quelle revealed that in the fifteen years since the end of the HARP programme, sophisticated guidance instruments, able to withstand the high G forces of a gun launch, had become available. He said these instruments could achieve guidance of unprecedented accuracy and that they could be contained in shells fired from large guns that offered "the possibility of delivering payloads intercontinentally or into orbit at extremely attractive costs". Quelle then detailed, for the first time, the real purpose of what he called "this workshop": it had been organized "to find out how this emerging technology can be most creatively exploited, as well as to understand its limitations, to identify the most important military objectives to which it can be applied and to map out a technologically sound course for achieving those objectives".

Two DARPA staff scientists, Dr. Al Brandenstein and Dr. Sherman Karp, said that a device about the size of a cigarette pack had been developed that could be placed in a projectile and fired from a 155-mm gun. The device would then guide the projectile directly to any fixed target over a range of about 25 kilometres. Now they asked Bull if it would be worthwhile developing a similar device to guide gun-launched projectiles across intercontinental ranges for distances of a thousand kilometres or more. Potential missions, they said, might include long-range attacks on bunkers, command and control centres or airfields. On the civilian side, such a projectile might be used, they suggested, to carry supplies into orbit for a space station.[1]

They were talking about Bull's dream. Yet as he ambled to the podium that November afternoon, his old friend Palacio was worried. Palacio had watched Bull making presentations over the last two years as he tried and failed to sell artillery systems to NATO nations. Remembers Palacio: "Bull had lost a lot of the magic. It had been kicked out of him by the South African affair. His lectures and his presentations had become dull. I didn't think he would impress the Americans." But suddenly Bull came alive. His history of Project HARP and the big guns built in Germany was sparkling and full of wit. He let his imagination soar, assuring the Pentagon scientists that intercontinental ranges were well within the scope of guns and that he already had the technology to put a payload into orbit.

He told DARPA that if they could provide the guidance system he could provide the ballistics expertise to build a supergun and projectiles. He showed slides of the Martlet missiles he had built for HARP and said that he could base new projectiles on those designs. He ended by suggesting the Pentagon consider building a supergun that would have a one-metre bore and a barrel about 150 metres long.

It was one of the best performances Bull had ever given. "I was very proud of him," Palacio says. "Everyone was enormously impressed. I realized that this was where Bull belonged. He performed best when he was working on the cutting edge of science."

DARPA asked Bull to make a formal proposal for building a supergun that could shoot payloads across oceans. The proposal was submitted early in 1986.

Bull was elated. He felt sure that it would be only a matter of months before he was called to Washington and assigned to produce the supergun. Bull received an acknowledgement for his proposal and was told it was under consideration. And that was that. The idea was shelved. "I guess they were looking for something more high-tech than a powder gun; they had other propulsion systems in mind," says Murphy.

Bull had always read for relaxation and as he became intensely involved in his own book, he concentrated on histories of the two world wars. On visits to Belgium, Mimi would see these histories piled high in the new apartment. She remembers: "He said that everyone should read about wars so they would know just how stupid political leaders could be and so that they would understand the horrors. He said that if everyone knew how terrible war was, there would be no more fighting. He said people would stop making the same mistakes."

Bull now picked up another pastime. He began to rent a car on weekends and drive out to the war graves around Ypres and Passchendaele, two hours west of Brussels. He became an expert on the battlefields, knowing exactly where breakthroughs had been made and drives had been stopped. But he spent most of his time on those pilgrimages simply walking through the rows of white crosses, reading aloud the names and ages of the fallen soldiers. "My God," he would say to anyone listening, "here's a kid of seventeen. I wonder who remembers him now." As he wandered around the graves he would try to whistle, most often "Lili Marlene". After a couple of hours reading the grave markers, tears would be streaming down his face, and it was time to go home.

How could a man who hated the sight of blood and who cried at war graves be so involved in the development of war machines? It was just another side of his complex and contrary nature. Defence, as he once said to Michel, was a right and a duty. Humanity was a warrior species and always had been. You are just as dead killed by a big stone thrown by a caveman as by a nuclear explosion. Yes, he thought about what happened when one of his full-bore extended-range shells, filled with high explosive, shattered into thousands of jagged white-hot steel fragments. If a piece hit you, it would probably kill you, at the very least tear a large lump of you away. It was true he had never been in a battle, nor witnessed one first hand. But weapons are not the problem, he would say, it is the men behind them.

Michel now says that, deep down, Gerry Bull was unhappy working in defence. Space Research Corporation was always a temporary solution to amass enough money to allow him to get back to Project HARP.

Towards the end of 1985, the main part of the Chinese contract was almost completed, and Beijing was very pleased with the work. Bull's guns had given them new confidence on their long border with the Soviet Union and encouraged them to take more of a chance on peace with Moscow. But for now the Chinese had no more assignments, and SRC needed a new source of income. The company tried to break into the Egyptian market – Cairo was looking for new artillery – but failed to win orders. There was much better luck with Yugoslavia and Spain. A major contract was signed with the Spanish company Explosivos Rio Tinto to design an artillery piece that later was designated FGH-155 (for Field Gun Howitzer). While this gun was basically the same as that produced by Voest-Alpine and Armscor, Bull redesigned the ordnance and carriage to reduce the number of moving parts by 30 per cent. "The simpler the gun, the less there is to go wrong and the longer it will last," he said.

For Yugoslavia, Bull provided analysis and calculations that allowed the Yugoslav Army to modify their old Soviet 130-mm M46 guns to fire Western 155-mm ammunition. The "conversion kit" supplied by SRC involved swapping the Soviet barrels for new Western-made 45-calibre barrels with a resulting dramatic increase in range when Bull's base-bleed ammunition was used.

By now Bull's third son, Stephen, who had graduated in electrical engineering from Laval, had joined the company in Brussels. Nervous and unsure of himself, Stephen was not trained in management and soon made himself unpopular with most of the staff. Where Michel had financial expertise and natural diplomacy to offer – attributes SRC badly needed – Stephen was seen as the boss's son without a real role.

And the harder he tried, the more mistakes he seemed to make. Bull was impatient; he would shout at Stephen in front of staff. It led to a drop in company morale and a great deal of family unhappiness. All of which was most unfair, for in fact Stephen was a hard worker, anxious to learn the business and support his father.

Stephen acted as Michel's deputy. First, the brothers struggled to keep control of the budgets and to take over all financial negotiations. But at best they could only half succeed, because their father always had access to the company cheque books and continued to spend freely from contract accounts on his personal research into Project HARP and the other big guns of history. And, in the end, clients wanted to deal directly with Bull. He had a legendary reputation for results. Perhaps more important, though, clients knew they could talk him into almost anything.

The second area that concerned Michel and Stephen was international law, arms embargos and the continuing American insistence that some of SRC's basic technology had been developed in the U.S. and was subject to U.S. technology-transfer regulations.

Dr. Bull grew impatient with Washington and didn't see the need to consult the State Department on every contract. But his sons insisted. They wanted to ensure there would never be another South Africa. It caused a lot of friction among the staff, and by mid-1988 the SRC office had split into two camps – those who supported Bull and his free-wheeling ways, and those who supported his sons and their insistence on controls.

The split was exacerbated by lack of money. The Chinese contracts had almost finished, although Bull was proposing a line of 203-mm self-propelled artillery that was generating interest in Beijing. The Yugoslav work was finished and the Spanish contracts were in their final stages. There were other small jobs in house, but a new major client was needed quickly. In mid-1988 the company fell two months behind in paying salaries to senior staff. "We were living hand to mouth," recalls Monique Jaminé. "But then a big cheque would come in from somewhere and everybody would get paid and we would have a party to celebrate. That place was like a family. You couldn't rely on getting paid, but Dr. Bull was like a big daddy and the staff would do anything for him."

At PRB they referred to SRC as "the professor and his students". The imagery pleased Bull. He liked the idea of SRC being a centre of learning, a sort of ballistics university. Still, the staff noticed that Bull was growing increasingly bad-tempered as the year wore on. His attempts to win a pardon seemed to have stalled. And, almost as significant for him, he had started to hear rumours that the Pentagon had decided to go ahead with his ideas for a supergun – but to cut him out of the deal. According to the rumours, work was under way at the Lawrence Livermore Laboratories in California on a gun that would be used to put payloads into orbit. He now faced the bitter prospect of being beaten on his own project. The Americans had chosen to go with a high-tech gas gun, rather than his proposal for a powder gun, but the concept was the same.

During the second week of November 1987, the switchboard operator at SRC had difficulty handling an incoming call. The caller politely insisted on speaking to Dr. Bull. As per instructions, the operator said he should write for an appointment, but the caller then asked for Bull's personal assistant. He was put through to Monique Jaminé. The caller identified himself as an official with the Government of Iraq, based at the embassy in Bonn. He said he wanted to invite Dr. Bull to visit Baghdad. Monique, knowing only too well the company needed new business, transferred the call to Michel.

Michel pointed out that it would be impossible for SRC to help with any weapons work while Iraq remained at war with Iran. The Iraqi official understood that, but felt the time had come to establish contact for future work, when the war was over. Michel, knowing how his father might jump at the opportunity, said he would need to discuss the prospects in much greater depth before Dr. Bull could become personally involved. The Iraqi then invited Michel to Bonn. A week later Michel and Stephen took an early flight to West Germany to make the first contact with Iraq since 1982.

They were entering a web that Iraqi leader Saddam Hussein had spun all over Europe, a web that had been positioned to capture the sort of military technology Saddam needed to lead the Arab world and to challenge Israel and the U.S. in the Middle East.

PART VI

Force Rules the World

"Force rules the world still,
Has ruled it, shall rule it;
Meekness is weakness,
Strength is triumphant ..."

"The Challenge of Thor"
from "The Musician's Tale"
Henry Wadsworth Longfellow

14

IN SEPTEMBER 1980, about a week before Gerald Bull reported for jail, Iraqi forces invaded Khuzistan, an oil-rich Iranian province whose Arab-speaking people were unhappy with the clerical rule of the Ayatollah Khomeini. Saddam Hussein had been supplying arms to Khuzistan rebels, and he claimed that the province, along his eastern border with Iran, was Iraqi territory that had been stolen years before.

The Iranians moved to reclaim their land with much stiffer resistance than Baghdad had expected, and within days a full-scale war was shaping up.

By the time Bull was settling into Allenwood Penitentiary, Iraqi jets were raiding Abadan, Iran's huge oil-refining centre, and columns of Iraqi troops shielded behind tanks and heavy artillery were on the outskirts of the city. As Bull used a glass of water – "The substance fitted the subject," he said later – to toast Jimmy Carter's defeat by Ronald Reagan in the November 4 election, the United States and the Soviet Union declared themselves neutral in this latest conflagration.

The Soviet Union, under Brezhnev, had invaded Afghanistan just nine months before, and the superpowers were in no mood to cooperate to help end the fighting in Iran. Indeed once it became obvious that world oil supplies would not be severely disrupted, Washington even saw some advantage in having the Iraqi and Iranian armies tied down.

In early 1981, as Bull was released, the Reagan Administration adopted an official hands-off policy towards the Iran–Iraq war, and senior officials were privately gloating that, as they saw it, two particularly nasty countries were blasting the hell out of one another. Western nations took a superior stance and banned the sale of weapons to both sides. However, the arms trade bows to no law, and as the war bogged down into a long and vicious affair, with Iran using "human waves" of young soldiers to attack fixed Iraqi positions, there was no shortage of supplies or suppliers.

In what became known as the Irangate scandal, members of the Reagan Administration secretly and illegally sold weapons to Iran in an abortive attempt to free U.S. hostages being held by pro-Iranian elements in Lebanon. The South Africans sold their G-5 artillery – based on Bull's designs – to both Iran and Iraq in exchange for much-needed oil. Indeed, that oil allowed Pretoria to stockpile fuel and nurse the country through the early part of the decade when the anti-apartheid movement was gathering international strength and the oil embargo was being enforced with more vigilance than ever before. At the same time, Voest-Alpine was also alleged to be selling its version of Bull's guns to both sides. Five or six years into the war, Iran had about 350 of Bull's guns, while Iraq was thought to have 400.

The guns had a significant influence on the fighting. Neither country had an effective airforce, and it was primarily a ground war involving massive movements of infantry. Artillery was vital for both sides to break up and stop the advance of the opposing armies. Bull's shells, with their high rate of fragmentation, proved to be particularly lethal in those sections of the border terrain that were flat and desertlike and where soldiers on the move had no cover. It was this experience with Bull's guns that later gave Saddam Hussein the confidence to defy allied armies after his invasion of Kuwait in August 1990. For Saddam's cannon were superior in every way to those in the Western arsenal. They were bigger, could fire further, faster, more accurately and with greater killing power. But, as we now know, the might of the coalition forces arrayed against Saddam was so great that he did not have the opportunity to put his best artillery into action in the Gulf War.

Unlike Belgium or South Africa, Austria had strict laws governing arms dealing, including one that barred all weapons sales to any state involved in armed conflict. In 1986 the U.S. State Department called in Austria's ambassador to Washington, Thomas Klestil, no fewer than ten times to show him CIA evidence, including satellite photographs, that GHN-45 cannon were being sold to Iran and Iraq. No action was taken, although later in 1989 an Austrian government investigation showed that between 1985 and 1986 some 110 artillery pieces and 41,000 shells were sold by Voest-Alpine to Iran and that between 1981 and 1983 some 100 GHN-45 howitzers were sold to Iraq. Directors of Voest-Alpine skirted the neutrality law by shipping the weapons through third countries, including Libya, but there was never any doubt about the real customer. It is widely believed in Austria that at least six top politicians were behind a scheme to increase state revenues by authorizing the sales. State prosecutor Siegfried Sittenthaler was later to say: "With these weapons, Austria sold its honour."[1]

Bull played no part in selling artillery to either side in the Iran-Iraq war, but he carefully followed news of the ebb and flow of fighting. The loss of human life appalled him, and he felt there were direct comparisons with the First World War. Yet as the death toll mounted he felt no personal responsibility. Cannon based on his designs were blowing hundreds if not thousands of men to pieces, but Bull later said: "I'm no more responsible than the guy who designed the trucks that carried the men to the front."

On June 7, 1981, about nine months after the war started, Israeli F-4 Phantom jets, armed with precision weapons known as smart bombs, destroyed the Osirak nuclear reactor 20 kilometres south of Baghdad, severely setting back Saddam's plans to develop – or so Israel said – nuclear weapons. Iraq had claimed that the reactor was for peaceful purposes only, and the Israeli raid received international condemnation. Relations with the U.S. were strained badly, not least because the Israelis had used American-supplied aircraft for the job.

Certainly, Prime Minister Menachem Begin had no regrets. Two days after the raid he said that if Iraq rebuilt a nuclear reactor capable of producing atomic weapons, Israel would "use all the facilities at [its] disposal to destroy that reactor". He said Israel would not tolerate any enemy country developing weapons of mass destruction intended for use against Israel, and that the raid had been conducted in "supreme, legitimate self-defence".

Iraq's supply of enriched uranium, some 12 kilograms delivered by France, was not damaged in the raid. And as he fumed, Saddam assigned his scientists to find another way to make nuclear weapons. What he needed was a weapons system so fearful that Israel would not dare repeat the Osirak raid. Thus Saddam ordered renewed efforts to develop nuclear, chemical and biological weapons. And just as important, he ordered work to begin on a missile system that could deliver his warheads with accuracy over long distances.

In 1984, at the peak of the gruelling fighting on the ground, large amounts of U.S. arms were being sold to Kuwait and from there shuttled directly to Iraq. The Stockholm International Peace Research Institute says that at this time Iraq was spending $14 billion a year on arms, half of its gross domestic product. Poland was providing tanks and anti-tank missiles; the Soviet Union sold MiGs and missiles; China chipped in with bombers and armoured personnel carriers; France sold Mirage fighters and Exocet missiles; and Brazil entered the market with multiple-rocket launchers. Without exception, every major weapons producer was selling something – and many were dealing with both sides while keeping up a front of "plausible deniability" by pretending to sell to countries like Jordan and Kuwait. And every major intelligence service in the West knew all about this so-called clandestine dealing.

When the Pentagon decided that Iran, with twice the population of Iraq, couldn't really lose, the U.S. began to "tilt" heavily towards Iraq. The fanatical followers of the ayatollah were prepared to make any sacrifice and in the long run were sure to wear down Iraq's resolve. But an Iranian victory might also mean that Khomeini's brand of revolutionary Islam would blaze through the Gulf nations and Saudi Arabia. Teheran would then control Middle East oil supplies and the future of Israel would be seriously threatened. The only satisfactory solution was for the war to end, but to end in a stalemate. Iraq was ready for peace, but Iran insisted that only the toppling of Saddam Hussein would end the fighting.

Thus, Reagan approved Operation Staunch, a scheme to cut weapons supplies to Iran while allowing them to continue to Iraq. Eventually, the thinking went, the Iranians would be forced into a peaceful stalemate. By now, both Iran and Iraq had opened weapons-buying offices in every major European capital. As part of Operation Staunch, all NATO countries were urged to close the Iranian operations. Britain, for instance, in 1987 closed down the London offices of the National Iranian Oil Company, an arms-buying front, but allowed its Iraqi equivalent to remain open.

The scheme only confirmed what Saddam Hussein had realized long before. This time, he was on the winning side of the international ploy, but the arms cut-off could just as easily have been directed at Baghdad. So, like South Africa, Iraq had to establish its own arms industry. Saddam believed that, after the war, he could build Iraq into the most powerful of all Arab nations. Saddam saw himself as heir to 5,000 years of Iraqi civilization and as leader of a new Arab confederation powerful enough to defeat Israel and control Middle East oil. But to get the other Arab nations behind him he had to demonstrate his strength and invincibility.

Starting in the mid-1980s, Saddam launched a campaign to invest in European companies involved in technology and machinery with potential military applications. The idea was to develop the companies, win their trust with generous orders, and then gradually transfer their expertise to Iraq. The overall scheme was assigned to Hussein Kamil, Saddam's son-in-law, who in due course became the minister for industry and military industrialization.

Kamil's deputy was Amir Saadi, a smooth and cultured diplomat with Western manners and ready charm.

It was Saadi's idea to call Gerry Bull in November 1987.

Space Research Corporation still had no manufacturing facilities of its own. Bull provided the drawings and the calculations and the ideas from which weapons systems were constructed by others. And the development of a new artillery system took a long time. Even working at Bull's remarkable pace, it had taken six years to perfect the 155-mm gun howitzer to Chinese satisfaction.

The Iraqis called SRC because Saadi knew of Bull's capabilities and of his reputation as a rogue genius. He knew of Bull's missile work at CARDE. He also knew that Bull had experimented with the characteristics of re-entry vehicles and missile nose cones. It was Bull the aerodynamicist who interested the Iraqis.

But when Michel and Stephen flew to Bonn that December, they hadn't been told that. The Iraqis at the embassy said they would pay all expenses if Dr. Bull and his sons would care to visit Baghdad. They wanted to discuss the long-term future and the rebuilding of their nation. In particular, they were considering a space programme that might interest Dr. Bull. They were looking for general discussions with a man they admired and respected. The Bulls were impressed.

When they returned to Brussels, Michel arranged a conference with the Belgian foreign ministry. The Belgians encouraged Michel to accept the Iraqi invitation with the strict understanding that SRC could enter into no weapons contracts until the war with Iran was ended. The officials felt the war would soon be over and suggested Iraq would then be a good customer. Their advice: "Go, but be careful."

15

IN JANUARY 1988, Gerry and his
two sons flew tourist class from Brussels to Frankfurt. There they
settled into first class seats on an Iraqi Airlines 747 for Baghdad. As
guests of President Saddam Hussein, they were pampered
throughout the three-hour flight. This was the sort of attention that
Gerry Bull liked best. Indeed, it prompted Michel to go over the
ground rules once again: this was an exploratory visit only, they
would enter into no agreements but merely investigate the possibility of long-term business opportunities once the war was over.
Bull was planning to develop a new artillery system. "Advanced
technologies – larger guns, longer ranges," he had told the Iraqis on
the telephone from Brussels. But as Michel explains, "My father was
a very enthusiastic man and he could easily get carried away. He had
this great ego, he thought he could do anything."

This time Michel, as the executive in charge of finance, was
determined that only he would negotiate the money side – should
contracts develop. SRC certainly needed business, but not at any
price. This time there had to be substantial profit. Gerry had so
much of himself invested in the company that he couldn't bear to see
it run down for lack of contracts. This made him vulnerable, and his
sons were determined to keep tabs on him.

They were met at the handsome Saddam International Airport
by a chauffeured car and driven down Saddam Highway, past
Saddam Hall and through Saddam Square to their luxurious rooms
at the Al Rashid hotel. On almost every public wall there was a

portrait of the heavy-eyed Saddam. "Sure, he is a dictator," Bull told his sons. "But the Arabs need dictators or they fall into political anarchy." That evening they walked under the palms that line the banks of the Tigris River, stopping for tea and talk at the outdoor cafés. Several customers spoke to them in English, and the conversations seemed open. There appeared to be general support for Saddam, and the people were proud that, even though he was brutal, he was not personally corrupt or greedy. The idea of strict but honest discipline appealed to Dr. Bull. He saw the bearded and beturbaned Iranian fanatics as "the bad guys". Saddam was fighting the ayatollah's mob, holding back the spread of revolutionary Islam, whose worst excesses Bull saw as comparable to those of communism. Also, the Americans were backing Saddam. And he knew from the arms world pipeline that "everyone" was dealing with Saddam. In this fight anyway, Saddam was "the good guy".

Bull had been pro-Israeli and had dealt with the Israelis fairly extensively in the early days of SRC. Since then he had travelled to Tel Aviv to give lectures on ballistics and had highly placed friends in the Israeli military. But he was not convinced that Israel should control all of the technology in the Middle East any more than the U.S. should control all the technology in the West. Also, he believed that Israel was responsible for spreading a great many false stories about Arab leaders. The Israeli propaganda machine made the Arabs sound like beasts. However, almost all of the Arabs Bull had met he liked. And had he not himself been a major victim of propaganda, slander and character assassination? As a result, he was inclined to give the benefit of the doubt to the underdog.

On their first full day in Baghdad the three Bulls were taken to the fortress-like offices of Hussein Kamil, who a few weeks later was to be appointed minister of industry and military industrialization. They were led through a series of offices filled with soldiers carrying AK-47 rifles and aides with .45-calibre pistols strapped to their belts. Kamil's chief aide and later deputy minister, Amir Saadi, was standing close by. Tea was served and the two Iraqis looked cool and efficient yet friendly in their crisp, well-tailored uniforms.

Straight off, Michel explained that for SRC to become involved with the current Iraqi war effort would be illegal and could result in the company's principals going to jail. And, Michel continued with a smile, the company had taken that path once before and had no intention of a repetition. Kamil quickly assured the Bulls that he had nothing illegal in mind. The war, he said, would be over in a few months. At any rate, he was no longer involved in the war effort but was now in charge of rebuilding the nation. The new artillery pieces that Dr. Bull was planning were obviously several years from operational use and so were of no relevance to the current war.

Nevertheless, said Kamil, Iraq was interested in the new artillery and once the war was over would almost certainly place orders. In the meantime, he would be grateful if Dr. Bull would give Mr. Saadi some broad outlines of what he had in mind. But first, Kamil invited the Bulls to tour Iraq with Mr. Saadi as a guide and consider what role SRC might play in rebuilding the country. Perhaps the company could supply engineering advice. For example, President Hussein was anxious to launch a civilian space programme and make Iraq the first Arab nation able to launch its own satellites. Would Dr. Bull be interested in contributing? Also, Iraq wanted to develop its domestic manufacturing facilities and to this end was looking to invest in European companies. Those companies could then be encouraged to train young Iraqis who would return home to open branch plants or subsidiaries. Would SRC be interested in looking for suitable companies for Iraqi investment?

Nor was Kamil all business. Turning to the Latin-looking Michel, with his heavy moustache and slightly hooded eyes, he joked that with a good suntan he could pass for an Iraqi. If they stayed long enough, said Kamil, Michel might end up with a wife. Michel laughed and said that would not be possible because he already had a wife. After a pause he added: "But maybe it would be possible because I understand that in your country a man can have more than one wife." A faint smile flickered across Kamil's face as he replied: "Sometimes." Then Michel remembered that this man was married to Saddam's daughter. A second wife would certainly not be very healthy for him.

That first meeting with Kamil and Saadi was friendly and pressure-free. There was not the slightest suggestion that Iraq wanted SRC to do anything untoward. Michel and Stephen were relieved. They were also delighted, because if Kamil was right and the war was soon coming to an end, there would be the opportunity for lucrative contracts, and perhaps also a chance to diversify out of the defence business. And both of the Bull sons wanted that. Customers employed SRC as a defence company for only one reason: Dr. Bull's legendary expertise. That meant that once he retired, the company was finished. But if SRC could diversify into general engineering or some other technical area for which experts could be brought on staff, the prospects might be very different.

Saadi proved a perfect host. He took the Bulls around archaeological sites and talked freely about Iraq's munitions capabilities. They were even taken to Al-Hillah, a top-secret military base near Baghdad where explosives were made and where they were told that Soviet Scud missiles were being modified to increase their range for use against Iranian targets. Working conditions appeared to be high, safety precautions were stringent and machinery was modern and kept in perfect condition. The Bulls were impressed.

On the fourth day Saadi met alone with Dr. Bull. He said he was very interested in Bull's ideas for bigger gun systems and said that Iraq would pay for development costs if SRC would start working on concepts right away. And then he moved on to what he considered the heart of the visit: Iraq wanted Bull's help with its space programme. Iraqi, Egyptian and Brazilian scientists had been working with some European "contacts", and they were convinced that a way could be found to tie together five Soviet-supplied Scud missiles to make the first stage of a three-stage space rocket able to launch satellites. But there were problems galore. The one that Saadi wanted to discuss now was the lack of a supercomputer.

The Brazilian scientists were saying that without one it would take years to design an airframe for the three-stage rocket. However, Saadi said, Dr. Bull had a reputation for getting things done quickly with minimum facilities. What they wanted from Bull was the calculations that would show them how much steel would be needed, how strong it should be and how it should be used to tie together the five Scuds for the first stage of the rocket. There were, Saadi stressed, no military implications to this whatsoever. They were asking only for Dr. Bull's considerable knowledge as an aerodynamics engineer to help launch a satellite. If he would agree to help on this purely scientific venture, Saadi would take him to Saad 16, the secret missile research station in northern Iraq where the engineers would provide the technical details he would need.

This was the kind of assignment at which Bull excelled. The boy rocket scientist of *Maclean's* 1952 article was excited. And this was non-military, a contract he could take without running into legal problems. Without consulting Michel or Stephen, he agreed.

Dr. Bull did not have access to a supercomputer and could not get such access. But from experience he believed he would be able to handle the mathematics that would enable him to simulate the thrust of rocket engines, and calculate the heat and pressure involved. He had completed similar assignments at CARDE without a supercomputer, and he knew that the sort of research he could provide would drastically cut development time, costs and the need for flight tests.

It was at this point that Dr. Bull introduced his passion. If Iraq wanted to launch satellites, he had the perfect solution – the supergun. Saadi already knew about HARP, and now Bull told him about the DARPA conference he had attended two years before and the rumours he had heard of the project going ahead at Lawrence Livermore. Bull said that for about $3 million he could make a supergun that would dwarf HARP and put a sizeable satellite into orbit. Furthermore, once the gun was established, it would be able to launch satellites for $2,000 or $3,000 a shot. Iraq could afford to "litter the skies" with satellites and could launch them for every Arab nation. True, the satellites would have to fit into the barrel of the gun and would be limited in size, weight and scope, but that might be perfect for short-term specific missions. And, Bull believed, he could beat the Americans to the punch and have the gun firing in a couple of years. Such a project, he told Saadi, was a lifetime ambition of his and, once successful, would bring with it enormous scientific prestige, publicity and praise for Iraq.

Saadi promised to consult about the supergun and recommend that Iraq back the project.

Almost as an afterthought, Bull told Saadi that if Iraq went ahead with the supergun, it would have to build at least one smaller prototype for testing purposes. That prototype could be used, Bull said, for nose-cone testing of the rockets needed for the space programme. He had after all conducted such tests for the Pentagon on his Highwater gun sixteen years before. Thus, he explained, the gun-launch system would complement the rocket-launch system. Indeed, this was the very two-prong programme he had presented to Canada and the United States more than three decades before. The gun would launch small satellites, the rockets would launch larger ones.

Saadi was more interested than ever. Money, he told Bull, was no problem. Iraq's oil exports, which accounted for 90 per cent of foreign earnings, had climbed to nearly three million barrels a day, just below the prewar level, and pipeline projects were on the verge of replacing the export routes lost when Iran closed Iraq's only southern port and Syria shut down a major overland export line to the Mediterranean. At the same time, said Saadi, the United States was now providing secret strategic help to Iraqi forces, giving them access to satellite intelligence. But once the war ended, the satellite intelligence would end too, even though Iraq would remain threatened by Iran and Israel and maybe even Syria. U.S. intelligence help had persuaded the Iraqi military that satellite facilities were essential.

On that first trip to Iraq, the Bulls stayed for about a week. On the flight home Gerry told his sons about the Iraqi request for help with calculations concerning the first-stage rocket of a satellite launching system. They agreed there was no reason why SRC should not get involved. Bull was going to do some initial calculations and then let the Iraqis know what he might be able to achieve and how much it would cost them. They decided to code-name the research Project Bird, and Gerry put Stephen in charge of its management. It was to be Stephen's first big job. The major development to emerge from the trip, however, was seen as the Iraqi interest in new artillery systems.

The trip, the Bulls agreed, had been successful. Immediate non-military work had been secured and there was the promise of big contracts for the future.

Dr. Bull in particular seemed to be in a good mood. There were probably two reasons. First, the prospect of a backer for his super-gun, something he decided not to share with his sons at that time. Second, he had found someone to improve the quality of his life in Brussels and take away some of the loneliness he felt when Mimi wasn't there. Hélène Gregoire was a wealthy, attractive, middle-aged and divorced French-Canadian who had been a family friend for years. Gerald Bull was finding her to be a lot of fun; she made him laugh a lot. Of course, he was still in love with Mimi, but Mimi lived in Montreal. Hélène was just a good friend, someone to add a little spice to his life. Still, he didn't think it prudent to mention her to his sons either.

He was in high spirits when they landed in Frankfurt and transferred to tourist class for the flight back to Brussels.

16

GERRY BULL had a reputation for enjoying the company of women and could be an incorrigible flirt. He had a way of maintaining eye contact for a moment too long, and his grin was of the kind that promised mischief. In the office he would write little poems for the women he knew best, calling them aside so that he could read them with exaggerated emphasis. "It was one of his best jokes," says Monique Jaminé. "Sometimes they would be funny, and sometimes romantic and sometimes sad." Gerry did not hand over his poetry; he read it and later threw it away.

His flirting was always tinged with humour, and women had trouble knowing if he was being serious. "Oh, there was nothing serious to it at all," says Monique. "It was just his way."

Gerry combined two features that made him attractive to some women. First, he was extremely attentive. He always had time to listen to problems and to offer well-thought-out solutions. And he was so generous. No matter who was involved, he would give his time and make the other person feel important. People mattered to him. Second, he was very vulnerable. He was obviously in need of being looked after. As one SRC secretary said, "You wanted to mother him."

For his part, Gerry seemed to find safety in numbers. He could flirt with half a dozen women at the same time, and enjoy them all, happy to be pleasing everyone. So those close to him quickly noticed when he appeared to develop a special relationship.

Hélène Gregoire was in her late forties, and she looked remarkably similar to Mimi, with short blonde hair and a flair for stylish, low-key clothes. She had two daughters and a hefty fortune left by her husband. The Bull family had known her for years; she was one of Mimi's friends. The Bull children looked on her as a surrogate aunt. "She happened to be in Brussels and he happened to be in Brussels, and it was natural they would get together," says an SRC engineer. When Gerry needed to take an escort to a party or reception, he would ask Hélène first.

And she was good for him. She didn't drink and frowned on those who did, so Gerry cut down his consumption. She encouraged him to go to church and was always willing to drive him out to the war graves for a Sunday stroll. She persuaded him to take her to the Cannes Film Festival and accompanied him to war museums in West Germany and France as he continued research on his book.

At any suggestion that something might be serious, that he might be having an affair, Gerry would become extremely angry. Hélène, he insisted, was just a good friend. It was ridiculous to think anything else. But eventually, Monique told Bull that he and Hélène had become an item of office gossip.

To counter the rumours, he organized a party for the senior staff at a smart Brussels restaurant. The party, he said, was for Hélène and her boyfriend, another friend of Bull's. Hélène would soon be getting engaged, Bull told his guests. "It was the most clumsy attempt to squash a rumour that I ever saw," recalls Monique. "Hélène didn't give a damn, and the guy she was supposed to marry was flirting with every other woman in the room. Hélène went home on her own." The next day Dr. Bull told Monique, "There now, you can see that Hélène has a real romance. I am just an old friend." She didn't bother to set him straight.

During the first week of March, Amir Saadi sent a diplomat from the Bonn embassy to talk with Dr. Bull. They met in Bull's third-floor office in the SRC building.

The white walls of Bull's corner officer at the back of the building were covered in family photographs and a collection of prints, many of them from China. A glass-fronted bookcase was jammed with technical reports. Bull had a large walnut desk. A walnut table surrounded by six chairs was pushed up against the front of the desk so Bull could conduct office conferences without leaving his seat. There was one problem with that. Bull's desk was entirely covered with reports and magazines and notebooks and newspaper cuttings. Some piles were half a metre high. He couldn't see over them. And it was often impossible to see him. It made communication rather difficult, but he refused to clean up.

In the far corner on an easel was a huge blackboard covered with mathematical equations. Bull had used it for calculations on a Spanish gun-testing programme. When the programme ended he so liked the look of the board that he refused to rub it out. By the spring of 1988, the board had been full of the same numbers for nearly two years. When he absolutely needed to use it, he would rub out only a small corner.

Now the Iraqi diplomat sat at Bull's office table and tried to talk with him through the jungle of clutter.

First, he wanted to know if Bull had made any progress on calculations to tie together the five Scuds. Bull told him he could provide the necessary calculations and would accept a contract, which should be negotiated with Michel and Stephen.

Second, the diplomat said that Baghdad wanted to go ahead with Dr. Bull's idea for a supergun. He did not, however, believe that such a gun could be built for the $3 million suggested earlier in Iraq. He said that Bull should propose a new budget to cover the building of prototypes and the full-scale gun, remembering that President Saddam Hussein would expect the gun to be in operation within five years.

Not since McGill University had agreed to launch the HARP project had Gerald Bull the scientist been so delighted. He had feared that his professional life would end without the dream of the supergun being fulfilled. At last it was going to happen. Five years was an impossible deadline, but he saw himself in a race with the United States and believed it could be done. And, when achieved, it would make the front page of every newspaper in the Western world and would confirm his reputation. It would overshadow the South African affair.

The Iraqi diplomat asked Bull to write a formal proposal. Saddam wanted him to start work on it immediately. A preliminary payment could be made within days, and a contract would be forthcoming as soon as the proposal was received.

That night Bull called three of his SRC staff experts at home and told them he was going to build the greatest gun in history. But Bull urged them into silence and secrecy. At the same time he began handing out surreptitious engineering jobs on which he could base an initial proposal. The work would have to be done away from the office, and Bull would pay for it in cash out of "discretionary" funds he would soon receive. For a code name, he decided on Project Babylon, although it went into the company books as a number, Project 839.

By mid-March 1988, negotiations were underway for a supergun treaty with Iraq. The contract was to be renewed annually for an indefinite period, though under its terms a substantial prototype had to be in place, in Iraq, within a year. Two full-size superguns would be built; one would act as a test bed while the other was to launch a first satellite by 1993. Funds would be paid into a Luxembourg bank every four weeks – after Baghdad received and approved a monthly progress report. A total budget of $25 million was agreed.

Iraq wanted no delays, and while the details were being settled they urged Bull to surge ahead. He needed little encouragement. He increased the amount of freelance work he was secretly assigning to SRC engineers. Dr. Christopher Cowley, a fifty-year-old British metallurgist and mechanical engineer with international experience on mega-ventures, was made project manager.

Cowley put together the original Project Babylon team, consisting of aerodynamicist Tony Slack; mathematician Graham Ingham; mechanical engineering draughtsman Michael Clark; and John Heath, a highly talented graphics man able to depict on paper the concepts of the senior scientists.

Bull told them initially that he wanted to put into orbit a payload of two tonnes, the minimum size for a useful satellite. The design and size of the gun were thus dictated by the payload. The team quickly decided that the bore would have to be one full metre. This would make the gun a truly phenomenal machine capable of firing a projectile the size of a telephone booth.

The Project Babylon team met at night in Bull's office. Whatever the final figures, they started the project knowing they were dealing with a gun that would dwarf anything that had been seriously considered before. The technical problems were immense.

Bull was at his best. His enthusiasm was overwhelming. He was certain that all difficulties could be solved. The barrel would be smooth-bore without rifling because the projectile would be rocket-assisted and would be fin-stabilized – they did not want it to leave the barrel spinning; it needed steady flight. For now, Bull simply wanted a gun design. This could not be just a bigger artillery piece. Totally new concepts were involved, and those working on it should know that they would gain a place in ballistics history.

But it was up to the engineers actually to design the gun; this was not the sort of detail Bull wanted to be personally involved with. He would start work on the projectile.

Says Cowley: "Bull was an incredible motivator. He never interfered, he never questioned you. He filled you with confidence. And he was always available."

Before the end of April, Cowley and his assistants had designed the supergun and its prototype and developed a formula for the extraordinarily strong steel that would be needed. Cowley's final specifications, backed by complex calculations, called for a supergun barrel a staggering 156 metres long. That's nearly as high as the Washington Monument, nearly three times as high as Nelson's Column.

Cowley wanted the barrel made in twenty-six sections to be bolted together through massive flanges. The barrel alone would weigh 1,665 tonnes. In addition, there were to be four recoil cylinders weighing 60 tonnes each, two buffer cylinders weighing 7 tonnes each and a 182-tonne breech. In all, the gun was 2,100 tonnes. It was to be bigger than a gunboat.

At the breech, the steel tube would be 30 centimetres thick and able to withstand a maximum operating pressure of 70,000 psi. The steel had a tensile strength of more than 1,250 Mega Pascals. The thickness of the barrel walls was to be staged down over the length of the gun as the pressure they would have to withstand fell. By the end of the muzzle they were to be 6.5 centimetres. Actually, to withstand the pressure, the muzzle section need only have been 12 millimetres thick, but the barrel also had to maintain a certain rigidity, and this introduced new structural problems. Explains Cowley: "When the gun recoils the muzzle end must be able to carry the load of all the other tubes below it, which are going in the opposite direction."

As a prototype for the two superguns, Cowley and his team designed Baby Babylon, or "the model", which was to be about one-third the size of the real thing. This gun would be 46 metres long with a 350-mm bore. The entire Baby Babylon barrel would weigh about 113 tonnes.

It was always envisioned that Baby Babylon would be placed in a permanent horizontal position and be used primarily to test what is called interior ballistics, the behaviour of projectiles and propellents inside the barrel. The gun was to be self-recoiling and mounted on rails, like the prototype for HARP that Bull had made years before.

While Baby Babylon would answer many questions about the functioning of the supergun, it could not be used to test the integrity of the entire system. For this, a full-size test bed was essential, and one of the superguns would serve this purpose. It too would be mounted horizontally and would be used to test the recoil system and the size of propellent loads needed to achieve required velocities.

Bull swore everyone to silence; Michel and Stephen must not find out about the supergun. Monique Jaminé was informed about the scheme and asked to handle the financial side. She would drive to Luxembourg every month to pick up the Iraqi cash.

Before the Project Babylon team had been working for a week, office gossip about the gun eclipsed the Gerry-and-Hélène rumours. SRC engineers were lining up outside Bull's office asking to get in on the job. Michel was told about the project by four different employees. He called Stephen aside, briefed him, and the two brothers marched into their father's inner sanctum determined to have a showdown.

Gerry Bull had never learned to take criticism, and now that his decisions were being questioned he became furious. Stephen sat at the back of the room saying almost nothing. But Michel would not be silenced. He insisted that his father come out from behind his piles of papers and sit at the conference table. And then Michel spelled out the facts as he saw them. SRC was able to survive in the defence business because it was a fringe company, not big enough to do any real harm. As long as it continued to produce only engineering drawings and concepts for artillery, it would be no significant threat to anyone.

However, if Dr. Bull was to produce his gigantic gun, he would attract international attention. SRC would come under scrutiny, as never before. No matter what Bull said about the supergun, no matter how strongly he proclaimed it was for the launching of satellites only, the enemies of Iraq, particularly Israel and Iran, would not believe him. They would declare it was a weapon of such fearful potential that it would upset the balance of power in the Middle East. There would be international condemnation, Michel said. He predicted that the satellite gun would be viewed as a weapon capable of shooting nuclear, chemical and biological warheads halfway around the world.

Bull tried to force a laugh, but it rang hollow. Project Babylon would not be seen as a weapon – was not a weapon – because it made no sense as a weapon. The gun would fire a two-tonne projectile into space, and the detonation in Iraq would be so great that it would register on seismographs in California. A 90-metre flame would shoot from the mouth of the cannon at every firing and would be picked up by every spy satellite. Within minutes of the first firing, every sophisticated military force in the world would know the exact coordinates of the gun. And the gun would be completely immobile – it could not be moved or protected. For, as Bull pointed out, the barrel was to be made in sections, and these sections would be so fragile in their alignment that even a small bomb dropped five kilometres away would throw them out of sync. Not only that, but this was a gun that could not be aimed. True, if the guidance systems that the Americans were developing could be obtained, then it might be possible to use the gun to fire on targets. But it would be fired only once, said Bull, because the counter-attack would knock it out.

No, he and the Iraqis could easily prove that Project Babylon was not a weapon. Still, it was essential to keep development secret because the Israelis and the Americans might stop its manufacture – because they didn't want Iraq to have spy satellites. There was enormous scope for the supergun to be misunderstood by foreign governments, and the pieces for the gun would have to be made in factories and foundries all over Europe. Iraq had nothing like the facilities that would be needed to build this project. It would be easy to stop Project Babylon for political reasons. Anyway, if the press got hold of the story they would aim for the sensational and portray it as a doomsday weapon.

Dr. Bull was insistent. Project Babylon would be the making of SRC and it would confirm his own reputation.

Michel remained unconvinced. The project could not be carried out in secrecy, he said. It was certain to leak. It was equally certain to be the ruin of SRC. The company would be seen as a threat to Middle East stability, and huge political pressures would be brought. There would be accusations of illegal technology transfers and criminal charges might be threatened. As SRC's managing director, Michel said it could end with him going to jail and that risk was not acceptable.

Struggling to keep his composure, Dr. Bull said that Michel and Stephen – who still had said nothing – could have their way. He would form another company quite separate from SRC and would conduct Project Babylon from there. SRC would not be involved. Furthermore, when the project was completed and the gun was declared a major scientific breakthrough, his sons would not share "in the glory", nor would they reap the financial benefits. Michel said that he could not stop his father doing what he wanted.

Before leaving that first session Michel again made it clear that he believed building Project Babylon for Iraq was a stupid and dangerous idea. This was not just a father-son argument. It was bitter and deep. And it wasn't over.

That afternoon, Dr. Bull had Monique draw up the papers to form a company called Advanced Technology Institute, or ATI, and within a few days he had rented offices just above the Bolivian Embassy, across town from the SRC offices. He had deliberately put several kilometres between SRC and ATI. Engineers were to complain long and hard about the commute through Brussels traffic.

The core team moved into the new offices, and Alexander Pappas, an SRC vice president and long-time Bull aide from the HARP days, agreed to act as a special consultant.

Bull registered the company in Athens because he wanted a European office close to the Middle East so his staff could "pop backwards and forwards to Iraq and to where drawings could be delivered easily". Says Cowley: "Athens was perfect because, like Belgium, Greece has very lax laws when it comes to exporting technology." As it worked out, the Athens office was used only as a post box.

The formal contract between Iraq and ATI for Project Babylon was not signed until June 10, 1988, but was backdated to cover the design work already completed.

Because the war with Iran was still underway, SRC could not enter into a legal deal to develop artillery for Iraq, but it was "understood" that once the war was over a contract for artillery would be forthcoming. In the meantime, a series of small research contracts involving the satellite-launching rocket were signed, as was a contract under which SRC would give ballistics training courses for Iraqi personnel.

Over at ATI, Cowley could hardly believe the freedom he was given. "Bull was a concept man, an ideas man," he says. Bull sought no part in what he called "the agricultural side" of the work – the mechanics, the materials, the manufacturing and processing technology. He left it entirely to the staff. Says Cowley: "Bull would plot out the concepts. He wanted certain payload weights travelling at certain speeds. He would be deeply involved in the mathematics and the physics." But once those concepts were settled, he moved out of the direct picture. "Bull pulled all of the different scientific disciplines together and somehow got them to mesh. He was just incredible. It simply wasn't possible to operate at anything less than your maximum potential. And yet he left everyone alone to operate in their own way. It sounds like a lunatic asylum being run by the inmates, but it worked brilliantly."

Bull told colleagues that once Project Babylon was in place in Iraq and ready for full testing, it would be made public. Scientists from around the world would be invited to inspect it and to witness the first gun-launching of a satellite. The publicity, he said, would be Project Babylon's security blanket. It would be fairly easy to prove that the gun was a scientific tool. And once that was proven, the Israelis would not dare to knock it out with an air attack because such an attack would be seen as an act of international vandalism.

Meanwhile, Project Bird was progressing. Bull had reached the point where he could discuss basic airframe problems for the first-stage rocket. And he was now asked for ideas on the second and third stages. A proliferating set of mini-contracts were issued by Iraq for work on all stages of the system, and by summer 1988 Iraq was rapidly becoming SRC's major customer.

Bull began to spend as much as a quarter of his time in Iraq, and it was agreed that as part of the need to keep Project Babylon secret, the Iraqis would set up an engineering and draughting shop for the project's exclusive use at a base just outside Baghdad. This meant that basic drawing and calculating could be done on Iraqi soil, lessening the chances that charges might eventually be brought over an alleged illegal transfer of technology. But highly skilled technicians were needed to back up the work in Brussels, and on Cowley's suggestion advertisements for "Design Draughtsmen to work Overseas" were placed in newspapers in the Bristol area, where Cowley had a home. About a dozen were eventually employed on the understanding that they would be paid in cash, there would be no health benefits or pension plans, and they would look after their own tax obligations. With overtime, they found they could make about a $1,000 a week, which was far more than any of them had ever made before. Although they were not officially informed, it soon became obvious they were working on projectiles. However, the high pay, excellent working conditions and the close relationship that nearly all the draughtsmen soon developed with Bull ensured they kept the secret – at least at first.

The speed with which all of this was happening was phenomenal. In two months ATI achieved more than a national government might have achieved in two years. "This was Bull's genius," says Cowley. "He could get the absolute best out of everyone. There was no room for jealously or pettiness."

Throughout May 1988, Cowley had been studying the technical press, looking for likely companies to make the supergun components. There was a Europe-wide arms embargo on Iraq, and since the uninitiated would regard the supergun as military, the project had to be disguised. In late May, Cowley offered a contract to Walter Somers, near Birmingham, for the "pipes" that would make up the barrel of Baby Babylon. The company, known for producing tank gun barrels, was told that the "pipes" were for a petrochemical project in Iraq, and they would have to be delivered within ten months.

Walter Somers needed the business but was suspicious that the pipes looked awfully like a gun barrel. Twice they questioned the British government's Department of Trade and Industry (DTI) and asked if an export licence would be needed. Twice they were told that a licence would not be needed. But that still didn't satisfy Walter Somers's managing director and chief metallurgist, Rex Bayliss. Bayliss contacted Sir Hal Miller, the local Conservative MP, and said the specifications the Iraqis were requesting did not match their stated use. Says Sir Hal: "The company is a Ministry of Defence contractor. They are not stupid." Sir Hal called the DTI, the Ministry of Defence and a branch of the British intelligence service. He told them everything he knew about the pipes. He told them Gerry Bull was involved, and he told them Rex Bayliss thought he might be dealing with a gun barrel. And Sir Hal was told not to worry, that Walter Somers should continue with the order.

A few weeks later, Cowley offered a contract for the "pipes" to make the actual supergun barrel to another British company, Sheffield Forgemasters, who had advertised their expertise in producing gun barrels capable of withstanding the corrosive effects of "advanced propellents". Forgemasters, concentrating on the export trade, had gained a reputation for high-quality products made to exacting specifications in the defence, oil, aerospace and power-generating industries. The project was said to be for "the polymerisation of polyethylene" at an Iraqi petrochemical plant. This time the deadline was two years. The contract was valued at £1.7 million.

Phillip Wright, the chief executive officer for Sheffield Forgemasters, wanted to accept the contract. His company too needed the business. But a couple of phone calls quickly confirmed that ATI was closely connected to SRC and that SRC specialized in the design of long-range artillery. And although neither ATI nor SRC had any background in the petrochemical industry, both were rumoured to be doing military business with Iraq. Not only that, the specifications for the "pipes" were so exact and demanding that they could be for little else than a gun barrel.

In June, Wright and a group of directors from Forgemasters and two subsidiaries, Forgemasters Engineering and River Don Castings, flew to Brussels to discuss the contract with Cowley. They asked him if the tubes had any military purpose and he answered no. Wright made it clear that he had doubts, and insisted that he would have to inform the Department of Trade and Industry to make sure no laws were being broken. Immediately after the meeting, Bryan Cookson, managing director of River Don Castings, telephoned the DTI from Brussels and was told there would be no problem with a petroleum-chemical pipeline for Iraq. It would not need an export licence.

Six more meetings were held between company officials and Cowley over the next few weeks as they negotiated over the specifications, including the absolute necessity that the bore on any one pipe match the bore on any other with no more than 0.5 millimetres difference.

Agreement was reached in July, and production of the fifty-two pipes, for two barrels, began immediately. But Wright remained so troubled by the ultimate purpose of the tubes he was making that he sent a full copy of the exacting specifications to DTI – where it was approved as a pipeline.

Detailed discussions with petrochemical scientists reveal that no one with any knowledge of the petrochemical industry could accept that such demanding specifications were necessary.

As if to emphasize that they were not acting in secret or doing anything that the British government had not been fully informed of, Forgemasters made a fifteen-minute video of the pipes being manufactured and announced they were going to use it as an advertising promotion. In the video, Forgemasters seemed to be waving a red flag at the government. "In size, toughness, and accuracy, these tubes are in a class of their own," said the promotion. The video explains that the company developed its own machine to bore the tubes. It says each section of pipe has flanges so that it can be bolted, via three guide holes, to another section "at key positioning points". "When bolted end to end, this ensures perfect bore alignment over the total length of the assembly." In a final ironic swipe, the video points out that the pipes can withstand pressures and temperatures twelve times greater than the maximums needed for the manufacture of polyethylene.

As sections of "pipe" were completed, Iraq arranged to pick them up from the Sheffield plant and take them directly to the docks for shipping. On pick-up, the Iraqis paid for the work completed with an irrevocable letter of credit.

The money also started rolling in to ATI. For the first time in more than a decade, Bull had a large budget into which he could dip. The money to publish and research his book on HARP and the German World War One big guns came out of the supergun budget. Nor in all the excitement had he lost his obsession with getting a pardon for the South African affair. Now, on the advice of General Arthur Trudeau in Washington, Bull employed William Gill, a Washington lobbyist, at $5,000 a month to help him fight for the pardon. No matter how often Michel and others told him it was a total waste of money and time, he refused to give up the idea.

As Projects Bird and Babylon got under way in Brussels, the Reagan Administration was helping Baghdad reorganize its elite military units. Furthermore, Washington was working out a military strategy that would allow Iraq to re-take the oil-rich Fao peninsula, where troops had been bogged down since 1986. The U.S. assistance included building a replica of the Fao peninsula for dry runs by the Iraqi army. On April 18, 1988, Iraq recaptured Fao in an attack that lasted less than thirty-six hours. The tide of the war had been turned and Iraqi troops pushed forward, taking more Iranian land than ever before. By August, Iran was forced to accept a United Nations ceasefire, and an uncertain peace was enforced. For all practical purposes the war was over, leaving Saddam Hussein firmly in power.

By the end of the war, Saddam's regime had spent its vast prewar foreign exchange reserve surplus and piled up debt estimated at $100 billion. But during the crucial final months of Iraqi assaults, Baghdad had captured at least 40 per cent of Iran's most sophisticated arms, including tanks and some of the Bull-originated 155-mm artillery pieces bought from South Africa and Austria. As a result, Iraq emerged in a position to dominate the Persian Gulf.

Throughout, Iran had been pictured in the West as the villain, and although Teheran had made several approaches to SRC for cooperation, Dr. Bull had always turned them away. He had joined Iraq's corner in the first place because he was understandably convinced that Baghdad had the backing of the NATO countries. But now Bull was shocked to find that, with the end of the war, the Western media began to expose Saddam as the "Butcher of Baghdad". Reports were printed that he tortured the children of political dissidents. Persuasive evidence showed that in March 1988, just as the supergun was being approved, the Iraqi military had dropped chemical bombs on Kurds in the northern Iraqi town of Halabja, killing hundreds of people.

Bull recalled how Washington had backed him in the early 1970s only to desert him towards the end of the decade, with the press printing allegations about him running guns. And Bull chose to disbelieve the allegations made against Saddam and to continue with his plans. He conveniently convinced himself that Saddam was no worse than a dozen other dictators and that he had more foresight and imagination than most.

By now the book on HARP and the Paris Guns was completed. It was privately printed by a German company and contained dozens of colour photos. Thousands of copies were shipped to Bull's office, and he sent them out as presents to almost everyone he knew. The military press received the book well, and in several prestigious military journals he got outstanding reviews. Without doubt he had uncovered more information about First World War German advances in artillery than had ever been printed. He was already busy on the next book, looking at German artillery advances in the Second World War and going into more detail on the HARP project. Eventually, a third book would detail Project Babylon. But that was years ahead. For now he threw a party to celebrate the first publication.

Monique Jaminé was in charge of arrangements. There were to be twenty people, all involved in the book, at a luxurious dinner at the Pavillon Louis Quinze. The editors were invited from Germany, Murphy and his wife from Baltimore, and Mimi was coming from Montreal. A few hours before the dinner, Bull told Monique there would be an extra guest – Hélène Gregoire.

Says Monique: "The last-minute change threw everything into disarray. It created so much tension." At the end of dinner, Dr. Bull thanked everyone for coming and outlined their role in the production of the book. When he came to Hélène, he said she was present simply because she was such a good friend. And Mimi added: "Yes, she looks after my husband when I am not here."

A few days later, Michel had another showdown with his father. Dr. Bull was starting to devote almost all of his time to Project Babylon, and Michel was still certain it would prove the ruination of the company. It had to be abandoned. Bull steadfastly refused, and Michel announced that in the circumstances he could no longer remain in Belgium. He would return to Montreal.

Michel had been his father's partner almost from the start in Brussels, and now the prospect of his leaving hit Dr. Bull hard. In many ways, Michel had been the bedrock of the company, the source of fiscal responsibility. But something had to give. Very well, said Dr. Bull, why not return to Montreal and run the financial side of the organization from there? Michel agreed, and the two men parted feeling that at least something had been settled.

PART VII

This is the Arsenal

"This is the Arsenal. From floor to ceiling,
Like a huge organ, rise the burnished arms ...
Ah! what a sound will rise, how wild and dreary,
When the death-angel touches those swift keys!"

"The Arsenal at Springfield"
Henry Wadsworth Longfellow

17

IN AUGUST 1988, Baghdad signed contracts with Dr. Bull to produce two new artillery systems. Both had been discussed at length since the February meeting and SRC engineers had completed extensive design work, but only now, with the Iran-Iraq war ended, was it legal to proceed. True to its word, Baghdad paid for work done before the contract was signed and in so doing established itself as SRC's major customer and asset. Bull was flying to Iraq every month, Michel and Stephen were frequently there, and at any given time two or three staff members from either SRC or ATI were in the country. Although the two companies and their projects were supposed to be separate, they inevitably overlapped because both staffs worked for the same boss – Gerry Bull.

All this activity did not go unnoticed. Bull was employing increasing numbers of young British draughtsmen. Arms trade insiders began speaking of "the old man and his children". And the image was not just fanciful. For as the new employees discovered, to work loyally for Bull was to be part of his family. One young Belgian couple working for SRC were being torn apart by financial problems lingering from their student days. Bull heard about it from another employee, paid off their debts to the tune of some $10,000, then told the newly-weds to get on "with being in love".

The sometimes crazy work schedule also contributed to the special "feel" of working with Dr. Bull. With no warning, he would suddenly assemble a team to solve a physics or aerodynamics problem. By lunchtime the team would be gathered at the conference table in his office. They would send out for sandwiches in the early afternoon and for Chinese food for dinner. Around midnight another snack might be ordered. Bull, the dynamo of ideas and solutions, would drive at the problem right through the night, inspiring those around him. And then the team, unshaven, dishevelled and exhausted, would retire to the Hilton for a ham and eggs breakfast. It was from sessions of this kind that some of the most inventive and progressive aerodynamic solutions emerged. Says one young mechanical engineer: "Bull expanded your thinking. He took you beyond theory and he knew by instinct what would work and what wouldn't."

As summer turned to autumn in 1988, Dr. Bull had plenty of problems to contend with. First, there were the gun systems for Iraq. SRC artillery had so far been designed to be towed around battlefields by armoured vehicles. But the Iraq systems were to be self-propelled. They were each to come in two units, a forward and a rear. The forward unit would be an armoured vehicle with a Mercedes-Benz diesel engine, and it would be coupled to a rear unit made up of the gun, a turret and a fighting compartment. The forward unit would be the same for both systems and would give the guns a maximum road speed of 90 kilometres an hour and a cross-country speed of 60 to 70 kilometres an hour. Both guns would also be on the same type of chassis and would have the same type of turret.

The South Africans, in one version of Bull's original 155-mm artillery piece had produced the G-6 Rhino, nicknamed the Kalahari Ferrari. Mounted on six two-metre-high tyres, and tied into a heavy militarized driving mechanism, it had proved successful in desert and bush operations. This was the sort of weapon the Iraqis now wanted, in two sizes. The first of these was to be a 155-mm gun, designated the Majnoon by the Iraqis. It was essentially an updated version of Bull's 155-mm towed gun, and it would incorporate many of the improvements built into the Chinese gun with emphasis on improved accuracy, particularly from slight design changes to the ammunition. The Majnoon was to weigh 40 tonnes and be fitted with an eight-metre-long barrel firing a 45.5-kilogram extended-range full-bore base-bleed shell. Its maximum range was being forecast at 38 kilometres, with a maximum rate of fire of four rounds per minute and a sustained rate of one round per minute.

The second self-propelled gun was to attract much more attention from the international community. At 210-mm, it would be the largest artillery piece in any army. The Iraqis had designated this system Al Fao (Majnoon and Al Fao were the names of battles in the war with Iran), and it was to weigh 44 tonnes. It was to be fitted with an 11.13-metre-long barrel to fire a 109.4-kilogram extended-range full-bore base-bleed shell with a maximum range of 57 kilometres. Its rates of fire were to be the same as the Majnoon's. Al Fao was to be the longest-range operational artillery piece in the world. Bull had been thinking about a 210-mm gun, and the development of ammunition for such a weapon, for about two years, yet he did not assign his engineers to start on hard design details until mid-1988. Normally, it would take about six years to develop such a system, but Saddam Hussein was in a hurry, and Gerry Bull was known to be quick. Even then, when Deputy Minister of Defence Amir Saadi asked Bull to have the gun systems ready for display in May, when Iraq planned to hold an international defence equipment exhibition in Baghdad, Bull blanched. He didn't say it was impossible; he said "something" would be ready, just so long as the Iraqis kept the money flowing. Saadi emphasized that the guns were to be presented as Iraqi in origin and that eventually they were to be made entirely in Iraq. Their development was to be confidential, and SRC was to stay far in the background. But for now, Saadi asked SRC to go one step further than was the company's normal practice. He asked not just for the design drawings but also for SRC to subcontract the manufacture of prototypes. Again, Bull agreed. Nothing seemed too big a job. The Iraqis, most particularly Saadi and Defence Minister Hussein Kamil, were enormously impressed. Saddam Hussein was constantly demanding the impossible, and Bull was one of the few who seemed able to deliver.

Bull's depth of interest and capacity to analyse and interpret new information made him a fascinating companion. Says one colleague: "He could talk about anything. He knew a lot about antiques and painting. I once heard him talk for an hour on animal husbandry, and everyone at the table was interested. The man didn't know how to be boring." After a visit to the excavations and restorations in Babylon, Bull was able to discuss Babylonian engineering with Saadi and compare it with the engineering of ancient Egypt. Saadi, who had become accustomed to dealing with narrowly focused scientists, was not only impressed by Bull, he became very fond of him. The Iraqi began discussing with him a wide range of the nation's rebuilding plans. For the first time since he'd left CARDE, Bull began to feel like an insider, only this was better because it almost seemed as though he was being included in the government's decision making. These people valued his opinions and advice. He felt wanted and needed, and he was eager to help wherever he could.

Bull liked to have a lot of discretionary funds at his disposal. Not that he was greedy. Indeed, money had no real value to him, and his whims were almost always directed towards helping others. Still, the more the Iraqis asked for, the more Bull was willing to give, and the more the Iraqis paid, the more cash-comfortable Bull felt.

In late August 1988, Saadi accompanied Bull on a trip several hours north of Baghdad to the military-industrial complex known as Saad 16, the top-secret home of Iraq's missile development programme. Although the schedule was tight, Saadi suggested a side trip. The present needed to be weighed against the past, he said, and he took Bull over to the east bank of the Tigris to visit the remains of Nineveh, the oldest city in Assyria.

Nineveh flourished under King Sennacherib, around 700 B.C., and was for centuries a centre of world learning and development. It was famous for one of the greatest libraries of antiquity, containing some twenty thousand tablets. Bull soaked up the colour and the drama of the past. And he pondered on the problems of history: How could so much achievement end this way? What had happened to the promise?

The brick and mud defences of the city contain fifteen gates, and Saadi shepherded his guest towards one of them to end the tour. Near the gate were two huge carved figures from the time of Sennacherib, and Saadi stopped below them. The two men gazed upwards in the dazzling afternoon sunshine at the figures – massive winged bulls. "Well," said Saadi, "you can see that you are not the first Bull to visit Nineveh." They laughed at the little joke, and then

Saadi became serious. "Dr. Bull," he said, "I hope that you will help Iraq to rise again, to once more be great ... "

It is not possible to know how much planning Saadi had put into his performance at Nineveh, but the effect on Bull was exceptional, for he was caught up in the romance of a civilization rising again from the dusts and sands of these desolate hills. Here was a challenge to which he could relate.

Saddam Hussein had invested more than $200 million in Western technology for Saad 16. Before trade restrictions made such sales illegal, American companies provided about 40 per cent of the equipment. Hewlett-Packard was believed to have provided computers for some fifty laboratories in the complex and other U.S. firms had sold a scalar analyser system, computer graphics terminals, measuring instruments and telecommunications and satellite ground-station equipment. France, Italy and West Germany had also been major suppliers. The German-Austrian company Gildemeister was said to have been the principal builder.

Technological supplies for Saad 16 became difficult to obtain after April 1987, when the U.S., Canada, France, West Germany, Italy, Japan and Britain signed the Missile Technology Control Regime. The regime banned the export of most missiles and their components.

Now, as they drove to the secret complex, Saadi complained to Bull that in effect the regime was meant to ensure that Israel could continue to develop missiles and rockets to launch satellites while the Arab world could not. He pointed out that years before, Israel had developed the Jericho I rocket, with a range of at least 950 kilometres, and that testing of a newer version, the Jericho II, with a range believed to be at least 1,400 kilometres, had begun in 1987.

During the early 1980s, the Soviet Union had provided Iraq with more than a thousand Scud B surface-to-surface missiles, with a range of about 300 kilometres. By cannibalizing other Scuds, the Iraqis had been able to modify the missile, increasing its engine power and fuel capacity and reducing the weight of its warhead. It had taken 300 Scuds to make 190 modified missiles, which were called Al-Husayn. They had a range of about 600 kilometres and generally would land within a kilometre of their target. This was not a missile to use against a specific building, but if general devastation of a city was the object, it would do fine; Al-Husayn would leave a crater the size of a large swimming pool.

Many Iraqi cities are situated along the border with Iran, and throughout 1987 the Iranians subjected them to a near-constant barrage of shells and rockets. Earlier in 1988, a few days after Bull's first trip to Baghdad, Iraq had announced that, with Al-Husayn ready, it was opening a "War of the Cities". Al-Husayn could reach most of Iran's major centres, whereas the Scud B had not been able to. Iraq proclaimed that it was going to fire its new missiles continuously until Iran stopped bombarding Iraq. This war within a war went on for fifty-one days, until Iran backed off. For the Iraqis, Al-Husayn had been an overwhelming success. The missile attacks, on six cities, severely undermined morale and caused a quarter of Teheran's 10 million citizens to flee into the countryside. Some 2,000 Iranians were killed and another 4,000 injured; psychological damage was inflicted on millions. Saddam Hussein was delighted, and it was this success more than anything else that caused him to demand an all-out drive for more advanced missiles with greater range, greater accuracy and greater warhead capacity. The War of the Cities had convinced him that missiles, whatever might be in their warheads, were the key to domination of the Middle East. In 1991 Saddam's first battle tactic in the Gulf War was to fire his modified Scuds at Israeli and Saudi cities.

In the fall of 1987, the Iraqis began working on an upgraded version of Al-Husayn, the more advanced missile to be called Al-Abbas. Development fell under the wing of Hussein Kamil and Saadi. Equipped with a Brazilian guidance system, Al-Abbas proved to be more accurate than Al-Husayn: it would reliably land within 500 metres of its target even at maximum range. Nevertheless, Al-Abbas was no more than a further-modified Scud B.

When Bull visited Saad 16, Iraq was working on three other missile systems. The first was a joint project with Argentina and Egypt, a missile known in the West as Condor 2 and in Iraq as Badr-2000. (Badr was the ultimate battle between Muhammad and the infidels.) Badr-2000 had an estimated range of 950 kilometres and could carry a payload of 450 kilograms.

The second missile system, Saadi told Bull, was quite different. This was the system for which they had earlier asked Bull to design a first-stage rocket, to put satellites into orbit. At least some of the satellites would be for surveillance and intelligence-gathering, Saadi said, and thus the system would have indirect military use. But there was no intention to fit the system with a warhead and use it as a weapon. However, he went on, there was another three-stage rocket in the works, this one intended as a weapon. It was to have a range of more than 1,600 kilometres.

Throughout the Iran-Iraq war, countries as disparate as China and France, the Soviet Union and the United States had supplied Iraq's military needs. Ronald Reagan had come to regard Saddam Hussein as a force for moderation in Arab politics. The Reagan Administration saw Saddam as the only Arab leader able to combat and control the religious and political fanaticism of the Ayatollah Khomeini in Iran and Moamar Qaddafi in Libya. Reagan ignored Iraq's domestic policies, re-established full diplomatic relations in 1984 (they had been broken to protest terrorism and torture) and authorized U.S. loan guarantees to underwrite the purchase of billions of dollars' worth of American grain and manufactured goods. American farmers and corporations who profited from the resulting Iraqi trade became a pro-Iraqi lobby working to keep the system going.

Oil-rich Kuwait was one of many Arab states alarmed by the Islamic revolution in Iran. Kuwait lent Iraq an estimated $15 billion to help finance the Iran–Iraq war. More significantly, it was a major transit point for the delivery of arms brought by ship through the Persian Gulf. Kuwait had no illusions about Saddam's fearful ways, but it saw him as the lesser of two evils.

Jordan, jammed between Iraq and Israel, had other problems. King Hussein allied himself with Saddam as a counterweight to Israel. He hoped that with the end of the Iran–Iraq war, Saddam would concentrate on economic development that would serve to boost Jordan's economy. King Hussein was more than pleased to act as a weapons conduit.

But as the Iran–Iraq war ended Saddam did not demobilize his forces. The Iranian revolution appeared much less of a threat to Gulf allies such as Saudi Arabia. And Saddam was making belligerent noises towards Israel. His drive to lead the Arab world took on ominous tones. Suddenly, he was seen as a major threat to U.S. interests.

Newly elected President George Bush started to pay more attention to the foreign and domestic policies of Saddam Hussein. It was quickly decided that the man was repugnant. His human rights record ranked with that of Idi Amin, and his thirst for power was unquenchable. Almost overnight, Washington switched from backing Baghdad to a new scenario aimed at limiting Saddam's power and even encouraging those who wanted to topple him.

The U.S. launched a campaign to force Argentina out of the Badr-2000 deal, and the Missile Technology Control Regime was being enforced with unusual ardour. Israel, the most powerful and resourceful military presence in the Middle East, had decided that, of its many enemies, Iraq was now the most dangerous. Israel's ruthlessly efficient intelligence service, Mossad, had determined by the summer of 1988 that Baghdad was again making serious progress towards building nuclear weapons while it already possessed large quantities of poison gas and even biological weapons. What Iraq *didn't* have was a large, reliable, accurate, long-range delivery system. Not surprisingly, the Israelis put the Iraqi missile programme at the top of their hit list.

In January 1988, Tel Aviv's strategy and methods became apparent when the Iraqis and the Egyptians together launched a clandestine effort to acquire restricted high-technology materials for missile development. The effort was under the direction of Egyptian Colonel Hussam Yossef, who opened an office in Salzburg, Austria. Yossef had a ring of agents in the United States, including Abdelkadr Helmy, an Egyptian-born U.S. rocket scientist. It was Yossef's assignment to acquire rocket-fuel chemicals, carbon-fibre materials, steel for rocket casings, telemetry tracking equipment and assembly plans for a tactical missile system. In fact, U.S. Defense Department analysts later concluded from Yossef's shopping list that the Egyptians and Iraqis were seeking to build their own version of the American Pershing II missile propulsion system.

During the first few months of the year, Yossef issued buying orders to his agents in the U.S. and funnelled to them nearly $1 million. The cash transfers were handled by a Swiss-based company headed by one Ekkehard Schrotz.

Helmy found it was not difficult to buy what Iraq needed in the U.S. just so long as the producers thought their products were going to be used within the U.S. The problem was getting the materials out of the country without an export licence. The solution was to smuggle them out aboard the Egyptian Air Force C120 that flew from Baltimore International Airport to Cairo almost every week.

Orders were being filled and the scheme seemed to be going smoothly, when Ekkehard Schrotz visited Grasse, France. He was safely in bed there, at 3:00 a.m. on May 27, when a bomb placed under the front seat of his Peugeot detonated by remote control. Hours later, a man claiming to represent an Iranian group called Guardians of Islam called the Agence France Presse news service in Paris to say that the bomb had been meant to punish Schrotz for aiding Iraq's missile programme. The message was clear: we could have killed you but decided to give you another chance. Don't make the same mistake again.

That same day, an anonymous informer tipped off U.S. Customs that Yossef was running an illegal ring to buy and smuggle restricted missile technology. He supplied Helmy's name and telephone number. The informer must have been known to the U.S. authorities because the information was taken seriously.

A tap was put on Helmy's phone, and on June 3, U.S. officials recorded a call from Yossef saying: "Certain people tried to do away with us. They put something in a company car and it exploded." Yossef doubted that it had anything to do with the Iranians. He said: "We suspect the ones next to us. The way the operation was executed by remote control indicates that the country next to us is the culprit."[1] Next door to Egypt is Israel.

By early June, Helmy and others had acquired 28 tonnes of rocket fuel, 195 kilograms of carbon-carbon fibre matting, which can be used as a protective coating for ballistic missile warheads and rocket motor nozzles, and forty sheets of military-grade high-nickel-content steel along with special forgings that would allow the Egyptians and the Iraqis to bend and weld large rocket motor casings.

On June 24, U.S. Customs officials arrested Helmy on charges of trying to smuggle restricted missiles components. He eventually pleaded guilty and was jailed.

It is not immaterial that Bull's visit to Saad 16 took place just three weeks after the smuggling ring had been effectively smashed. He was there at a time of set-back, and the Iraqis were looking for whatever help they could get to speed their lagging missile pro-grammes. Before Bull left Saad 16, he promised to redouble his efforts on Project Bird.

Home again, Bull found Cowley well advanced with placing orders for supergun parts. Some small pieces had been contracted out to companies in West Germany, Spain, Italy and Greece, but the major manufacturing orders were going to Britain, where Cowley knew the market.

Meanwhile, gossip about the formation of ATI and the expansion of its staff and rumours about Bull buying steel parts for Iraq were spreading through the Belgian arms industry. There had been inquiries from Bull's old partners at PRB. It was only a matter of time before the stories spread to foreign embassies, where the military attachés were sure to pick them up.

Bull knew that if he made Project Babylon public he would jeopardize its future. On the other hand, if he tried to maintain the secrecy it would only deepen suspicion that he was hiding a super-weapon. He decided to tell the whole story to the intelligence agencies that would be most directly concerned and leave the next step to them.

Bull arranged a meeting with his PRB contacts and gave them full details of the supergun. Further, he asked them to accept an order to make a propellent for Project Babylon. Always in need of busi-ness, PRB agreed, and Iraq arranged to place the contract, using Jordan as a middleman. Bull reasoned that by involving PRB in the project he would stop them spreading stories through the industry. However, he guessed that PRB officials would protect their own interests by quickly informing the Belgian government intelligence service.

By early September, Bull had contacted friends with the Israeli embassy in Paris and briefed them on Project Babylon. Bull insisted that the project could not be mistaken for a weapon and that it had no other use than to launch satellites. The Israelis listened politely and suggested a meeting might be arranged later for further discussions.

A week after the Israeli meeting, Christopher Cowley of the Project Babylon team arranged through his own contacts for a meeting with British Intelligence officers. Bull felt that he had to inform British Intelligence because the bulk of the gun was being made in England and MI6 was sure to be informed by Belgium and Israel. Bull thought he would gain more credence if he told them himself. Says Cowley: "I was in the room when Bull briefed MI6. He told them everything." Again, there was very little reaction.

About the same time, Bull informed his long-time Washington colleague General Arthur Trudeau, the former head of U.S. Army Intelligence. He gave him full details of Project Babylon to be passed on to the Pentagon.

As the weeks went by and supergun production proceeded, Bull began to feel easier again. The Israelis did not call him to ask for further consultations, and the British did not stop work on the barrels. It seemed to Bull that the West didn't care about Project Babylon – although he was sure they would all want superguns once he proved how well and how cheaply his idea worked.

18

NOT UNTIL much later did Gerald Bull understand the significance of his visit to Saad 16 in the summer of 1988. And by the time he realized, it was too late. For by then he was too deeply involved, both emotionally and technologically, to extricate himself quickly. And by then he was being trailed by gunmen.

But back in the early summer of 1988, Bull was still safe. True, he was designing ever more deadly artillery systems for Baghdad, and he was working on the supergun. Yet in the murderous netherworld of Middle East dealing, these actions did not cause the enemies of Iraq any great discomfort. Conventional artillery could be purchased on the open market, and if Bull didn't sell it others would. As for the supergun, the war rooms of the Middle East agreed that it wasn't a weapon. It couldn't be aimed, it was vulnerable to counterattack, and it was years away from firing. Sources say that Israeli scientists who examined Project Babylon decided that it would never put a spy satellite into orbit because no high-resolution camera could withstand the shock of a gun launch. The supergun, the Israelis believed, was a dead end for Saddam Hussein, and they were glad to see him pour money into its development.

So until he visited Saad 16, Bull was as safe as any other arms developer. But that changed during the visit, for Bull casually stepped over the line that separates conventional from unconventional weapons. It changed when he sauntered with seeming disregard into the sights of those determined to keep large and accurate missile systems out of Saddam's hands – at any cost.

As so often in the past, a variety of mixed emotions and motivations led Bull into trouble. He felt an empathy with the Iraqis' "us against the world" perspective. He was fond of saying that there was nothing he could do to upset the balance of power in the Middle East because there was no balance to upset – the military scales had been so heavily loaded in Israel's favour by the U.S.

During his visit, Bull was introduced to a group of Brazilian scientists and was briefed on what he was to perceive as "the sorry state" of the Iraqi missile programme. To his surprise, he learned there was no original Iraqi research going on. The only success achieved, with Al-Husayn and Al-Abbas missiles, had come as a result of cannibalizing the Soviet Scud-B missiles. And even that had been done by foreign scientists, mostly West German and Egyptian. Saad 16 was an extraordinary development, full of the most advanced Western technology, but the Iraqis didn't even know how to use some of the laboratory machines. He quickly concluded that many of the Iraqi scientists were poorly trained and the technicians didn't know their jobs. "It's a disgrace," Bull told his colleagues in Belgium. "Those poor bastards don't even know how to make a screw."

Now Bull was told that Iraq was on the verge of pulling out of the Badr-2000 project – the two-stage ballistic missile – because the Argentinians had failed to produce the guidance system they had promised and the Egyptians had not come up with the high-tech construction materials they were supposed to supply. The project was well behind schedule. Saddam was tired of hearing excuses and wanted to concentrate on projects over which he had more control.

The Brazilians had come to Saad 16 on enormous salaries to train Iraqi physicists and work directly on the development of Al-Abid, the three-stage rocket system Saddam hoped would launch a satellite and the system Bull had earlier agreed to help develop. But that day, from Saadi, and now again from the Brazilians, he had learned that yet another three-stage system was in the works, and this one, to be called Tammuz I, was to be a ballistic missile capable of delivering warheads to targets at ranges of more than 1,500 kilometres. Al-Abid and Tammuz I were being given top priority at Saad 16. New connections were being explored with French and West German companies.

The Brazilians knew about Project Babylon and questioned Bull on his progress. He was full of enthusiasm and optimism, playing down problems and promoting breakthroughs. Before the evening was over he had lifted the spirits of the rocket scientists. The Iraqis were pleased. In the course of a few hours Bull had not only been able to inspire but had also offered a stream of suggestions for new approaches to problems.

Bull knew little about electronics, so he could be of no help with missile guidance systems. He knew almost nothing about the payload for missile warheads, so he could offer no help in the development of nuclear or chemical weapons. But he knew a great deal about the design of missile airframes and nose cones. And, after a day of being fawned over in the Saad 16 laboratories, Bull made no secret of his expertise. In fact, he almost certainly exaggerated.

Much later, one of Bull's engineers overheard a conversation that indicated Bull had led the Iraqis to believe he had played a central role in designing the Minuteman missile. It wasn't that Bull set out to tell lies; he just got carried away when he was the centre of attention. It had happened so often before – like the time Michel heard his father telling colleagues he had helped to set NATO policies.

But this was far from the innocence and harmless digression of drawing-room boasting. For Bull was now in desperate company. He was in a complex surrounded by 30-metre-high earthen walls, with batteries of anti-aircraft missiles sprouting from the perimeter. The buildings were all low and widely spaced to limit damage from a bombing attack.

And the Iraqis lapped up his every word as Bull addressed the issue they most wanted to hear about: missile design and nose cone technology. Israeli intelligence sources believe that when Kamil first invited Bull to Baghdad it was to find out what he knew about missiles. The advanced artillery systems and the supergun were bonuses.

There seems little doubt that along with the bravado and swagger, Bull told the Iraqis about his missile experience. Not only that, Bull still had all the data from his extensive studies on re-entry vehicles. The information was eighteen years old, but it was better than anything the Iraqis could gain access to. Furthermore, as part of his latest research to design a projectile for the supergun, Bull was again directly involved in nose cone development. He was still in only the most rudimentary stage of projectile design, but already he was concerned about shapes, speeds and the carbon-fibre materials he would need for construction.

Professor Steve Fetter, a University of Maryland expert on missile design, explains: "The most technically challenging part of delivering a ballistic missile payload is getting that payload to re-enter the atmosphere." And the most critical part of a re-entry vehicle is the nose cone because it experiences the most heat and the most stress.

To withstand temperatures of several thousand degrees Centigrade, nose cones are made from carbon-fibre materials. And because it is known that Third World nations like Iraq are trying to build ballistic missiles, the necessary carbon-fibre materials are restricted.

Part of the most modern carbon-fibre nose cones is designed to evaporate as the cone re-enters the atmosphere at more than five kilometres per second. This process is known as ablation, and it helps the re-entry vehicle protect the warhead it is carrying. In ablation, the carbon changes directly into vapour, and as it does so the nose cone changes shape. This is critical because the shape of the nose cone determines its direction and thus is vital for accuracy. The most accurate nose cones are those that survive ablation still pointed. But they are also the most difficult to design. The greatest challenge to nose cone designers is being able to predict the shape of the cone after re-entry.

Bull agreed to give a series of seminars for Iraqi scientists on nose cone design. He also agreed to help with calculations to assist in the second- and third-stage separations of the satellite-launching missile. In so doing, he must have known that a space-launching vehicle can easily be used to launch warheads.

At the same time that Kamil was ensnaring Bull into helping develop the missile programme, he was involving other scientists (particularly West Germans) in the development of nuclear and chemical weapons. Small front companies had been set up all over Europe to buy restricted parts so Iraq could secretly build its own gas centrifuges, devices that transform cheap uranium ore into uranium 235, the basis of a nuclear bomb. Bull was never included in Iraqi discussions of nuclear weapons, but he knew that Saddam had ordered a crash programme to perfect at least one nuclear device. According to informed speculation within the European arms trade, Saddam was willing to use the device on an Iranian city to end the Iran–Iraq war. But American assistance ended the war before the device was ready. Now he wanted nuclear weapons as a threat to everyone else in the region. Saddam was quite prepared, indeed anxious, to let the world know that anyone who crossed him would risk terrible retaliation.

But nuclear breakthroughs were slow in coming. Bull believed the Iraqis to be at least ten years away from nuclear weapons and thought they would equip any missile that he worked on with a conventional high-explosive warhead.

Just how close Saddam Hussein really was to developing nuclear weapons before the massive coalition air strikes against his nuclear facilities in the Gulf War in January 1991 remains uncertain. Many American experts believed he could have developed at least a small nuclear arsenal by 1995. In any event, Bull seems to have put the nuclear equation out of his mind when he returned from Saad 16 to Brussels.

Aside from the complex mathematical calculations needed to design a missile body and nose cone, a supply of carbon-fibre material would be needed if cones were to be produced. And by early September, Bull was becoming involved in an effort to buy a factory able to produce the very materials needed.

It seems likely that Bull knew about Al Arabi Trading, a Baghdad-based company British Intelligence believed was under the control of Hussein Kamil. MI6 also believed that as minister for industry and military industrialization, it was Kamil's major assignment to perfect nuclear weapons and a fleet of ballistic missiles able to deliver them.

In 1987, Al Arabi Trading bought Technology Development Group (TDG), a British holding company with offices in London. TDG quickly acquired a new board of directors from Iraq, including Dr. Fadel Kadhum, a former official with the Nasr State Enterprise for Mechanical Industries. Later, Dr. Kadhum was to be named in the British parliament as an Iraqi military intelligence officer. He was closely monitored from the moment he arrived in London.

Under its new owners, TDG became extremely active. Within weeks it began a successful effort to buy Matrix Churchill, a manufacturer of high-technology lathes. Some 11 per cent of the shares of Matrix Churchill remained in the hands of the British management, but the rest were Iraqi-owned. Following the Iraqi takeover, the bulk of orders came from Baghdad along with a team of young engineers who were taken on staff for special training.

Over the next year, Matrix supplied lathes to Iraq in three orders that were worth £19 million, and later the company accepted a £26-million project to establish a die-forging plant in Iraq. This last project was funded by a letter of credit from the Atlanta, Georgia, branch of Banco Nazionale del Lavoro, which was later discovered to have improperly sanctioned $3-billion credits to Iraq.

Some of the computer-controlled lathes went to the military-industrial complex at Al-Hillah, south of Baghdad. Christopher Cowley saw them being used there to make Bull-designed 155-mm artillery shells. Other British machine tools, suitable for making the outer casings of missiles, were supplied through TDG to the Saad 16 complex.

It is not clear how Bull first heard about the Lear Fan factory in Newtownabbey, near Belfast, Northern Ireland, but by September 1988 he was looking into possibly acquiring it.

Michel Bull was in Montreal at the time, and so Dr. Bull made initial inquiries on his own. The plant, which contained state-of-the-art machinery for the manufacture of advanced composite and carbon-fibre aircraft components, had been idle since 1985, when Lear Fan had gone bankrupt.

Some six months before Bull showed interest in the property, F.G. Wilson (Engineering) Ltd., which makes diesel-power generators, and incidentally had Iraq as a customer, had bought the machinery and the plant for just over £1 million. They had then advertised the machinery for sale. Says F.G. Wilson, the chairman: "We eventually found a Belgian company for the equipment, but they were only interested if they had the factory as well." The Belgian company was, of course, Dr. Bull's Space Research Corporation.

Stephen shared his father's enthusiasm for the property, but Michel was less sure. He knew about the Lear Fan failure and doubted his father could do any better. But he also remained conscious of the need to diversify away from defence contracts. And most important, he was looking for a business he could handle independently of his father once he moved back to Montreal, a move he now planned for 1989. He flew the company Cessna to Belfast to investigate.

He was surprised to find the plant had everything he was looking for, and the technology captured his imagination. "Here was a factory that could be revamped in a couple of months," he says. The idea was to reopen the factory as a production point for composite and carbon-fibre materials for the aeronautical industry. From his own research Michel knew that many of the major airlines were replacing their ageing fleets, that new aircraft were using more and more composite and carbon-fibre parts and that there was a shortage of producers. "The plant was perfect, the market was waiting, the opportunity was tremendous," says Michel.

Wilson asked £3 million for the package, and the Bulls, not knowing how much Wilson had paid just a few months before, accepted. Michel drew up a business plan and concluded they could go ahead if they had £3.4 million cash and grants of about £2 million from the Industrial Development Board. The board assured Michel that if he could put the rest of the package together the grant money would be forthcoming. SRC had few spare funds, but Dr. Bull said that he could put in £500,000 from the ATI supergun account.

On his next trip to Iraq, to handle financial negotiations for Project Bird and the two gun systems, Michel introduced the subject to Kamil. The minister explained that it was Iraqi government policy not to invest directly in foreign companies. However, he suggested that Michel approach Technology Development Group. This company, he said, was controlled by Iraqi businessmen who might help.

It quickly became obvious to Michel that the London group had close ties to the Iraqi ministry and that they would do what the minister wanted. TDG agreed to become partners with a Bull subsidiary company called SRC Engineering, registered in Geneva, to form a third company, to be called CANIRA Technical Corporation (CAN for Canada and IRA for Iraq). CANIRA then formed another company, SRC Composites, with a share capital of £3.4 million and used this company in the attempt to re-launch the Lear Fan plant.

In his 100-page business plan, Michel identified SRC Engineering as a Swiss company, part of the SRC group of companies. He wrote: "The Group is basically an engineering group active in the field of mechanical engineering, aerodynamics, ballistics, aerospace, and other related subjects." The description carefully skirted the fact that the SRC group was almost exclusively involved in the design of artillery. But if the true nature of SRC was masked in the business plan, TDG was in head-to-toe disguise: it was described as "an English company with offices in London". There was no mention anywhere of Iraq.

Michel insists that in private conversations he told the Industrial Development Board that his partners were connected with the Government of Iraq. It didn't seem to make any difference to the board, for they still indicated there would be no difficulty in getting a £2-million grant. As the year grew to a close, the deal seemed certain to go through, and Michel had never felt better about his career prospects.

While Michel was delighted with developments, his father was increasingly concerned with reports from Lawrence Livermore Laboratories in California that the U.S. was proceeding with its own supergun. The Americans had decided not to power their gun with the conventional propellent powders that Bull favoured, but were using a gas gun. Bull had worked with such guns at CARDE and later at McGill but had abandoned them as inferior to standard propellent guns.

In a gas gun the driving force is obtained by igniting a mixture of methane gas and air to compress hydrogen gas in a chamber. The projectile is propelled by the hot, high-pressure hydrogen as it ruptures a diaphragm and expands with a furious blast of energy into the vacuum of the launch tube. John W. Hunter, the Livermore physicist in charge of the supergun project, said that the technology was not complex: "It will work like a high-performance BB gun."[1] According to initial calculations, the gun being worked on at Livermore would fire a projectile weighing about two tonnes. Much of that weight would be taken up by a motor needed to direct the payload in orbit, by a nose cone to shield the payload and by a metal sabot to make the projectile fit the one-metre bore of the barrel. Eventually a payload of some 350 kilograms could be sent into space. The launch speed would be about six kilometres a second, sufficient to allow projectiles to escape the earth's atmosphere.

It was particularly galling to Bull when he discovered that the American project had been officially designated as the Super High Altitude Research Project, or SHARP. The Americans seemed to be going out of their way to say they were going one up on HARP – Bull's High Altitude Research Project. Bull believed the Pentagon had deliberately chosen the name to goad him.

According to the rumours that reached Bull, and that later proved to be true, the U.S. had allocated a budget of $1 billion for preliminary SHARP research and was considering a budget of $6 billion for development if the initial work indicated that production was justified. Such a budget far outstripped Bull's $25 million from Baghdad. But, as always, Bull believed he could work on a fraction of what it would cost a government bureaucracy.

The initial plans called for SHARP to dwarf Bull's gun not only in budget but also in size. Where Bull's barrel was to be 158 metres long, the Livermore barrel would be 700. In addition, the breech and the tube used to pump up the gas pressure would be a massive 3.6 metres in calibre and another 800 metres long. Thus, the entire gun would stretch 1,500 metres.

Bull was determined to be the first scientist to launch a payload into space with a gun. After all, it was his idea. The way he saw it, he was in a race with Livermore. And he also knew that another type of gun known as a coil gun was being developed at Sandia National Laboratories and that a rail gun was being developed by the U.S. Air Force, all with the idea of eventually shooting payloads into space. Thirty years after he had first proposed the idea, the Americans were at last becoming interested. It currently costs $10,000 to put a kilogram of payload into space using the Space Shuttle. Using a gun, that same kilogram can be boosted into space for about $600. And to build a space station, thousands of tonnes of material will have to be transported beyond the earth's atmosphere. The savings in using a gun are potentially phenomenal.

Bull could see that his dreams were being justified, but there was a major risk that he would be left out.

19

GERRY WENT back to Montreal to be with Mimi for Christmas 1988 while Michel stayed in Brussels, working on the Lear Fan business plan. But before leaving, Bull asked his son for a private meeting, away from the office.

The supergun deal had caused a major rift between father and son, but ever since Michel had made the decision to relocate to Montreal the atmosphere between the two had improved greatly. They dealt with the supergun by not mentioning it. Also, the Northern Ireland project had them excited; they were in full agreement about the potential of that scheme.

As 1988 had progressed, the Western press had carried more articles about the savagery of Saddam Hussein. His regime was being exposed as murderous and fiercely ambitious for increased regional power. Saddam had become, in a matter of months, the latest Hitler, and Iraq a pariah nation. But Gerry Bull and his son did not believe it. They had seen before the wheeling and dealing governments use to shape public opinion. As criticism of Saddam grew, Dr. Bull recalled with ever more passion how the American government had encouraged him to deal with South Africa and then – purely to pander to the anti-apartheid lobby – had let him go to jail, and done nothing as he was labelled a racist and a gun-runner.

Bull preferred to judge by his own experience. And his experience of the Iraqis was nothing but positive. As far as he was concerned, they had been open, friendly and generous. Saddam, he concluded, was the victim of vicious propaganda just as he himself had been. He was certainly not going to turn his back on Iraq just because Saddam was trying to pull the Arab world out of the squalour and backwardness into which it had sunk. Sure, Saddam was a dictator, but that was what the Arabs respected. And as for human rights – well, that was a highly selective argument. Look what Jimmy Carter's human rights policies had done for Iran. No, the human rights cry was no more than a political ploy. Gerry Bull, employing his own code of honour and loyalty, would stick by Saddam.

And now there was another incentive: the Lear Fan factory. In effect, the Iraqis were offering to give SRC half of the new business in return for management and development services. It was not so much a magnanimous gesture as it was one of convenience and purpose.

Before the supergun affair, Dr. Bull had shared everything with Michel. But since the forming of ATI he had started not only to keep secrets from him but also to deceive him to avoid arguments. And there was an element of deception underway with Lear Fan, for Bull had been attracted to the company perhaps chiefly because the carbon-fibre it was able to produce would be perfect for the nose cones of the Martlet IV projectiles he needed for Project Babylon. And Bull had no other way of getting that carbon-fibre.

There was more. Bull knew that the real reason the Iraqis were prepared to invest in the old Lear Fan plant was that they saw longer-term possibilities of the company providing nose cone materials for their ballistic missiles. Bull mentioned none of this to Michel and Michel continues to insist that his father wanted the plant only for the most legitimate of reasons. Michel does not believe his father intended to use the plant to divert carbon-fibre to Iraq.

Michel believed the Iraqis wanted a share of Lear Fan as a base to train their own engineers in carbon-fibre and composite manufacture. After all, these were the products of the petrochemical industry, the very industry Iraq wanted to develop. Once they had the experience – and Michel guessed that would take ten years – the Iraqis would open their own factories in Iraq. In the meantime, the

Lear Fan factory could be developed into a financially secure operation that would allow the Bull family to diversify and get out of the weapons industry. It was the ticket that would finance his father's return into full-time scientific research.

But now as father and son sat at the bar of a small hotel for their private talk, there were other problems to solve. Although Michel refused to discuss Project Babylon or ATI with his father, he remained open to giving management advice.

Dr. Bull was worried about Christopher Cowley, the project manager for supergun. Cowley knew his job and had completed advanced work, both technologically and commercially. However, there was a personality problem. Bull said Cowley's arrogance was upsetting the Iraqis and the harmony of Project Babylon was threatened. Michel said the solution was to fire him. "If I fire Cowley," said Bull, "he will tell everybody about Project Babylon." It was a sour dilemma. While Project Babylon was common knowledge among the world's intelligence agencies, it remained hidden from the public sector. Bull feared that if Cowley told the press, Project Babylon would be stopped. At the very least there would be a public inquiry in Britain. Then, said Michel, you must accept his personality quirks as part of the price of doing clandestine business.

Bull wanted his son to offer to take Cowley back into SRC on some kind of special project, and if necessary to invent one for the purpose. But Michel wouldn't take that route: he had problems of his own caused by his father's slapdash hiring policies. Earlier that year, Dr. Bull had employed a mathematician at SRC who was proving to be a disaster, annoying the staff and making mistakes. Michel wanted Dr. Bull to fire him. But Bull, who hated to upset anyone, refused. A few days after his meeting with Michel, Bull returned to Quebec for the holidays, and Michel discovered that the mathematician had made an error on a small contract, the sort of mistake that cost the company's reputation dearly. Furious, Michel called his father in Montreal with details. Dr. Bull said he would think about it. The next day he called and said: "I've been considering your problem ..." Michel cut in: "Just stop right there. It's not my problem, it's *your* problem." "Anyway," his father continued, "the best thing you can do is fire that guy and get him out of the office right away."

Early in the new year, Michel asked the man to resign. He asked for, and was given, a few days to clear out his office. That evening Bull, who was due to return to Brussels the following day, called Michel to see if the deed had been done. But now Bull said he would need to stop off in London on unspecified business. He called Michel from London: Had the mathematician gone? In the end, Bull stayed away for a week rather than risk bumping into his fired employee. "You see, my dad was really soft about things like that," says Michel. "He could never fire an employee and he couldn't say no to a client."

While in North America over Christmas, Bull had visited Washington again and talked with General Trudeau, who was by now in his late seventies and in poor health. Bull wanted to write Trudeau's biography. He also wanted to talk with William Gill, the lobbyist who was supposed to be helping secure a pardon. Work for Iraq was keeping Bull busy, but never a day passed without him giving some thought to the prospects of a pardon. Trudeau and Gill kept the idea alive and encouraged him to believe it possible.

On this occasion, Bull also wanted to discuss a new concept with Trudeau. He told him that in designing Baby Babylon, Cowley had discovered that the steel alloy ATI had developed was strong enough and light enough to produce a gun with a much-reduced recoil. Furthermore, the lightness meant that the 45-metre-long barrel of Baby Babylon had a certain manoeuvrability. Although Baby Babylon was being made as a prototype to be mounted horizontally on rails, it would be possible to design a similar gun with a barrel of about 30 metres that could be elevated and aimed. Bull was faced with an unexpected prospect. It would be possible to modify Baby Babylon into a weapon: an artillery piece with a fantastic range. Preliminary calculations showed it might fire a conventional shell for 750 kilometres. Using the technology available to Washington, it would be possible to develop a guided rocket-assisted shell with even greater range and with pinpoint accuracy.

It was never very difficult to sell General Trudeau on the value of long-range artillery. He had been one of the earliest and most enthusiastic backers of HARP. And he was now as excited as Bull about the prospects for a modified Baby Babylon. Surely such a gun would be eagerly accepted by NATO. In fact, Trudeau thought it might be the breakthrough that would force the U.S. to open its arms once again to Gerry Bull and welcome him back where Trudeau believed he belonged – as a senior scientist with the Pentagon.

Trudeau agreed to sound out the U.S. Army for an initial reaction to the Baby Babylon gun, and in early 1989 Bull again travelled to China. He discussed Project Babylon as a satellite launching system, but Beijing expressed only limited interest. The Chinese decided to wait and see if the system operated well for Iraq.

Returning to Brussels, Bull found the office in a flap. The Iraqis were still insisting that prototypes of the 155-mm and 210-mm self-propelled guns be ready for display at the Baghdad International Exhibition for Military Production in May 1989. Work had been completed on prototype barrels, but design details for some ballistic components had not even left SRC's drawing-boards. Still, Bull had promised something would be ready, and now he abandoned substantial progress on the systems in favour of show.

Bull told his staff to concentrate on simply getting out a framework for the systems, something that would look complete from a distance. Visitors would have to be kept at arm's length and no one would be allowed to inspect the turrets. The guns would be no more than empty shells, but the appearance of new systems would be achieved.

French, German and Spanish arms companies had been subcontracted to manufacture parts for the guns, and during the first three months of the year the parts were rushed to Bilbao, in northern Spain, where the Spanish firm Forex assembled them. In late March one 155-mm and two 210-mm prototypes were ready, though only in "empty shell" form. To save transportation costs, Bull had arranged for some minor parts of Project Babylon that were being made by the Spanish engineering company Trebelan, to be shipped to Bilbao as well.

Three years earlier, when SRC had been doing a lot of business in Spain, Bull had moved Luis Palacio to an office in Madrid. Palacio had stayed in Spain in an effort to drum up more business. Now Bull asked him to help arrange for the guns to be flown to Baghdad. Palacio found two planes that were available and big enough to handle such a cargo – one heavy transport belonging to the Republic of Ireland, and a Soviet Antonov An-124 transport. The Soviet plane was considerably less expensive to rent, but Palacio strongly advised Iraq to use the Irish aircraft because the Soviet plane would attract attention.

But the Iraqis disregarded his warning and put their budget first. The giant Soviet aircraft was considered so unusual that its arrival was worthy of a news item on a Spanish TV station. The cargo was made to sound mysterious enough to alert every intelligence service operating in Europe.

And there was something else that Palacio didn't like. When the Iraqis rented the plane, they would have been required to supply exact details of the cargo it was going to carry. The crew would need such details to plan their loading schedule. And once the crew knew the nature of the cargo they were bound to inform Moscow that it involved unusual armaments. Moscow, Palacio believed, would be interested enough to put a specialist on the plane to examine the items closely. And at the very least, the KGB would follow that up in Baghdad by demanding full details of all Iraqi business with SRC and ATI. Unless, of course, the Iraqis had already supplied such details. Either way, the use of the Soviet plane meant that the KGB knew, or very soon would know, about Bull's work for Iraq, including Project Babylon.

Palacio presumed from Iraq's action that Baghdad was no longer concerned with keeping the project under wraps, that the "secret" of Project Babylon was by now so widely known within the intelligence community that Iraq didn't feel it was worth the extra money to give it a little more cover. Still, Palacio was shocked. Using the Soviet plane had been a defiant gesture, and it worried the careful Palacio because it meant his old friend and boss Gerry no longer had even the pretence of cover. "I thought it was stupid and dangerous," says Palacio. "Nobody seemed to be looking out for Gerry."

Palacio had started to hear about Project Bird, and what he heard – about the first stage of a rocket – frightened him. There was, says Palacio, a "really big problem" with that. The first stage of a satellite rocket and the first stage of a ballistic missile are pretty much the same thing. And anyone helping a country like Iraq with missiles would be on very dangerous ground with the Israelis. "A three-stage missile could be a direct threat to Israeli security, and they won't tolerate that."

Meanwhile, Bull had heard from a disappointed General Trudeau. Pentagon reaction to Bull's idea was at best "cool". Mikhail Gorbachev's new Kremlin policies had led to a much lower "threat perception" from Moscow, and military budgets were being cut. There was neither the money nor the will available to research and develop new artillery, no matter what its range. Furthermore, Pentagon insiders couldn't see any clear role for Bull's gun. Whatever its range, rockets and missiles already in the arsenal would do the job just as well.

Bull felt the Pentagon was being short-sighted and almost certainly influenced by a prejudice against himself. But he didn't have time to brood because the Walter Somers Company in Birmingham had completed work on the "pipes" that made up the barrel for Baby Babylon. The breech and other parts had been completed by companies in Germany, France and Spain, and all the pieces had been shipped to Iraq, where they were assembled on railway tracks, with the gun in a fixed horizontal position, pointing at a mountainside about one and a half kilometres away.

The site was a remote area to the north west of Mosul near the village of Bir Ugla, not far from the Saad 16 complex. Before the Baghdad International Exhibition opened in May, Baby Babylon was being regularly fired. The propellent, derived from a nitroglycerine-based solid and specially made by PRB in Brussels, was shipped to Jordan under the guise of ordinary artillery propellent. Jordan acted as a post box and rapidly passed on the exotic mixture. In one test, a section of the Baby Babylon barrel was ruined, or "blown", when too heavy a charge was used. But the section was quickly replaced by one of the spares Cowley had ordered.

By late spring, Cowley had the prototype firing slugs into the mountainside at speeds of about three kilometres per second. But as test firings continued, the flanges connecting each of the tubes that made up the barrel began to leak, allowing propulsion gasses to escape.

A special seal was needed and ATI contracted with the

British high-tech company DESTEC, based in Lincoln, to fly an expert to Iraq to do the work. DESTEC was told the tubes were part of a petrochemical project and managing director Stewart Mac-Lachlan checked with the Department of Trade and Industry and was given the go-ahead to accept the job. Bull should by now have been ready to start testing models of the actual projectile he intended to use to put a satellite into orbit. In fact, he was lagging far behind on the projectile front. He had plenty of drawings, and books filled with calculations, but construction had not even begun. As so often in the past, Bull had oversold his speed. The technical problems involved with the projectile were vast. He knew now that they were going to take months more to solve.

Bull was planning a larger version of Martlet IV, the ultimate HARP projectile he had designed but never built at McGill. His initial calculations called for the projectile to leave the barrel of Project Babylon at something less than three kilometres per second and travel to a height of 27 kilometres, when a first-stage rocket would ignite. This rocket would take the projectile to 48 kilometres, when a second-stage rocket would kick in. At 80 kilometres a third and final rocket would be activated to take the satellite payload to 105 kilometers. By then the projectile, or what was left of it, would be moving at close to nine kilometres per second, with an altitude of 1,700 to 2,000 kilometres, and would move into a fractional orbit. At the right moment an insert motor would fire, pushing the vehicle into a final orbit, which would take it a maximum of 4,600 kilometres from earth. No radio control was needed to guide the rockets through their manoeuvres or separations – it was all to be done by automatic timing, and that would greatly cut the cost of ground facilities.

Eventually, Martlet IV would evolve into Martlet V, able to launch heavier satellites to more distant orbits. But, to start, Bull believed Saddam would be happy to put anything into space, even if it was of no real practical value. For as Bull was constantly saying to Saadi, "Think of the prestige."

The projectiles would leave the barrel of the supergun wrapped in a series of sabots designed to protect the Martlet rocket fins from damage. Preliminary testing with the 350–mm prototype proved, however, that the sabots Bull had made from aluminium were too heavy. New studies showed that carbon-fibre sabots were needed. There was now more reason than ever to get the Lear Fan factory into operation.

The Iraqis had a perfect method to pressure Bull to produce Martlet IV. ATI payments were made each month on the basis of a progress report. If the progress was not sufficient in Iraqi eyes, the payment would be withheld. But Bull needed the money to keep his company going, and now, fearing a cut in funds because of delays in producing Martlet IV, he played the super-artillery card.

He told Saadi and Kamil about the possibility of producing a Baby Babylon spinoff that would make current artillery look like catapults. And they expressed all of the enthusiasm Bull had hoped for from the Pentagon. They told him such a system would bolster their defences along the border with Iran, where their superior air force would be able to provide protective cover. And they authorized Bull to begin preliminary studies, on the understanding that Martlet IV would be delayed.

PART VIII

The Cataract of Death

I see the Past
Lying beneath me with its sounds and sights ...
And hear above me on the autumnal blast
The cataract of Death far thundering from the heights.

"Mezzo Cammin"
Henry Wadsworth Longfellow

20

THE MONTH BEFORE before Dr.
Bull and Michel were to leave for the international exhibition in
Baghdad, Bull came into SRC looking worried and irritable. He
called Monique Jaminé into his office and closed the door. It was the
week in which he had found the rented film taken out of the VCR
and placed on a side table. He told her about it and also mentioned
other things that seemed to be out of place. He was sure someone
had been in the apartment and had been through his belongings.
Monique laughed and said he must be imagining things; he must
have rewound the video himself. "Oh no, I'm not crazy and I know
what I did," he insisted.

For years, Bull had presumed that his telephone was tapped and
his mail often intercepted and read. "It comes with the territory,"
he would tell friends. Anyone dealing in arms, designing weapons
for China and Iraq, must expect to be closely watched by intelligence services. Luis Palacio says that Bull's luggage was so frequently "lost" when he travelled that he always carried with him on
the plane a spare set of underclothes and toiletry items. "The bags
would usually turn up next day, after the CIA or MI6 or Mossad or
maybe all three had gone through them," says Palacio.

A few days after the video incident, Bull again called Monique
into his office. He had returned home the night before to find some
of his furniture rearranged and a new set of water tumblers in his
cupboard. His old drinking glasses were gone. The new ones had
nothing special about them, but they were quite different from the

glasses that Mimi had bought for the flat a year or so before. An armchair had been moved, leaving behind the indentations in the carpet where it once had stood.

This time Monique took him more seriously. She was a regular visitor to the apartment. She sometimes did Bull's grocery shopping for him, and she knew everything in the kitchen. Sure enough, the drinking glasses had been changed.

Bull decided not to tell the police. To do so would involve too much explanation and invite investigation. But this was very unsettling. Bull was certain, and Monique reluctantly agreed, that someone was deliberately leaving clues so that he would know his apartment was being entered.

Nothing had been taken – except the drinking glasses, and they had been replaced. On both occasions when Bull believed someone had been in, several hundred American dollars and several thousand Belgian francs had been left on the dressing table beside the bed. Dismissing therefore the possibility of a common thief, Bull and Monique decided that it had to be agents from an intelligence service. And it was Monique who suggested that maybe they were sending a message, and that the message was a not-so-subtle warning. Were they telling him, she wondered, that he was vulnerable and that they had access to everything, even his home? Although Bull said that no conclusion could be reached, Monique could see that, for the first time in all the years she had known him, Daddy Bull was frightened.

The Baghdad exhibition in May 1989 was a big success. The international military press was fascinated by the new artillery, and Hussein Kamil was greatly pleased by all the attention directed at the 210-mm self-propelled gun. He was also delighted by the progress being made by Baby Babylon. Initial tests showed the system to be living up to every promise. Kamil assured Dr. Bull that Saddam Hussein himself knew of the work and wanted to express his thanks. Soon, said the son-in-law, Dr. Bull should meet the president in person.

No one paid much attention and it wasn't mentioned in the military press, but on display at the exhibition without explanation or announcement was a 1.5-metre-long scale model of Project Babylon. It was an unobtrusive unveiling.

Almost every Western nation had one or more military experts at the exhibition. It is the job of such experts to look out for the unusual, and those who spotted the model and asked about it were personally briefed by Iraqi officials. While it is not known how many such briefings took place, it is reasonable to assume that by the time the exhibition closed at least all of the NATO countries were sharing what they had been told and had been invited to the first firing of the gun scheduled for 1993.

Soon after the exhibition opened, Dr. Bull told Saadi about the mysterious happenings at his apartment. The deputy minister was sceptical at first. Could a girlfriend be playing a joke? Maybe Bull was just confused ... Once convinced that there was no innocent explanation, Saadi took the situation seriously. He offered to provide a live-in bodyguard, someone to be with Bull at all times. But to Bull the very notion was ridiculous. He lived in a one-bedroom apartment and his lifestyle was totally unstructured. How could he take a bodyguard around the war graves on his weekend walks with Hélène? It would rob his life of intimacy and privacy. Anyway, there were some SRC dealings Bull did not want Iraq to know about. For example, that he had himself informed Israel and Britain about Project Babylon. An Iraqi bodyguard would also be an Iraqi spy, thought Bull.

If he would not accept a bodyguard, Saadi suggested that SRC should immediately form its own security department. He questioned Bull closely and found that security precautions were minimal at SRC and ATI. Something should be done at once, he said.

Knowing that Bull, by nature, would be slow to trigger anything so bureaucratic as a security system, Saadi consulted Michel. He offered basic advice and said that at the very least the company should appoint a security officer and instigate a screening system for visitors to the office. Saadi was pleased to learn that Bull normally did not drive a car and that there was no regular pattern to his journey between the office and his apartment. In a separate talk with Bull, Saadi urged him to encourage those who drove him home at night to take different routes. Says Michel: "We appointed a guy who was already on staff to look after security and we tightened things up around the office. But my father didn't alter his lifestyle in any substantive way. He was fatalistic. 'If they want to get you, they'll get you,' that's what he said."

The day after the security talk, as Bull and Michel toured the exhibition in Baghdad with Saadi, Bull stopped in front of a display case of small arms, Beretta automatics made under licence in Iraq. A number of the guns were gold-plated and displayed in hard-sided briefcases designed to carry them. Bull, who loved gadgets but had never actually fired a handgun, stopped and ogled. "Hey," he said to Saadi, "maybe I should get one of these."

Saadi said something to one of his aides, and later in the afternoon Dr. Bull was presented with a heavy briefcase covered in maroon leather. Inside, nestled in specially built compartments, were two gold-plated Beretta automatics. One was a rather large and heavy 9-mm, the other was a more compact and easily concealed 7.65-mm. Built into the case was a compartment containing twenty-five bullets and cleaning instruments for each weapon. When Saadi saw the look of envy on Michel's face he asked him what he would like. "Oh, something good," said Michel. The deputy minister left the room for a moment and returned with another gold-plated 9-mm automatic.

Back at the hotel that night, Dr. Bull had Michel explain just how the guns functioned. They were real collectors' pieces, glistening in the light from a bedside lamp. Bull spent the next hour twirling his guns on an index finger cowboy-style and practising quick-draw methods with the guns pushed through his belt or into the top of his trousers. They were great toys, and Bull thoroughly enjoyed an evening playing with them. Nor were they a trivial gift, for the golden guns were later valued at about $10,000 each.

But, like so many toys, the guns soon lost their attraction and a week or two after his return to Brussels, Bull put them in the company bank vault and never looked at them again.

On another front, Michel's plans for SRC Composites were progressing apace. By now he had attended conferences in Britain, France, Belgium and Germany on composite manufacturing and was becoming something of an expert. He had also consulted with potential suppliers, customers and the banks that would be needed for operating capital. In every area he was finding support. The final boost came in a letter dated May 21, 1989, from Feargal McCormack, a project manager with the Industrial Development Board of Northern Ireland. Just so long as the company's final business plan proved positive, McCormack confirmed that he would be prepared to recommend that the development board approve grants totalling just over £2 million. By the end of May, the deal was sealed, and SRC Composites – jointly controlled by the Bull family and the Iraqi government – bought the Lear Fan plant and its high-tech manufacturing equipment.

In July 1989, at an exhibition in Birmingham, a consultant approached DARCHEM Composite Structures Ltd., a Huntington-based company specializing in the production of high-tech carbon-fibre products. He asked DARCHEM to make a prototype carbon-fibre drill guide for use in the petrochemical industry. According to DARCHEM managing director Tony Broad, the consultant subsequently introduced DARCHEM to SRC in Brussels and to British engineer Tony Philbey who was handling the drill guide contract. Philbey explained that SRC had recently bought the Lear Fan factory in Northern Ireland and expected to have the factory in production within a year. He said that once the factory was operating, SRC would produce the carbon-fibre drill guides for itself. But in the meantime, a prototype and a small number of examples would be needed. DARCHEM agreed to produce the drill guides for delivery to Belgium. But in August 1989 they read in the trade press of an Iraqi link with the Lear Fan factory and informed SRC that in the circumstances an export permit would be required. Tony Broad asked Philbey for more information about the use of the drill guides and Philbey cancelled the order. It was Gerry Bull who decided not to provide more information – for the so-called drill guides were not what they seemed: they were in fact the sabots that he needed for his Martlet missiles.

Not surprisingly, the development board came in for public criticism when the Lear Fan purchase figures emerged. In a depressed area where every penny counted, how could they possibly have let the property go to F.G. Wilson for £1 million in 1988 if SRC Composites' purchase now showed it was really worth £3 million?

Richard Needham, minister of economic development for Northern Ireland, said the property and the equipment had been valued by independent experts and the selling price to Wilson had been thought reasonable and fair. Just why SRC Composites was willing to pay so much more than the established market value was a mystery. Perhaps the Iraqi involvement had something to do with it. In the circumstances, Kevin McNamara, the shadow Northern Ireland secretary, instructed the development board to send a full report to the Foreign Office and ask for advice on SRC Composites.

British Intelligence had a collection of fat files on the situation. There were extensive background reports on TDG, and SRC had been watched closely for twenty years. When SRC had asked permission to land a light plane in Belfast the year before, British Intelligence knew. They had followed the saga throughout but had done nothing to stop it.

Just before the development board asked for guidance, however, British Intelligence officers had met with their American counterparts to discuss the Lear Fan sale. The request for the meeting, which took place in London, had come from Washington. At the meeting, the Americans produced a copy of Michel Bull's business plan. Towards the back of the plan, on page 94, under the heading "Production Capabilities", was something Washington found very disturbing.

Said the plan: "The factory has the complete capability to produce composite parts and assemblies using hand lay-out methods. The fully environmentally controlled clean room spans over 40,000 square feet [3,600 square metres] and is supported by fully refrigerated storage facilities. The Company has plans to acquire filament-winding capabilities in the near future."

British Intelligence was aware of the paragraph, and it was also aware that Michel had been quite openly making inquiries in the high-tech world about the possibility of buying a filament-winding machine. Those approached about costs and availability had immediately informed their own contacts in the British government. Similarly, the European office of an American company had been indirectly asked about the possibility of supplying a machine, and it had informed the U.S. Department of Commerce, whence the news had gone to the CIA for investigation. And that had led to the London meeting.

Filament-winding machines are listed among equipment and technology restricted by the Missile Technology Control Regime. They are used for making the nose cones of missiles. Anyone trying to buy a filament-winding machine is certain to attract a lot of interest.

Michel says he had made inquiries about such a machine because he wanted SRC Composites to be ready to produce anything the aircraft industry might need, and filament-winding machines are not only used for missile nose cones, they are also used to make radomes, the protective housing for radar antennae on some aircraft. And there was a chance that an order for radomes would be received.

During the summer of 1989, Michel moved his family back to Montreal and set up a one-room office near his new home. Fit and athletic, he spent weekends at the family compound in Highwater. One Sunday morning, while jogging through the woods, he fell and broke his ankle.

By now SRC Composites had a staff of nine in Northern Ireland and was just waiting for the government grants to be approved and bank loans to go through before hiring factory staff and starting production. In fact, it was to settle on a date for a full factory start-up that Michel made the journey to Belfast in mid-August. He was on crutches. After the lengthy trip he was exhausted by the time he reached the SRC Composites offices in the old Lear Fan factory.

"The second I hobbled through the doors, the staff told me that the development board had turned down our application for grants. There was a letter from them saying that the Foreign Office had advised them not to go ahead because they thought we were going to use the factory to help Iraq build missiles." Michel was genuinely flabbergasted. "I had worked my balls off for nine months on this project and all along the development board had been great – really cooperative. They had worked as hard as I had worked. I couldn't believe this." But when he tried to call the friends he had made at the board, none of them would speak with him.

Michel contacted the Foreign Office in London and begged them to reconsider. He offered to pay for a full-time government inspector to be stationed in the factory, someone who could watch everything and ensure that no materials or missile technology went to Iraq. He offered to hunt for new investors to replace the Iraqis. "The British government was well informed about my father's supergun project," says Michel. "They knew he was getting the barrels made in Britain under false pretences. And now they thought he was trying to pull a scam with the Lear Fan factory. For me, it was devastating." The Foreign Office refused to give Michel a hearing or to reconsider their position.

Michel called the four local banks that had been willing to help, but they had already been contacted by the development board and would no longer assist. "They had pulled the plug on us. This had been our chance to diversify. It was our chance to get out of the defence business. I would have been in charge of that factory and I would never have allowed missile materials to go to Iraq. But no one would listen to me."

He phoned his father in Brussels and passed on the bad news. Dr. Bull's reaction was to carry on with the project anyway – they had the factory, they had the technology. If they couldn't get grants or local bank support, they would find the money elsewhere. Michel refused, "I said, 'No, Dad, we are closing this down. We can't fight the government on this one. If we try to go ahead they will label us as a bunch of arms smugglers and kill the project with a smear campaign. Best to cut our losses and get out.' "

Michel could not understand or accept why the British government had decided to allow the project to continue for so long or progress so far if they were opposed to it.

In September, Kevin McNamara wrote again to Richard Needham, asking this time why the development board grant had been turned down. Needham said in his reply: "The Foreign Office advised that the involvement of Iraqi-backed companies in the consortium was itself a possible source of concern. The FO said that Iraq was known to be involved in an advanced ballistic missile development programme in cooperation with other countries including Argentina. Composite materials which the former Lear Fan factory produced could be used in ballistic missile and other weapons systems. The FO went on to say that the U.S., as a member of the Missile Technology Control Regime, was committed to do all that it can to prevent proliferation of such missiles. The Government would not wish to see public funds being used to assist in the acquisition of sensitive technology which could be relevant to missile development programmes in Iraq or in a number of other countries."

It is curious that Needham chose to stress that *the United States* was committed to preventing missile proliferation. Britain was also a member of the Missile Technology Control Regime and surely under the circumstances a statement of its own commitment should have been enough, without mentioning the U.S. But, sources say, the U.S. was mentioned because it was U.S. pressure – made obvious at the London meeting – that forced Britain to act. The development board had wanted to make the loan because, despite the circumstantial evidence, board staff were convinced that Michel Bull did not intend to sell restricted materials to Iraq. And British Intelligence, the holder of all the background information, was also prepared to allow the business to proceed because it felt it was better to have Iraq involved in a project it could monitor than in one it could not.

Indeed, according to one source briefed on the London meeting with the Americans, British Intelligence already had a contact in the SRC Composite management. This individual, or "asset", had co-operated with Intelligence for years and had fallen into place at SRC Composite by chance. He had been hired because of his legitimate expertise and background. And London was certain that he would act as an inside source, keeping Intelligence informed of any suspicious developments. Nevertheless, Washington was concerned that nose cone materials could slip through and was not prepared to take the risk.

Significantly, Michel Bull was soon able to sell the Lear Fan plant and equipment to Short Brothers, the Northern Ireland aircraft and missiles company, for £3.5 million. The profits from the sale were split with TDG; SRC in Brussels made about £50,000 from the deal after expenses had been paid. The sale proved that Bull had been right all along about the value of the property. But it was only after he had seen the potential and it had been made public that Short Brothers became interested.

21

AS SOON AS Bull arrived back from the Baghdad exhibition, he checked his apartment carefully. There were no signs of anyone having been there since he left, and that came as a big relief. While Bull's office was a wilderness of paper and his clothes were often untidy, he was meticulous at home, keeping everything exactly right, down to straightening the Chinese rug to make sure it was in perfect symmetry with the fitted carpet and that the coffee table was centred. The flowered print cushions on the small sofa and armchair were always exactly in place and plumped. He rarely cooked much for himself – "He could live on ham, cheese and bread for a week," says Monique Jaminé – but when plates or glasses were used they were promptly washed and put away. He knew at once if things had been moved.

Within a week of his return, he scurried into the office about 10:00 one morning and again called Monique for a closed-door meeting. He had spent the night before out of town but had stopped in at his apartment that morning before coming to the office. There, he'd found the door leading from the dining room onto the balcony wide open. Not only that, but some boxes he had stored on the balcony had been moved. He had already checked, and the cleaning woman had not been for a week. He had not opened the balcony door for weeks, not since he had put those boxes out there. He had left that door locked from the inside. There was no sign of anything being forced. Nothing else seemed to have been moved or taken. Not even the most careless or sloppy of secret agents – if indeed secret agents were involved – could possibly have left the balcony door wide open by mistake. If he had any doubts before, he was now sure that someone was sending a signal, and the signal was meant to be frightening. This was not a prank. Someone was trying to scare him. It must be connected, he told Monique, with Project Babylon. If he had to guess, he told her, he would suspect the Israelis. They were the super-pros in this business. But he had a lot of friends in the Israeli military. He had produced shells for them, he had provided free consulting work whenever they asked. They had often called him for advice on ordnance problems. He had informed them about Project Babylon and they hadn't told him to stop. What else could they want?

The Iranians and the Syrians, Iraq's other enemies, might want to end his work for Baghdad. But from what he knew of Middle East intelligence operations, this was far too subtle for Teheran or Damascus. They tended towards the Chicago gangster school. If they were after him, it would take the form of a masked man with a machine gun opening fire from a car.

No, if this was an intelligence service at work, Bull thought, it was the Israelis, the Americans or the British. The Americans were anti-Iraq. It was possible the CIA might try to scare him. But the British were interested in him only because Project Babylon's parts were being made in England. There was no reason for the British to frighten him: they could stop Babylon any time they wanted.

And so Bull narrowed it down to either the Israelis or the Americans. In either case, there was nothing he could do but wait for something else to happen.

In early spring, Christopher Cowley's contract with Bull ran out, and the two men agreed to part company on friendly terms. Cowley was ready to go: he didn't care for Brussels and his work on the supergun was finished. If Cowley had only been a little less ready to tell others what to do, Bull would have fought to keep him. As it was, he let him go and hoped he would keep Project Babylon secret. Bull informed the Iraqis that Cowley would no longer be involved and almost in passing mentioned that there might be some danger that Cowley would talk to the press. Later, Bull told Monique that the

Iraqis had offered to kill Cowley if that became necessary. "Dr. Bull was very frightened for Cowley," says Monique.

During his life as a weapons scientist, Bull had encountered a lot of extraordinary behaviour. But never before had anyone offered to kill someone if they became a problem, and never before had his own home been entered or invaded. Dr. Bull began to worry that he was getting too deeply into dangerous dealings from which he might not be able to extricate himself. Normally he would have consulted with Michel, but his son refused to discuss anything connected with Project Babylon.

Dr. Bull put one of Cowley's colleagues in charge of coordinating delivery of supergun parts. He was to order outstanding pieces and ensure that the rest, particularly the barrel, progressed on time. The first major assignment was to order the breech for the supergun and parts for its hydraulic system. Bull feared that British companies might be overloaded and told Cowley's successor to look elsewhere. Orders were placed with the Von Roll works in Switzerland and with the Società delle Fucine steelworks in Italy. The companies were told the parts were needed for a civil engineering project.

In early June 1989, Bull's bank in Switzerland told him they had received a strange request from SRC's accounting department. The bank was being asked to provide full details of all accounts connected with SRC and ATI, along with details of all personal accounts of all members of the Bull family. Bull's account manager felt he needed approval directly from Dr. Bull before such information could be released. Bull's first reaction was extreme anger. That some snoop in his own accounts department was poking into his personal and corporate finances was intolerable. But as he started to hunt for the culprit, his anger turned to puzzlement and then to that uneasy feeling he was learning to live with, the tension of fear. There were at least twenty employees with access to the company's computer system, and it was impossible to know which one of them had made the request. As a result of the expanding Iraqi account, SRC and ATI had employed some thirty new people over the last year. They were engineers and scientists, draughtsmen, accountants and secretaries with no particular loyalty to the company or to Bull. Bull decided that he had better presume there was a spy in the office. And if someone on staff was looking into his finances, they were probably also looking into his work.

On the advice of the Iraqi deputy minister, Michel had tightened security. SRC's full-time pilot was given the added job of security chief. Access to the building was more tightly controlled, and a system was devised so that visitors had to pass at least three secretaries before they could reach Dr. Bull's private office. The secretaries were instructed to stop all strangers and to call the security chief if anyone tried to reach Bull without a confirmed appointment. The laissez-faire office protocol that had allowed even junior draughtsmen access to computers containing details of most if not all company projects was abandoned. Now only the most senior and trusted employees had access to all the information. The rest of the staff had access only to the information they needed for their specific jobs. But Dr. Bull knew, and told his senior vice presidents, that if they had been duped into employing a trained intelligence agent, that agent would soon learn to penetrate the new system. The company should now consider that nothing was safe and that nothing was secret once put into the computers or written down and put into the files.

For his own part, Bull had always kept the paperwork on his most sensitive subjects close by him. These papers went into the large black canvas shoulder-bag he carried everywhere. Stuffed so that the stitching was under constant stress, the bag usually weighed about 10 kilograms. And it never left Bull's sight.

In midsummer, Dr. Bull went to Iraq for nearly a month. Baghdad was having major problems with their three-stage missile system and they wanted his engineering advice. This time, he worked under stringent security conditions at two bases, Al-Iskandaria and Al-Anbar. His work was almost entirely concerned with the first stage of the missile. He was showing the Iraqis not only how to tie five Scuds together safely; he was also showing them how to ensure the Scuds would be coordinated to produce a maximum thrust.

While Bull was away, Michel borrowed from Monique the key to his apartment. His father had a large collection of CDs, and Michel wanted to tape some of them before returning to Montreal. Most of the CDs were American country music that Michel didn't like, but there were some French recordings of Edith Piaf and Jacques Brel. Michel taped these one afternoon and returned the key to Monique.

When Dr. Bull returned from Iraq on a sunny afternoon, he went directly to his apartment. As he walked into his bedroom, he saw something that alarmed him. He backed out of the room and called a taxi to the office, where he ushered Monique into yet another closed-door meeting. "I could see by his face that he was frightened," says Monique. He asked her to drive him back to the apartment at once for a full inspection.

Says Monique: "It was just a single very long black hair, one strand, that was all, and it was draped across the top of the white bedspread. The way it was, you couldn't miss it." The bedspread was in perfect order, pulled straight and tight just as Bull had left it a month before. The rest of the apartment had not been touched. Michel had left the CDs as he had found them.

The Iraqis had suggested to Bull that he keep a log of all strange happenings; they had told him to change his routines, to use different restaurants to vary his comings and goings, and to keep a special watch to see if he was being followed. The advice, meant to shore up his security, had the effect of making him more nervous. The black hair shook Dr. Bull badly. Back at the office he questioned Monique about everything that had happened while he had been away. Only then did she remember that Michel had been in the apartment.

Bull called in Michel. "Have you had a woman in my apartment?" he demanded. Michel swore he had not. He had been there for a couple of hours, alone. But Dr. Bull wouldn't accept his son's word and started to shout. Michel became as angry as his father. He stormed out and wrote a memo denying in the strongest terms that he had taken anyone to the apartment. "I felt so strongly about this," says Michel, "that I needed to put my emotions in writing. I felt so disappointed that my father wouldn't believe me. He was desperate to find an explanation for that long black hair. I made an easy target because, yes, I had been to the apartment. I even said to him, look, in view of all the stuff that has been going on, if I wanted to take a woman somewhere, which I don't, the very last place I would pick would be your apartment."

The incident again caused strains between father and son at a time when Bull was having trouble finding peace anywhere outside Iraq.

The black hair occurrence brought to an end the series of obvious entries into Bull's apartment. Much later, Belgian police were to tell the Bull family that they were almost certain foreign agents had been in Brussels throughout 1989 monitoring SRC. While no one knows for sure, it seems probable that the watching and the warning of Dr. Bull was – like the Iraqi missile system – a three-stage affair. And the first stage had just finished. Attempts to stop Bull dealing with Iraq through nonspecific threats had failed. Those agents directly involved may have been withdrawn at this point and new teams sent to replace them.

We may never know the details, but sources familiar with intelligence operations speculate that the Bull affair would have been run from Brussels by a senior agent. He, or she, would have controlled at least four field agents – one of them a woman – working in two separate teams. In addition, the master agent would have infiltrated someone, most probably a woman, onto the SRC staff, perhaps as a secretary. And now the operation was moving into the second, more sinister stage.

Meanwhile, by late summer Sheffield Forgemasters had ready the first of the giant sections that were to make up the barrels of the two superguns. Bull was nervous as the parts started their journey to Iraq. At the last moment they could be stopped, just as the grants had been stopped on the Lear Fan factory. But the parts were allowed to pass. The Iraqi minister Hussein Kamil was excited by their arrival, and the pressure on Dr. Bull to start test firings quickly was increased. There was no chance of that, however, because Bull had still not solved some of the gun's major problems. For example, he still didn't know what he was going to do about calculations that showed the propellent powder would cause extensive wear on the barrels every time the gun was fired. It was possible, he realized, that the barrels might wear out after only a dozen firings. One solution involved disposable liner tubes for the barrels. Such tubes would narrow the bore, but they would also take the brunt of the wear. Getting them made, however, might be a lengthy and costly business.

Nor had Bull finished the design work on the Martlet IV projectile. The Iraqis were getting a gun for which projectiles existed only on paper. Bull knew he would never meet the deadlines he had promised Iraq for satellite launchings. What he *had* achieved in a remarkably short time was amazing, but he had promised what was impossible and now his achievements were taking on the tone of failure because he seemed to be so far behind. To ease some of the Iraqis' pressure over Project Babylon, Bull became more receptive to work on their missile problems. In effect, they were blackmailing him. To buy time on supergun, he had to work on the three-stage missile.

The Iraqis had another project, too, for Dr. Bull. They had been greatly impressed by PRB, the Belgian company providing the propulsion powder for Baby Babylon. Bull had told Deputy Minister Amir Saadi that PRB was in poor financial shape and according to gossip within the arms trade was up for sale. But, more than that, Bull said that in the new era of superpower diplomacy most nations were making severe cuts in their defence budgets. Competition was becoming intense among Europe's arms-making companies and some of them were bound to fold. Now was the time, Bull said, to buy into the best of these companies and combine them into one entity producing superb quality products. If action was taken quickly and cleverly, he said, it would be possible to dominate the European arms manufacturing industry within a few years. And the place to start was with PRB. The Iraqis liked the idea and authorized Bull to go ahead with his scheme – starting as he had suggested with PRB.

When Bull had tried to buy the Lear Fan factory he had sought guidance and advice from Ted Tylee, a Brussels businessman who specialized in technology-transfer problems. Now he asked Tylee, a former Rhodesian, to help again. But Tylee had been shocked by the collapse of the Lear Fan deal and the allegations he had begun to hear about Bull being a pawn for Baghdad. He says: "From the first moment that I met Gerry Bull I liked him immensely. But when he asked me to become involved in a possible takeover of PRB I said to him, 'Look, Gerry, I would like to know the real nature of your business and what you are doing.' " Bull gave Tylee a copy of his book and said that ever since his days at McGill he had wanted to develop a big gun that could put satellites into space. He told Tylee that at last he was building the gun and offered him whatever details he wanted. "Gerry made no secret of that whatsoever. In fact, he discussed it in great detail. Remember, I was not a close friend, I was a business associate. He made no secret of working for Iraq and he made no secret about making the satellite gun. At least in Brussels, everyone in the arms industry and everyone who knew Gerry knew about the gun."

By chance, Tylee knew senior officials at the bank that was handling the sale of PRB and was able to talk with them informally. Yet as soon as he told them that his client was Gerald Bull, the bankers said they weren't interested. "I pressed them very hard for the reasons, and it turned out they were connected with Gerry having been sentenced to a jail term ten years before." He went back to Bull, heard his version of the South African affair and then approached the bankers a second time. After a good deal of pressure, the bankers agreed to a meeting between the most senior officials at PRB, themselves, Tylee and Bull. "The meeting went very well," says Tylee. It was decided that Bull should draw up a formal proposal to buy PRB and that the proposal would be used as a basis to open negotiations. The proposal was completed and submitted, and not another word was heard. "They just never got back to us," says Tylee. Whenever inquiries were made, PRB and its bank said the proposal remained under consideration.

In September 1989, PRB announced it had been taken over by Astra Holdings, a small British munitions and fireworks group. Bull couldn't believe it at first. Astra was too small and lacked the experience to make a success of PRB. He concluded that they had accepted the Astra bid over his own for political rather than business reasons. Bull recognized the deal had gone against him because of his ties to Iraq. But he had also been stung by the bankers' reaction to his prison record. His obsession to fight for a pardon became even stronger.

22

ON AUGUST 17, 1989, there was a large explosion at Al-Iskandaria, the military base 60 kilometres south of Baghdad. During the first week of September news began to leak to the outside world. One report appeared in the London newspaper *The Independent*, and it quoted Middle East sources as saying that seven hundred people had been killed in the explosion, including Egyptian engineers helping on a missile project.

On the day that report was published, a group of British journalists left London as guests of the Iraqi government to tour Iraq and see its postwar rebuilding accomplishments. Among the journalists was Farzad Bazoft, a 31-year-old Iranian national who lived in London and worked freelance for *The Observer*. Bazoft was desperate for the sort of scoop that he hoped would secure him an *Observer* staff job; as a freelance, he was living on the edge of poverty. Earlier that summer, he had developed a relationship with a British nurse, 51-year-old Daphne Parish. Parish had a strong attraction to the Middle East and had accepted a job working in an Iraqi hospital. Bazoft planned to meet her in Baghdad.

By the time he arrived in Baghdad, Bazoft knew about the reported explosion at Al-Iskandaria. Saddam Hussein's government was refusing to comment, beyond saying that reports of seven hundred dead were total nonsense. Western diplomatic sources confirmed there had been some sort of an explosion, but no one outside the highly secretive Iraqi military seemed to know its cause or extent. Bazoft saw the explosion as the scoop he needed. If he could prove that large numbers had been killed and show that nuclear or chemical weapons were involved, it might just be enough to win him the *Observer* job.

He asked the Iraqi government press office about the explosion and was brushed off. They refused to take him out to Al-Iskandaria. At this point Daphne Parish turned up with her own transportation, a small ambulance. This is what Parish says happened next: "Many journalists in Baghdad had been to the explosion site. Farzad had made inquiries to go to the site and they told him to take a taxi, which he didn't want to do because in his experience cab drivers never tended to get him to the right place. I said that I would take him, as I had a couple of days off. We drove down there and looked at it from the outside and drove away. Farzad saw a heap of what looked like coal dust on the side of the road and said he wanted to take some of it. I gave him a bottle for a sample, which he took. He also picked up a rock and an old shoe. I felt, 'This is what journalists do.' I didn't think there was anything strange about it."[1] In Baghdad. Bazoft talked openly about his exploits, and they quickly came to the notice of the Iraqi secret police. On September 15, Bazoft and Parish were arrested and charged with espionage; it was alleged they were Israeli spies.

There was never any question that Bazoft had driven to a sensitive military plant in an effort to find information that the Iraqi government wanted to keep hidden. It was never in doubt that he had taken soil samples and picked up roadside garbage. Nor was there much question about what he intended to do with the samples – he was going to have them analysed in a laboratory to see if they contained any trace of nuclear or chemical fallout from the explosion.

Bazoft's defence was always a matter of motive. He claimed that he was engaged in legitimate investigative reporting – but from the Iraqi point of view that amounted to exactly the same thing as espionage. The way Saddam Hussein saw the case, Bazoft had tried to gather secret information and intended to use that information in such a way that it would be available to the enemies of Iraq. It didn't matter to Saddam that the information might fall into Israeli hands as a result of being published on the front page of *The Observer*.

In countries like Iraq, accused spies are almost always found guilty, and the punishment is death. Thus the arrest of Bazoft and Parish was treated with justifiable drama in the Western press, and Saddam's military programmes came under increased attack. The entire incident was of great concern to Dr. Bull. From accounts he read in the *International Herald Tribune* and *The Financial Times* – the two newspapers he read every day in Brussels – and from what the Iraqis told him when he asked, Bull decided that Bazoft was indeed a spy rather than a journalist. Bull believed he had been working part-time for some section of British Intelligence and would probably end up with a long prison sentence. Bull thought Parish had simply been foolish. She would get a short jail term. But in the meantime, attention was focused on the Al-Iskandaria base, where Bull was helping the Iraqis with their missile programme.

Bull asked Amir Saadi about the explosion and was told that there had been a very bad and unusual accident. Bull knew the Iraqis were safety-conscious and careful at Al-Iskandaria. However, propellent powder for artillery shells was prepared there and experiments were under way with rocket fuel. Even in the most careful of explosives factories, accidents happen. What occurred, Saadi said, was that a batch of high explosives had blown up as a result of an accident involving a faulty electrical connection. At the very moment of the explosion, a vehicle loaded with more explosives happened to be passing, and a second explosion was triggered. As Bull well knew, most of the buildings at Al-Iskandaria were single-storey and widely spaced, so the damage and deaths would be restricted to the original building and the road outside. As Bull also knew, large numbers of people are not involved in the manufacture of high-explosive materials, and he accepted Saadi's word that no more than twenty had been killed.

Still, news of the explosion and the arrests further increased the tension and pressure that Bull now felt working for the Iraqis.

In October, Bull received a call from an Israeli friend in Paris, who asked for a meeting in Bull's Brussels office later that week. The man was connected with the Israelis Bull had earlier informed about Project Babylon, and Bull was relieved that at last it was going to be talked about.

"As I understand it, three Israelis turned up for the meeting," says Luis Palacio. "Bull closed the door and the meeting was strictly private. No one else was in on it. It lasted for an hour or two and when it was over everybody had long faces. Bull didn't tell me what it was all about, but it's not hard to guess."

Palacio and other senior SRC officials were concerned about the meeting. Later, Dr. Bull told Michel that the Israelis knew everything he was doing. Palacio and others believe the Israelis used that meeting to tell Bull they were aware that he was assisting Iraq on its missile programme. "They probably told him to stop," says Palacio. He adds: "You couldn't order Bull to do anything. He didn't take orders. He wouldn't have given them any assurances."

American intelligence sources agree that it seems likely the Israelis used the meeting to remind Bull that Israel considered ballistic missile development by Iraq a direct threat to national security. Says one source: "The Israelis wouldn't issue any kind of threats. At a certain level, it was probably very friendly. But Bull would know he had been warned."

Whatever happened at that meeting, it must have generated a certain tension because all of those close to Bull know that it took place. "Right after the meeting, when the Israelis left, Bull was laughing because we had some Iraqi visitors on the second floor and the staff was busy making sure that the two groups didn't meet," says Monique Jaminé.

Luis Palacio had developed extensive contacts of his own in the arms trade, especially in Spain. In November, about two weeks after Bull's meeting with the Israelis, he was working in his Madrid office when he received a call from a Palestinian contact who suggested a meeting. The Palestinian had connections to well-known arms dealers and was respected as someone with substantial knowledge of the Middle Eastern netherworld. At the meeting, the Palestinian told Palacio that he had heard the Israelis had decided to "wipe out" Dr. Bull. No details were given. Just how the Palestinian would know such a thing, Palacio could only guess. Was it possible the Israelis had hired an Arab gunman for the job? If they intended to kill Bull, they would want to use someone who could not be traced back to Tel Aviv.

"This was not something to be ignored," says Palacio. "The same day that I got the information I wrote to Bull telling him everything I had heard and that the source was substantial. I advised him to take the information to Saadi and ask for advice. And I remember that, I ended my letter by telling him to take good care of himself."

A few days after receiving Palacio's letter Bull was in Iraq again and, following Palacio's suggestion, he showed it to Saadi. The deputy minister told Bull he need not worry about assassination by the Israelis. "If they killed one of our guys, then we would kill one of their guys and there would be no stopping the cycle. It would just go on and on with killing after killing," said Saadi. Bull should be careful and the increased security precautions in Brussels should continue. But, concluded the Iraqi, there was no need to worry.

Saadi was wrong. There was every reason to worry. That very week two men, medium-sized with dark hair, olive complexions, and strong accents, called at the business office of the Cherridreau apartment complex in Uccle where Bull lived. They were looking for an apartment to rent and said that the size was not as important as the location. They loved the area and wanted to be in the Cherridreau. A one-bedroom unit was available in the building to the right of the one where Bull lived and the men said they would take it. They left one month's rent as a deposit and supplied references for the management to check while the lease was being prepared. In the meantime, the management provided the men with a key to the apartment and to the main security door because the new tenants said their decorator would need to gain immediate access to plan a colour scheme. And that was the last the Cherridreau management ever saw of the two men. To the management's surprise, the references turned out to be false. As far as the management could tell, the men never returned to the apartment they had asked to rent. The Brussels police were later to believe that the men had made a good deal: one month's rent for the security key that opened the front door of all three Cherridreau buildings.

Bull was failing to respond to direct warnings and now the intelligence operation entered its third and final stage.

In mid-November, Bull flew to Montreal, picked up Mimi and drove down to Washington for a testimonial dinner to honour

General "Art" Trudeau. During the ten-hour drive Gerry told his wife for the first time about Project Babylon. "He said he had built this gun for Iraq and that it would soon launch a satellite. Gerry said that launching a satellite would win the Iraqis all the respect they needed to lead the Arab world. He said it was a peaceful way of putting the Iraqis on top." Bull told Mimi that only the Iraqis had the vision needed "to pull the Arabs into the twentieth century". He made it sound as though he were engaged in an historic humanitarian mission.

Gerry told Mimi that Project Babylon was developing well. Says Mimi: "I was surprised that he thought it could be done so quickly because HARP had taken so long to develop. But he said the Iraqis were sick of war and wanted nothing but peace. And he believed the satellite would be a force for peace."

Mimi was pleased with the idea of Gerry working for peace, but it wasn't the only thing that made her feel good during that long drive to Washington. During short periods of silence when conversation lulled, she noticed Gerry making the sign of the cross. "After we were first married I learned that Gerry used to say his prayers on the way to work in the car every morning. He didn't make a fuss about it, but you would see him crossing himself. And so there he was, still saying his prayers in the car. He had a firm belief in God."

The Trudeau dinner was to be held at the Chevy Chase Country Club, where Gerry and Mimi always stayed in Washington. The afternoon before the dinner Gerry went to see his old friend. The general was in very poor physical health, though his mind remained as sharp as ever.

Bull and Trudeau had talked a lot on the telephone over the last six months. They had decided that at the very least they should give the prospect of super-artillery a wide exposure and they should do it in such a way that other NATO nations might become involved if they so wished. Between them, Bull and Trudeau had prepared an article. While it did not mention Project Babylon, it detailed the possibilities of a new family of artillery based on Project HARP. Under General Trudeau's byline, the article was to appear in the December issue of the American military magazine *ARMY* under the headline: "Project HARP: An Idea Whose Time Has Come?"

Now Trudeau had an advance copy of the magazine. In the article Trudeau said that with the removal of the Pershing and cruise missiles from Western Europe there was a critical need to strengthen NATO's conventional deterrent capability. It could be done, he argued, by using super-long-range artillery based on the old HARP guns developed in the 1960s by Bull and Charles Murphy. Bull had provided Trudeau with figures on his latest research for the Iraqis, which showed that a purpose-built 40-centimetre gun with a barrel approximately 30 metres long could fire a rocket-boosted shell with a 270-kilogram payload for an "astonishing" 1,850 kilometres; a 90-kilogram payload could be accurately fired almost 3,200 kilometres. Trudeau wrote: "One suspects a preliminary study could be on the NATO command desk within a very short time."

Bull did not tell Trudeau about the Iraqis. And in fact there was little to tell. Since alerting them earlier in the year to the possibilities of a military gun evolving from Baby Babylon, he had been so busy with Iraq's satellite rocket that he had neglected the super-artillery concept. As with Martlet IV, nothing existed but drawings and calculations.

The Trudeau dinner was a great social success, and the Bulls were introduced to a group of retired U.S. military officers who invited them to a ball being organized for Mardi Gras in New Orleans the following February. In the midst of the party, Gerry accepted. But he was already having second thoughts as they drove back to Montreal the next day.

There was something else to talk about on that trip, however. Gerry revealed that after his discussion with Trudeau the day before, he had met with "some other guys" who had told him there was new evidence concerning his South African conviction. According to Bull, the evidence showed the shells that were supposed to have gone to South Africa from Montreal never in fact left the Montreal docks. This development, Bull said, was enough to crack wide open the government's case against him. For if the shells had never left Canada, there was no basis for most of the charges. And that would be enough to petition for the entire prosecution to be reopened and dismissed. Bull was no longer interested in a pardon;

now he wanted the whole business to be wiped clear, with a government apology thrown in. Mimi did not question him about the source of the new evidence or about the "guys" he had met with. She explains: "He became so upset and so agitated when he talked about the South African conviction that I always avoided the subject and tried to move on to something else."

They did not travel directly to Montreal but made a short detour to visit the Keeles in Kingston, Ontario. Gerry had always kept in touch with his cousins, and now Bob Keele and his sister Jesse were as pleased to see him as he was to see them.

Two days later, Gerry flew back to Brussels, and he was in the SRC office on December 5, 1989, when Iraq announced that Al-Abid, the three-stage satellite-launching rocket, had been tested that day at the Al-Anbar Space Research Base. Film of its launch was shown on Iraqi TV. The event took the West by surprise. It had not been realized that the Iraqis were so far advanced. Within three days the U.S. Defense Intelligence Agency said the Iraqi rocket did indeed seem capable of putting a satellite into orbit. U.S. State Department spokesman Richard Boucher said: "We have long been concerned about the destabilizing effects of the spread of ballistic missiles and missile technology, especially in areas of tension such as the Middle East." Seth Carus, an expert on Middle East weapons capabilities at the Naval War College, in Providence, R.I., made a telling point: "The simple reality is that if you are going to build a rocket which can put a satellite in low earth orbit, you have a rocket which can reach intercontinental range."[2] In other words, the satellite-launching rocket was also a ballistic missile capable of striking anywhere in the Middle East from sites hidden anywhere in Iraq.

The Iraqi rocket announcement and film caused something of a sensation in military circles around the world. Said the *Washington Post*: "Iraq's new capability is likely to bolster its efforts to become the leading Moslem military power in the region, eclipsing Iran and Syria, with whom Baghdad has tense relations."

Bull had provided significant help for the rocket launch. He not only showed the Iraqis how to tie five Scud missiles together for maximum thrust, he was also able to correct major design errors made by Iraqi engineers as a result of faulty measurements taken from a wind tunnel – which he discovered to be malfunctioning – at Saad 16.

However, the Al-Abid test was not the great success that Iraq announced. Only the first stage of the rocket functioned properly, as seen on TV, taking it to about 12,000 metres. The second and third stages failed to separate. The second stage was to be powered by two Scud B rocket motors, while the third stage was of Brazilian design and, in Bull's opinion, unreliable. Problems with first- and second-stage separation could be solved without great difficulty, but the third stage of the rocket system contained fundamental errors that Bull did not think could be rectified. What was needed before the next test, Bull told his close colleagues, was a redesigned third-stage rocket. It would take too long to design from scratch, and so Bull suggested to the Iraqis when he visited Baghdad in mid-December that he might try to persuade China to sell them a third-stage device. The Iraqi government had already tried that tactic and been turned down, but Bull said he had some close personal contacts in the Chinese military and that his intervention might make all the difference. In reality, Bull had no such contacts. As a result of his artillery work for Beijing he was friendly with some senior officials, but he had no influence on policy.

There was another major problem with the Iraqi missile. It used liquid fuel which was nowhere near as efficient as solid fuel. The Iraqis had the facilities to make solid rocket fuel but they couldn't find anyone to sell them the components. Again, Bull said that he would ask the Chinese to help.

One of Bull's problems was that he couldn't stop himself from exaggerating his own importance. The Iraqis must have known that Bull couldn't change Chinese policy on something as significant as missile sales, but Hussein Kamil was glad to let him try.

Bull had not intended to get any further involved with Iraqi missiles. In fact, he had been thinking that maybe he should pull out. Without ever meaning to, he had just talked himself deeper into the Iraqi mire.

23

BULL RETURNED to Montreal for the Christmas of 1989 and was back in Brussels for the New Year. He travelled to Iraq in early January and found that most of the barrel sections for Project Babylon had been delivered. They were being transported to a site north of Baghdad in the Jabal Makhul mountain range near the town of Baiji on the river Tigris. Massive excavation was taking place in the side of a mountain. Bull had originally planned for the supergun barrel to be elevated with cables and a steel structure resembling a suspension bridge. But computer tests by the ATI team in Brussels showed this type of device would not stop the barrel from buckling and twisting every time it was fired. Instead, the gun was to be built into a solid framework, every other tube had a large bearing around it, and the whole structure would run up the mountainside. The very lift of the land would provide the barrel elevation; it would simply follow the terrain at an angle as close to 45 degrees as possible.

Each time the gun fired, there would be a recoil force of some 30,000 tons. That recoil load was to be transferred back through the buffer cylinders to the recoil cylinders, to supporting girders and finally into a base of reinforced concrete that was to be sixty metres deep. The gun would recoil at a speed of about 12 kilometres an hour, but all 30,000 tons of that movement would have to be stopped in the space of two and a half metres. "You can see the immensity of the engineering problems if you think of the gun as a long train travelling behind a large locomotive," says Christopher

Cowley. "The train is not travelling fast, just 12 kilometres an hour, but imagine having to stop it in two and a half metres without a derailment." Imagine also the size of the propellent that would be needed to fire this gun: ten tons of propellent for every shot. The plan was for it to fire its satellite-bearing missile southeast over the length of Iraq and on over Saudi Arabia and the Indian Ocean and into orbit. Bull had determined there were wind currents blowing in the right direction to help. But he still didn't have Martlet IV off the drawing-board, and no further practical advances had been made on the super-artillery. He was nervous that the Iraqis might cut his monthly payments, and to maintain their confidence Bull stressed to Saadi that he would be in China within weeks and he would try to negotiate a third-stage rocket vehicle.

Saadi questioned him closely about his security worries and was pleased to learn that the incidents inside his apartment seemed to have stopped. But Bull was not so comforted as Saadi. He had an uneasy feeling that the warnings had simply moved into another stage. No one seemed to have been in his apartment since the meeting three months before with the Israelis from Paris. However, he had since received notice via Luis Palacio that he was on a hit list. And Bull's thinking on that was changing too. He now believed that the Israelis had deliberately planted the hit list story with Palacio's Palestinian contact, knowing that the contact would tip him off. In other words, it was a more severe form of warning.

Bull now also knew what the warnings were all about. They did not concern Project Babylon or any form of artillery. They concerned the Iraqi missile programme. Palacio had told him how dangerous it was, and he knew that Palacio was right. But Iraqi contracts were keeping his company alive, and without them he would go bankrupt.

That February, Bull returned to Canada and he and Mimi flew down to New Orleans for the Mardi Gras celebrations. The weather was terrible. Flights were cancelled and they arrived too late for a first-night dinner. A storm continued into the next day and the major parade was cancelled. Still, there was a big celebration that night, and Gerry and Mimi enjoyed it enough to be happy they had made the effort. They made firm plans to spend two weeks together at the house in Spain that April, and Mimi returned to Montreal while Gerry stopped off in Washington on his way to Brussels to "meet with some guys". Mimi thought it had something to do with the South African case and the shells that were supposed to have stayed in Montreal, and she didn't ask any questions.

About a week later Bull was in Beijing, were he linked up with Michael Chang, his old friend from London. They were going to Manchuria to inspect the gun systems Bull had designed and to discuss the possibility of a new contract. Says Chang: "I knew that Bull had been suffering from exhaustion. He was very tired and he had told me earlier in the year that he had arranged for a medical check-up. When I first saw him in the hotel lobby in China I asked him about the check-up. He said that all was fine and I said, 'Oh, so you are not going to die.' And he replied, 'I would not be too sure about that.'"

Something in Bull's tone alarmed Chang, but it was part of the ground rules that made their relationship a success that neither ever asked probing questions of the other. And so Dr. Bull's remark was never followed up.

The Chinese were pleased with Bull's existing gun systems, and they were open to discuss new proposals. Dr. Bull had brought with him the article from *ARMY* and urged the Chinese military leaders to consider such long-range guns. The military men could not believe that such large guns with such long barrels would be mobile, and they insisted that in fixed positions they would be too vulnerable to counter-fire to be effective for more than the first day or two of any battle. But they kept copies of the article and promised to give it further thought.

Bull now moved on to Iraq's missile problems and asked the Chinese military personnel if they would sell Iraq a third-stage rocket for the Al-Abid system. The Chinese would not even consider it. For one thing, they quickly told him, Iraq had not paid for military equipment delivered long before. And there were political factors to be weighed, such as U.S. relations. A period of increasingly warm ties to Washington had ended on June 4, 1989, when roughly a thousand unarmed students had been massacred in Tiannamen Square. Since then Beijing had been trying gradually to rebuild the relationship, and in the current mood the sale of a rocket to Baghdad would only be a step backwards. Despite this firm turndown, Bull went on to ask the Chinese if they would supply Iraq with the components to make solid rocket fuel. Again, they refused.

As Bull and Chang sat together in a hotel in a place in Manchuria that Chang describes as "the darkest hole in hell", Bull began to reveal some of his deepest worries. He told Chang he was frightened. Says Chang: "He said to me several times, 'You must help me to get out of Iraq.' "

Bull told Chang that all of the work he was doing for Iraq was falling behind schedule at least partly because the Iraqis themselves had so little technical ability and couldn't put the projects together even when all the pieces were in place. He said they had involved him in trying to solve their missile problems. Some months earlier, Chang had seen the warning letter from Luis Palacio. He had advised Bull to go at once to the Israelis, and not the Iraqis, to discuss the problem. Now he asked Bull if he had done anything about it. Bull mentioned the meeting with the Israelis but gave no details.

Bull then told a story that deeply disturbed Chang. He said that when he was in Washington, after leaving New Orleans, "a young guy one of the Pentagon types introduced" had told him he was in danger. To Bull's surprise the young man knew a great deal about his background, including the whole South African case. "The guy seemed to be telling me that at one time there was a plan to kill me and that I should be very, very careful," said Bull.

Says Chang: "I told Gerry that his conduct was making him more and more dangerous to the Israelis. I was very scared for him. It seemed to me that he misunderstood what he was told in Washington. Gerry thought they were saying that there had been a plan to kill him ten years before at the time of the South African case. I don't think they were saying that at all. I think they were saying that there was a plan to kill him now. Gerry was getting yet another warning. All this talk of Gerry being killed, everybody seemed to know. He was getting so many warnings, and he wasn't doing anything about it."

On the long flight to Brussels from China, Bull read in British newspapers that two days earlier, on March 15, Iraq had hanged Farzad Bazoft, the *Observer* journalist. (Daphne Parish, the British nurse arrested with Bazoft was sentenced to 15 years but released after President Kenneth Kaunda of Zambia made an appeal on her behalf in July 1990.) Bull later told Michel that even though he was sure Bazoft was a spy, the hanging was a terrible mistake. It was certain to heighten the international condemnation of Iraq, and it made Bull even more determined to ease away from the regime of Saddam Hussein. But Bull didn't know how he was going to do that.

He had too much to drink on the plane in the hope that it would help him sleep. But he couldn't sleep. He presumably thought about the warnings he had been receiving and of Saadi's words about one side not killing the other's men because that would only lead to reprisals. Well, Iraq had just killed Bazoft ...

Arriving in Belgium, Bull did not go directly to his apartment. Michel was in Brussels that weekend and tried to phone constantly. Bull had become so frightened of the apartment that he would find any excuse to stay away from it, and within the SRC offices it was believed he was staying with Hélène Gregoire.

When Michel did eventually reach his father later in the week, Dr. Bull said he had been in the apartment all weekend but had taken sleeping pills and must have slept right through the ringing of the phone.

Two months before this, Luis Palacio had heard that Abu Dhabi, one of the small Gulf oil states, was in the market for an artillery system. They wanted to buy the South African version of Bull's 155-mm self-propelled gun but for political reasons could not deal with Pretoria. Palacio had talked with defence officials in Abu Dhabi and found they had contacts with a German-owned factory in Turkey where the gun could be made. They were interested in buying design plans from Bull. When Palacio told Bull about the development in January, Bull had seemed very excited, even though "it was still a long-shot deal". Normally, Bull would not have shown interest until the deal was much further along. But when Palacio told Bull they had been invited to inspect the factory in Turkey, Bull had seemed anxious to go, which was unusual. "I think he wanted to get out of Brussels, to spend as little time as possible there," says Palacio.

Palacio and Bull met in London's Heathrow Airport on the morning of March 19, 1990 to fly together to Ankara. They were early for the flight and were sitting in the lounge drinking coffee when Palacio looked up to see a man walking away with his coat. "I shouted after him. He came back and apologized and said he had taken the wrong coat, but when I saw the coat he had left behind it didn't look anything like mine. And I thought that maybe it was deliberate and we were the subject of intelligence surveillance." On the flight Bull and Palacio had aisle seats, across from each other, and Bull fell into conversation with an English businessman who turned out to be interested in one of the Spanish companies SRC dealt with. Bull enjoyed the conversation and in the course of the flight drank three glasses of Cointreau. "That was very unusual for him," said Palacio. "I think he was drinking because he wanted to relax and also because he had been telling me earlier about the break in his South Africa case. He really believed he was getting somewhere with that business." In Ankara they found that Bull's suitcase had been "lost". "It was no surprise to me," says Palacio. "It just confirmed what I thought earlier: we were being watched."

There were meetings that evening with the prospective client, and the next day Palacio lent Bull a clean shirt and they toured the factory. A dinner had been arranged for that night. "Bull's bag had been found in London – it never left. But that evening Bull said that he felt too tired to attend the dinner and was going to spend the night in his hotel room working on some papers he had brought with him. He was talking about doing a biography of General Trudeau, and I think he was working on that."

Early the next morning, they flew from Ankara to London. Palacio left his boss at Heathrow to rush for a plane to Madrid while Bull went to find his bag from the airline. In Brussels by early afternoon, he did not go to his apartment but again spent the night elsewhere.

The next day, March 22, he was in the office early, and around 10:00 Christopher Gumbley arrived. Six days earlier, Gumbley had resigned as managing director of Astra Holdings, the company that had taken over PRB the previous September. Gumbley left Astra over a complex affair that was unrelated to PRB.

Gumbley and Bull talked until noon, went for lunch, returned and spent most of the afternoon in further deep discussion. During the day Dr. Bull called Michel in Montreal at least three times. He told Michel that Gumbley was seeking help in a plan to sue PRB through the Belgian courts. Bull remained hurt and angry about the way PRB had treated his own takeover proposal and was inclined to help Gumbley.

The previous July, Astra Holdings had raised £33 million from a share issue to finance a planned expansion into foreign markets. Some £21 million had been spent buying PRB on the understanding that the company would make a £2.3-million profit in 1989. As it turned out, PRB suffered a £12-million loss, throwing the future of Astra into doubt. PRB, which employed thirteen hundred people in five factories, had been sold to Astra by a company called Gechem, a subsidiary of the giant Belgian group Société Générale de Belgique. By March 1990, Astra was convinced that it had been sold a dud and that Gechem had not made available all the relevant facts at the time of sale. For its part, Gechem claimed that Astra had had ample opportunity to gain full information about PRB before the deal went through.

In October 1989, Astra officials had begun examining PRB's order books, and they found a contract for "unusual" types of gun propellent that Tony McCann, the business executive who took over from Gumbley, later said "could only be used in conjunction with a very large gun".[1] Specifications for the propellent had come from ATI in Athens early in 1988, and the end-user was supposed to be Jordan. This had to be a lie because the arms world knew that Jordan had no guns anywhere near big enough to use such a propellent. Astra officials guessed immediately that the real end-user was Iraq, and they informed the British government.

Now Gumbley was sitting in Gerald Bull's office pleading poverty and spilling out the background. Bull felt sorry for Gumbley. And he also saw a way to get back at PRB by supporting Gumbley's private legal suit against PRB officials for not revealing the full extent of the company's financial troubles. Late in the afternoon, Bull called Monique Jaminé into his office.

Says Monique: "Whenever Dr. Bull wanted to give away money without Michel or Stephen finding out, he would use me because I handled the ATI budget and his sons didn't have access to that. But also I felt responsible for the money and I wanted to save Dr. Bull from himself. Dr. Bull called me in and said, 'Monique, this poor guy has a lot of problems and he has lost his job. I want you to give him £15,000.' And I said, 'That is impossible. We have all the salaries to pay and we don't have that much money to spare.' But Dr. Bull said, 'Well, get it quickly. He needs the money by next week. You will have to find it. In the meantime he doesn't even have enough money to get home to England.' And then Dr. Bull went over to his jacket and got out a big roll of money. He always carried a great deal of money. And he gave about $2,000 to Gumbley. And then Gumbley left."

About an hour later, Dr. Bull asked Monique to drive him home.

24

THE FIRST DAY of spring had been cold and wet in Brussels with the clouds hanging low and grey. Night had come early, and it was already quite dark at 7:15 when Dr. Bull and Monique Jaminé left the SRC offices.

At 62, Dr. Bull was the classic rumpled professor, more at home with students and chalk dust than he was with tailors and suits. He always wore a tie but he couldn't stand to have anything tight around his neck, and for most of the time the knot was pulled down below the open top button. While in the office he hung his suit jacket on a peg and wore a comfortable old blue cardigan. Though it was thin at the elbows, he wouldn't let Monique replace it. More often than not, his shirt was bagging loose from his trousers and the tails often flapped free. Despite all this, Dr. Bull still had a streak of vanity. Before putting on his navy-blue raincoat that evening he had spent a minute in a bathroom straightening himself out. His shirt and tie were neatly in place when he asked Monique if he looked all right. She remembers: "He was always messy by the end of the day. He didn't care. But that night he wanted to look good, and so I knew that he must be seeing Hélène."

As Monique and Dr. Bull stepped out into the street, he was huddled inside his raincoat, the bulging black canvas bag weighing down his right shoulder. There was a chilly west wind, and he complained about the damp, miserable cold as they scrambled to avoid puddles in the parking lot. Dr. Bull pushed his bag into the back of Monique's Renault station wagon and climbed into the passenger seat. With the rush-hour over, the streets were nearly empty as they started out for his apartment, windshield wipers set slow to deal with the drizzle.

The barren offices of state power are well away from tree-lined Uccle, with its quiet street-corner cafés and old mansions. Normally, Monique would have driven down the rue de Stalle towards the Square Georges Marlow, but there was road construction at the intersection, and besides she remained mindful of what the Iraqis had said about choosing different routes and avoiding patterns. So she drove instead through the side streets and squares that gave Uccle its character. She was not in a hurry, even though Dr. Bull seemed anxious to get home. Obviously, she thought, he was late for his date. But Monique wanted to talk about Gumbley and the prospect of giving him so much money.

"We can't afford it," she told him. "Besides, it makes no sense. It won't do us any good if he wins a case against PRB." But Bull had made up his mind and was stubbornly determined to go ahead. "We almost had a fight," says Monique. "It was a matter of honour to Dr. Bull. He had said that he would give the money and so, no matter what, he was going to do it." Bull started to raise his voice, and Monique backed down, thinking it would be better to wait for another day when he was in a more receptive mood.

He had been travelling almost constantly over the last few weeks, and Monique worried that he would have nothing to eat in his apartment. "He never thought about food at the office, and I almost had to force him to eat. He would go all day with nothing but sweets and chocolates. And so I asked him if he wanted to go shopping for food." Now grumpy after the dispute, Bull said he had everything he needed. But after a moment he added: "I have no bread." Monique pulled over at a bakery and dashed in to buy the big crusty *pain de campagne* loaf that Bull liked best.

Monique was concerned because Bull seemed to be so tired. He had been that way for a long time, under so much pressure. The travelling and the intensity of his work had started to leave him exhausted. Indeed, over the last few months he had been jotting down some deep-rooted feelings. On scraps of paper pushed to the back of his desk drawer or left on the top of his bedroom dresser, he was keeping a disorganized diary. "My body aches," he wrote after one trip to Iraq. On another note to himself he said, "I'm so tired I don't know if I can make it through the day."

Monique was pleased that he was going to Spain with Mimi for a vacation the next month. That was one reason he was carrying so much money. For stuffed in his pockets that night were twenty thousand American dollars, in large currency bills. Some of the cash was for Spain and some was for Mimi to pay for repairs to the front drive of the family home in the Montreal suburb of St. Bruno. But Bull always carried a lot of money. He paid all personal expenses in cash, believing that it would bring him better service. Hotel bills, air fares, restaurants – they were all paid in cash as Bull shuffled around the world.

Monique began to regret that she had mentioned Gumbley. It had upset Dr. Bull at a time when he didn't need any more upsets. She tried to cheer him by calling him Daddy Bull, a pet name he liked her to use. She was enormously fond of her boss.

Bull loved comic situations and practical jokes, like the cleverly made Belgian 1,000-franc notes that were going around the office with his portrait printed in the middle. He enjoyed nothing better than plotting and planning elaborate escapades to raise a laugh. Almost everyone who ever worked for Bull remembered above all else, above the high salary and the professional freedom, above the demands to stretch the scientific frontiers, above all this they remembered the fun.

And so as the car twisted its way through the narrow side streets towards that quiet corner of Uccle where Bull lived, Monique told him about Madame D.

Madame D., tall and slim and handsome in her mid-thirties, had applied for a personnel job with SRC the year before. Michel had turned her down. He had discovered, he said, that she had a reputation for seeking promotion by sleeping around. She would be a disruptive force, he said. When Michel left Brussels, Madame D. applied again, and this time she got the job. Monique told Dr. Bull that while he had been away in Turkey, Madame D. had asked her out for lunch. And Madame D. had insisted on ordering more and more wine, until she became quite tipsy.

By now the car had turned left into avenue François Folie where Bull lived. The whole journey had taken no more than fifteen minutes. They were driving over the wide gravel road leading through the landscaped gardens and lawns and up to the front door of his apartment building when Monique reached her punch-line. Madame D., the reputed vamp, the unscrupulous flirt, the object of Michel's pious concerns, had asked Monique to have an affair. She was a lesbian.

Dr. Bull exploded with laughter. It was just the sort of story he loved, filled with potential for a jape the next day. "Just wait until we get to the office tomorrow," he chortled.

Monique was still conscious of the events of last summer, when someone had been entering Daddy Bull's apartment. She was still frightened for him, and she thought he too remained unsure of the place. When the weather gets better, though Monique, maybe we will find him somewhere else to live.

"Look, you have a lot to carry, maybe I should come up," she offered. "No, no no," Bull said. Monique realized Hélène might already be there, waiting for him.

Dr. Bull got out of the car. He pulled his weighty bag from the back seat and hoisted it onto his shoulder while he tucked the bread under his arm. He had to struggle to get his keys out of a trouser pocket to open the security door.

Monique watched from the driveway as he let himself into the building and walked towards the elevators. Those hunched-forward shoulders were shaking the whole way. He was still laughing to himself about Madame D.

Dr. Bull's apartment was number 20, on the sixth floor. And all the way up in the little mirrored elevator he would have been plotting a practical joke for the next day.

The apartment building was modern, tasteful, efficient and understated. The units had a self-contained air to them. It was a place where you could live for years without knowing a neighbour. The two elevators ran up the back wall of the building, with the elevator shaft protruding into the hallway on each floor, leaving a two-metre-square alcove on both sides.

On the sixth floor the hallway walls were of rough red bricks and the carpet had a warm, autumnal tone. The apartment doors were yellow. The reds and the rusts and the yellows combined for an anonymous, quiet effect, a feeling of refuge, just right for a hide-out.

As Dr. Bull ascended, the hallway was dark. But the opening of the elevator doors automatically switched on a light. Bull was a minute or two late for his date and was probably scurrying.

He turned immediately left into the alcove and fumbled with the keys at his apartment door. It was awkward with the heavy bag and the bread.

At that instant, someone stepped out from the alcove on the other side of the elevator. That someone had been waiting there in silence, and in the dark, and would have been completely hidden to Dr. Bull as he stepped off the elevator. And that someone now had a silenced 7.65-mm pistol in his hand.

The chances are that Bull not only didn't see him, he didn't hear him either. In all probability he died still laughing at Monique's little joke.

Five shots were fired from about a metre away, and they probably came no more than a second apart. The first bullet passed through the back of Bull's skull, travelled through his brain and exited high on his forehead, through the thin silver hair that had been carefully combed to hide a bald spot. The next three shots went into his upper spine and neck. The last bullet was fired again into his head.

Of the two other apartments on the floor, one was occupied. But no one heard anything. However, a woman on the floor below was startled by the noise of Bull's body and the bag as they crashed forward together into the door. She thought someone was moving furniture.

Police believe the killer left through the door leading to the stairs. He did not bother to look in Bull's pockets. The US $20,000 was untouched. There was to be no pretence that this was a robbery. It was a murder with a message. The killer slipped down the stairs to the ground-floor foyer.

Avoiding the front door of the building, he took a rear exit into the gardens and walked through the shadows of that early spring night, out of the apartment complex and vanished into the web of narrow brick-paved streets. He must have passed a car driving in, the one carrying Hélène Gregoire.

She parked, let herself into the building with her own key and took the elevator up. When she saw Bull's body lying in a heap in the doorway, she screamed. The neighbour downstairs heard the cry.

On the edge of hysteria, Hélène let herself into the apartment and stumbled towards the telephone. She thought Gerry had suffered a heart attack and through the gasps of her panic decided not to move him. She called an ambulance first and then called the concierge, pleading with her to go to the front door immediately to wait for the paramedics. Hélène then dashed back to Gerry Bull and cradled his face in her hands, speaking to him in French. She noticed the blood on his forehead and thought he must have scraped against the rough brick walls as he fell. It was then she remembered that Bull's doctor lived in the same apartment complex.

The paramedics arrived first. Under the impression that Bull had suffered a heart attack, the first paramedic bent over him and gently moved his feet. As he did so an empty brass cartridge rolled from under a leg. Startled, the ambulance man stepped back. At that same instant, a second paramedic put his hand behind Bull's head to cradle it into a more easy position. That hand came away wet with blood. As the body was moved slightly, three large blood stains showed on the carpet. Mystified, the paramedics began to pump Bull's chest.

At this point, Bull's doctor arrived. He passed his thumb over the wounded forehead and saw at once that it was a bullet hole and that his patient and friend was quite dead.

The doctor called the police.

The timing had been perfect, the execution precise and the assassin professional. Dr. Gerald Vincent Bull lay dead on a rust-coloured carpet on the sixth floor of a garden apartment building on the southern outskirts of Brussels. Some of the best brains had just been blown out of Saddam Hussein's war machine.

Bull had taken few precautions. His home phone number was unlisted and a company name, Giltaur, was on a plastic strip glued to his letter-box. He operated openly from his office. There were no guards, and although he lived and died for guns, he would no more have carried one than he would have pinned a rose to his lapel. He was an easy target.

It took the Belgian press a day to catch up with the story. On March 24 *La Libre Belgique* ran one paragraph on an inside page. The uninspired headline read: *"Meurtre d'un Americain"*.

25

AFTER THE POLICE had been summoned to Gerry Bull's apartment, Hélène Gregoire called Stephen's home. Stephen was in Iraq, negotiating payments for Project Bird, but his wife, Johanne, rushed to the scene. Since Michel had returned to live in Montreal, Stephen had become closer to his father and had become deeply involved with the Iraqi dealings. During 1989 he spent 105 days in Iraq.

The Belgian police called Michel's home in Montreal and reached his wife, Danielle. Michel was at his small office located nearby, and Danielle drove through the snow to tell her husband that his father had been assassinated. "It was the worst moment of my life," says Michel.

It was around midnight in Iraq when Michel reached Stephen in the Al Rashid Hotel in Baghdad. Awakened by the phone, Stephen was groggy when he picked up the receiver to hear his brother say, "Dad is dead."

"If this is a joke, it isn't funny," said Stephen.

"Do you think I would joke about something like that?" replied Michel. "He has been shot in the head."

Stephen went into shock. He couldn't talk, he couldn't think. He heard Michel saying he would make flight arrangements to get him back to Brussels. And there was nothing else to say. The last few months had been among the best of Stephen's life. For the first time ever, his father had started to listen to him. They were actually talking together, getting close, and Stephen had wanted that badly.

Michel made the twenty-minute drive to his mother's home in St. Bruno. She was out shopping, buying a frame for a photograph of Gerry. The photograph had been taken back in the HARP days, but she hadn't seen it before. It was one of the pictures that had turned up while Gerry was researching his book.

"I knew something was wrong the moment I saw Michel," recalls Mimi. He told her, and they collapsed into each other's arms.

SRC had an English-born engineer in Baghdad, and a few minutes after Michel's call the engineer arrived at Stephen's room with a bottle of whisky. He insisted on sitting up for the rest of the night with Stephen, and Stephen was grateful. He didn't want to talk, but it was good to have someone in the room. When the engineer went to sleep at about four o'clock, Stephen covered him with a blanket.

About seven the deputy minister, Saadi, arrived. He was driving his own red Mercedes, and he was alone. He put his arm around Stephen and helped carry his luggage. Stephen found him a comfort. On the drive to the airport, Saadi said the minister, Saddam's son-in-law, was shocked and angry. And he assured Stephen that if the Bull family needed anything, the Government of Iraq would do whatever it could to help. Stephen started to sob. After a long silence Saadi said, "We should have know better ... there should have been more security ... we should have had your father watched and guarded." That reminded Stephen of a conversation with his father a few months before. Stephen had asked about the threats, about the letter from Palacio. Dr. Bull had replied that it was no good having guards because there was no way to stop the sort of people involved. "If they want to kill me, they will kill me. I can't stop them." And Stephen remembered that his father had been grinning.

It was 6:30 p.m. when Stephen arrived in Brussels. Two Belgian detectives met him off the plane and he was driven directly to police headquarters. An inspector, cold and impersonal, said Stephen must answer questions but before they began was there anything he wanted to know. Stephen asked how his father had died. The inspector said he had just received the autopsy report and Dr. Bull had been shot five times from behind. "When I heard that, when I heard they shot Dad five times, it was like electricity going all over my body. I started to cry." The inspector did not wait for Stephen to compose himself but carried on with the autopsy findings. There was no doubt, the inspector said, that this was a professional job. No one had seen anything, no one had heard anything.

The police questioned Stephen for three hours before letting him go home. They kept pressing for exact details of the work Dr. Bull had been doing for Iraq. "We are so small," Stephen kept telling them. "We are nothing, we are a tiny cog, our work is insignificant."

Hélène Gregoire had been of very little use to the police. The first officer on the scene was a member of the narcotics squad. He had suspected that drugs might be involved, especially as Dr. Bull was carrying so much cash. The policeman was rather rough with Hélène. It was 9:00 p.m. before Belgian intelligence agents turned up. They said it was a "political" killing and held out little hope of ever solving it. By then Hélène could hardly remember anything that had happened. She couldn't remember finding Dr. Bull or any of the details. She kept repeating that she had been late for their dinner date and that if she had been on time maybe they wouldn't have shot him because she would have been there. Or maybe, she said, they would have killed her too.

The Bull family gathered in Brussels, but Gerry's body was taken home to Montreal for burial. There were some 600 people at the funeral and they came from all over the world. Among them were professors from sixteen different universities. On his tombstone they carved the motto he adopted as his own: "When reason sleeps, Justice is badly served".

That may well have been true of Gerry Bull. He was a man of technology, unable to deal with politics. "Technical matters drove him," remembers his friend Dr. Alfred Ratz. "He could understand that there might be technical obstacles to be overcome. But he could not understand why there should be silly political or administrative obstacles. Or why his projects should be permitted to be blocked by ignoramuses. His ideas were his life-blood. So he connived to pursue them in any way he could."

Ratz adds: "He never seemed to give in to the bureaucrats. He died unbowed. He died a free man. Of how many of us could that be said?"

Belgian intelligence refused to tell Stephen exactly what was in Dr. Bull's canvas bag. Stephen believes the bag, which the agents took away with them, contained all of the significant drawings and calculations for Project Babylon and Martlet IV. It is likely the bag also contained the relevant contracts because they could not be found elsewhere. Suspecting a spy in the office, Dr. Bull left nothing there. The police did find in the bag a log that Dr. Bull had been keeping about the strange happenings in his apartment. Along with the log was the memo Michel had written after the incident with the black hair. They questioned Monique Jamine at some length about the incidents Bull had discussed with her.

On March 28, six days after Bull's murder, Customs officials in London and New York announced the success of a complex sting operation in which they had caught Iraq trying to smuggle forty American-made devices for triggering nuclear weapons. The devices, known as capacitors, are restricted high-technology items that Iraq needed for its nuclear weapons development. They had been illegally bought in California and shipped via Britain. Along the way, Customs authorities had switched the real capacitors for dummies. When the London end of the Iraqi smuggling ring turned up to collect them, they were arrested. In all, six people were eventually apprehended. The arrests, capping an eighteen-month undercover operation, were quickly associated in the media with the assassination of Dr. Bull. One British newspaper alleged that Bull "was the only person who could have spotted that agents had swapped the triggers for identical dummies". The idea was a flight of journalistic fancy, for Bull was hopeless when it came to electronics. He knew nothing about capacitors, and no one directly involved with the smuggling operation has seriously suggested Bull was connected to that scheme in any way.

Nevertheless, the allegations brought Bull's links with Iraq to public notice. At the same time, military analysts, particularly in Israel, proclaimed that Iraq would not have expended so much effort to get capacitors if it were not well advanced with its nuclear weapons programme. After all, you don't need a trigger until you have something to fire. Experts began to revise their estimates about the likely date by which Iraq would possess nuclear weapons.

Before the capacitor sting most analysts in the West had believed it would be 1998 at least. But now analysts in Washington and Tel Aviv were saying Saddam might have his finger on the nuclear button as early as 1992. It was recalled that the last time Saddam had been close to nuclear arms, back in 1981, Israel had bombed the reactor. Now Iraq was said to be working with a secret underground nuclear facility and speculation was rife that Israel might move against that facility. On April 2, Saddam launched his own pre-emptive strike in the form of a chilling threat: he would scorch "half of Israel" with advanced chemical weapons if Tel Aviv sent war planes into his territory again. The very next day, Israel put Ofek-2, its second spy satellite, into orbit. The Iraqis knew about Ofek-2; it was one of the reasons so much pressure had been put on Bull to help with the three-stage rocket programme. Saddam had wanted to equal the Israeli performance. There was little hope of that now.

On April 11, 1990, some twenty days after the murder of Dr. Bull, British Customs seized eight sections of the Project Babylon barrel. They were packed in huge boxes, ready to leave Teeside docks in northeast England, and they were the last of the fifty-two sections that made up the two complete barrels for the supergun. The manufacturers claimed they were parts for a petrochemical pipeline, but their true nature very quickly emerged as did their links to Dr. Bull. It is almost certain that British Customs were informed about the barrel sections by MI6 and that MI6 was goaded into action by Mossad. Both the British and the Israeli agencies had known about Project Babylon almost since its inception. Both agencies knew that with the death of Dr. Bull the project was finished. The Iraqis could not have continued on their own even if they had all of the parts for the gun, which they did not. For the gun was not the most important part of Project Babylon. There are many engineers around the world – such as Christopher Cowley – who could design the gun. The secret of Project Babylon was Martlet IV, the projectile capable of taking a small satellite into space. Dr. Bull was one of the few scientists capable of designing that sort of projectile. And Dr. Bull hadn't finished it. It existed only on paper and even then not in its entirety. At the time of his death, Bull still had not solved some of the most compelling problems of Martlet IV. Stephen, who had discussed this with his father, says it would probably have taken another ten years for Project Babylon to put a satellite into orbit.

It now seems highly unlikely that the Iraqis will ever proceed with this project. However, unless the U.S. space budget is drastically reduced, the American supergun will be in action before the end of the decade.

Curiously, Iraq denied that it was ever working on a supergun. Mohamed Mashat, Iraq's ambassador to the United Nations, wrote in *The New York Times* on May 4 that "many lies have been told about Iraq". He went on: "Then came the story of the 'super' pipes that, when assembled, make a 'super' gun capable of launching 'super' shells. The only super thing about this story is that it is a super lie. The 'super' pipes made under British licence are to be used in a petrochemical complex."

As the British Customs inquiry progressed, independent of British Intelligence, Peter Mitchell, former managing director of Walter Somers, and Christopher Cowley were arrested and charged with exporting prohibited equipment. It was alleged that they both knew exactly what they were doing when they became involved with Project Babylon. Customs also began in-depth investigations of at least eleven other British engineers, some employed by Bull, some by the companies that manufactured gun parts. But in November 1990, all charges were dropped and the case was closed.

The decision not to proceed was taken at the highest levels of Margaret Thatcher's government. The reason seems clear. The defence would have argued that the British government had known from the start about Project Babylon and had done nothing to stop it. Such arguments – and Cowley says they would have been backed by documentary evidence including letters from the Belgian government dated late 1988 – would have constituted a major embarrassment for Downing Street.

Why did the British government allow Project Babylon barrels to be made in Britain and also allow SRC and the Iraqi government to come so close to buying the Lear Fan factory? The answer lies in the economics of trade. At the time of Dr. Bull's assassination, Britain was selling £450 million worth of goods a year to Iraq, which amounted to a £357-million surplus in Britain's favour. And with Iraq's vast oil wealth, there was every expectation this situation would improve. Iraq had billions of pounds to spend on reconstruction after its war with Iran, and in the words of Christopher Cowley: "Every European government wanted a share of the cake." Richard Murphy, the top U.S. State Department diplomat concerned with Middle East affairs for most of the 1980s, says: "We all saw Iraq in the postwar era as a very valuable market for our business communities. Potentially it was an enormous market once it got out from under the load of war debt it had accumulated. And most experts predicted that would happen in three to five years."

Britain envisioned trade with Iraq booming by 1995. It was going to become a major customer. Downing Street did not want to upset Baghdad.

The perceptions changed on August 2, 1990, when Saddam invaded Kuwait. Before the end of the month the U.S. and its allies – led by Britain – were sending air and land forces into the Gulf to push Iraq back. The UN Security Council authorized war and on January 16, with Iraq still refusing to withdraw, waves of allied warplanes flew north.

The U.S. and its allies had complete control of the air and for the next forty days and nights they bombed and blasted Iraqi positions. On February 24 the U.S. and allies launched their ground war and in the space of 100 hours they broke what was left of Saddam's army and drove it from Kuwait. The Iraqis suffered an estimated 100,000 casualties and desertions ranged from 30 per cent in some units to 60 per cent in others. Saddam's long range artillery – the 400 guns based on Bull's designs – were hardly fired. For the gunners were not only wanting, they were missing. Which does not mean that artillery has been toppled as king of the battlefield. It simply confirms that when one side has overwhelming air superiority, ground forces cannot cope.

But none of this was being forecast even as close as April 19, 1990, four weeks after the assassination of his father, when Michel closed down the offices of Space Research Corporation and dissolved the company. All staff were paid off, assets were sold, and the Bull family tried to consolidate. Monique Jaminé paid off debts and then closed out ATI and the Project Babylon accounts. She was able to send $187,000 to the Bull family. Bull left about $300,000, mostly from insurance policies. Iraq had been slow in paying its bills, and Stephen spent weeks in Baghdad trying to get what was owed. Closing the company meant that outstanding contracts were not being fulfilled, however, and Stephen realized the Iraqis might have claims themselves.

Stephen was negotiating in Baghdad when Saddam invaded Kuwait. He got out as quickly as he could, and after a family conference it was decided they would write off whatever was still owed.

In his last conversations with Saadi, Stephen was told that Iraqi intelligence had investigated and was convinced that Dr. Bull had been shot by agents of the Israeli Mossad. Stephen was further told that the Israelis would not have acted without consulting the CIA, because Dr. Bull was an American citizen and Israel relies heavily on U.S. aid.

A few weeks after that, an official in the Austrian intelligence service, a man who wishes to remain anonymous, contacted the Bull family through an intermediary. He had been a long-time friend of Dr. Bull. In fact, Bull had sent him a copy of his book with a warm dedication in the front. The Austrian told the Bull family that he had made his own inquiries and discovered that Mossad was responsible for Dr. Bull's death but that they had discussed it first with U.S. intelligence officials. At least some of those discussions, he said, had taken place in Frankfurt.

In private discussions, British and Belgian intelligence sources also say the murder was the work of Mossad. The CIA says it knows nothing about it. But one CIA official, speaking on the strict understanding that he not be named, says it is the general understanding of Western intelligence agencies that Mossad gave the order to kill Bull. They did so as a warning to other foreign scientists not to help the Iraqis with a missile system that could eventually be used to deliver nuclear or chemical weapons against targets in Israel. But the CIA official insists that Mossad did not inform Washington before the killing.

What did happen, he says, was this. The Israelis did not want to kill Bull. They wanted to scare him off and stop him working on the missile system. They made sure Bull knew he was in danger and they hoped it would be enough to persuade him to retire. American agents in Europe heard Bull was under threat and discussed it with their Israeli counterparts. "What you had was agents talking to agents, and it was all gossip and rumour."

But someone in Washington knew about the gossip because they warned Bull, the month before he was killed.

That warning, we now know, was Bull's last chance. He could still have saved his life if he had moved into immediate retirement. But he no longer had time to think it over, for the hit team was in place with orders to kill at the first secure opportunity. The site of the killing may well have been decided weeks before. The gunman was probably positioned to act, waiting for the right moment, for at least a month. Most probably there were four people directly involved on the last night. One would have been watching for Bull and Monique to leave the office and would have radioed a signal ahead to the others, waiting at the apartment building. Learning that Bull was on his way, one team member would have been posted behind the wheel of the getaway car parked nearby. One would have been positioned somewhere off the foyer on the ground floor of Bull's apartment building and would have signalled to the hit man that Bull was on his way up, alone. If Bull had been accompanied or if there was the slightest risk of someone else becoming involved the hit would probably have been postponed.

All members of the field team would probably have been spirited out of Belgium that night. They may have left by different routes – road, rail or air – while the murder weapon would have been dropped off at a safe house to be returned to head office via the diplomatic bag.

Obviously, much of this is speculation, for Mossad will never admit to committing an assassination. But something similar to the above scenario occurred. Of course, we are left with loose strings and unanswered questions. For example, why did the hit team need another key to the security door in November? Earlier in the year they appeared to have free access not only to the building but to Bull's actual apartment. And how much did the United States actually know about the killing? Could the CIA have stopped it? Did they choose not to?

Says Michel: "We don't know for sure who killed my father. But among the things that I find very hurtful is that the media seems to think that if the Israelis were responsible and if they killed him because he was working for Iraq, then it's okay. In other words, that they had some kind of right to do it. Now if the Arabs had killed an American or Canadian citizen, for whatever reason, there would have been outrage and there would have been inquiries and investigations. The Americans, the Canadians, have done nothing to solve my father's murder. It is as if Ottawa and Washington have sanctioned the killing. If that is true, then it stinks. No one had the right to shoot my father in the back."

Sitting in the sunny conservatory behind her home in St. Bruno, nearly a year after her husband's death, Mimi Bull was reflecting on what was best about Gerry. She said: "No matter who you were he would give you the impression that you were important. He always found time to listen to the problems of others, and if there was anything he could do to help, then he would to it. And there was something else that you couldn't miss. He loved to laugh.

"For his failings, well, I would say that he was impatient. He wanted to do a lot in a short time. And he was too trusting, he was easily deceived."

Mimi, cushioned by her large family, has recovered remarkably well. "Gerry once told me that he was on a hit list, but I didn't know if he was serious," she says. "I never had any real idea that his life was in danger." He had told her nothing of the recent threats. "I suppose he wanted to protect me. He didn't want me to worry." Mimi visits the house at Highwater often and continues to develop her talent for watercolour painting. She has kept the house in Spain and together with her friend Hélène Gregoire spent a holiday there in the winter after Gerry's murder.

Hélène regularly has a Mass said for Gerry in Brussels. Michel has bought a large modern house on the south shore of Montreal and is looking for a new business. He says he will never again work in defence. Stephen has stayed in Brussels and is running a computer company.

Michael Chang is philosophical. He points out that Bull died instantly, without anticipation or pain. "And most important of all, and I thought this before Saddam Hussein's invasion of Kuwait, he was taken away without having to face the potential horrific consequences of his actions." With the invasion of Kuwait, the intelligence agencies would have exposed Bull's work for Iraq, he would have been subject to great criticism, his company would most likely have been closed and ways might even have been found to prosecute him. Dr. Bull could never have survived an ordeal like that. Says Chang: "If one is religious, one might think that God was kind to him. Maybe in the end Gerry was still favoured and smiled upon."

While clearing his father's desk, Michel found a page of company notepaper on which Dr. Bull had copied a poem. Bull's handwriting could deteriorate to a scribble, but this was done neatly: every word was legible, there was something of a schoolboy quality to the evenly formed letters. The page was below a pad on the top of the desk that was covered as always with great piles of technical materials. But despite the crush of documents, Michel noticed that the way his father had arranged it, there was easy access to the poem.

The poem was "The Canticle of Brother Sun", by St. Francis of Assisi. Or rather, it was the canticle as Gerry Bull remembered it fifty years after learning the lines at his Jesuit boarding school in Kingston, Ontario. The exact wording of the final lines was not quite right, but the spirit of the poem was perfectly preserved. He may have been using it as a prayer. Wrote Gerry Bull:

> Praise to You, my Lord,
> For those who forgive one another in Your Love
> And who bear sickness and trials,
> Blessed are they who live in peace.

NOTES

Notes to Prologue

1. Interview with Monique Jaminé, Brussels, December 4, 1990.
2. Interview with John Pike, Washington, January 8, 1991.
3. *U.S. News & World Report*, June 4, 1990.
4. Bakshian, Aram Jr. Introduction to Curt Johnson, *Artillery: The Big Guns Go To War*. (London: Octopus Books, 1975.)

Chapter One

1. Braddon, Russell, *Roy Thomson of Fleet Street*, (New York: Walker, 1966).
2. Interview with Gordon Bull, Stirling, Ontario, September 20, 1990.
3. *Maclean's*, March 1, 1953.

Chapter Two

1. *Maclean's*, March 1, 1953.
2. Interview with Reverend Joe Driscoll, S.J., Vancouver, August 14, 1990.
3. Tennyson, Alfred, Lord, *Tithonus*.

Chapter Three

1. *Maclean's*, March 1, 1953.
2. Patterson, G.N. "Report on Visit to CARDE: July 24 to August 4, 1950," (National Archives of Canada).

3. Green, J.J. Confidential letter dated August 29, 1950. (National Archives of Canada).

Chapter Four

1. Cassar, Joe. "The Mirrored Spectrum: Velvet Glove." (Ottawa: Ministry of Science and Technology, 1973).
2. Bull, G.V. Lecture delivered at the opening of the Galbraith Building, University of Toronto, March 7, 1961.
3. Cassar, Joe. See note 1 this chapter.

Chapter Five

1. Bull, G.V. Private papers for the years 1955–56.
2. Skol, Walter, "Missile Defence Goal of Scientists." *Toronto Star*, April 18, 1958.
3. Interview with Charles Murphy, Baltimore, August 13, 1990.

Chapter Six

1. Bull, G.V. Private papers for 1961.
2. Tupper, K.F., Confidential memorandum dated February 25, 1966. (National Archives of Canada).
3. Orr, J.L., Secret memorandum dated March 4, 1966. (National Archives of Canada).

Chapter Seven

1. Orr, J.L., Secret memorandum dated February 8, 1966. (National Archives of Canada).
2. Brown, R.K., Secret memorandum dated February 9, 1966. (National Archives of Canada).
3. Arpin, Claude, "Ottawa Clobbers McGill's HARP." Montreal *Gazette*, November 15, 1966.

Chapter Eight

1. Hemingway, Sam, "Rare Act of Congress Aided Space Research Chief." *Burlington Free Press*, December 17, 1978.
2. Bull, G.V. Private papers for the year 1977.

Chapter Nine

1. Stockwell, John, *In Search of Enemies* (New York: Norton, 1978).
2. Bull, G.V. Private papers for the year 1976.
3. Malone, William Scott, "Space Research Official Defends South Africa Ties." *Burlington Free Press*, October 21, 1979.

Chapter Eleven

1. CIA Interagency Intelligence Memorandum entitled "The 22 September 1979 Event." Released under the Freedom of Information Act.
2. Younghusband, Peter, "The Nuclear Bullet." Montreal *Gazette*, April 5, 1980.
3. Rae, Robert J., "P.W. Botha and the Space Research Corporation." Released under the Freedom of Information Act.

Chapter Thirteen

1. Proceedings Intercontinental Cannon and Orbiter Technology Workshop. DARPA/STO. November 4–5 1985.

Chapter Fourteen

1. Wise, Michael Z., "14 Austrians Convicted of Arms Sales to Iran." *Washington Post*, February 2, 1991.

Chapter Seventeen

1. Tyler, Patrick E., "High Link Seen in Cairo Spy Case." *Washington Post*, August 20, 1988.

Chapter Eighteen

1. Henderson, Breck W., "Livermore Proposes Light Gas Gun For Launch of Small Payloads." *Aviation Week & Space Technology*, July 23, 1990.

Chapter Twenty-Two

1. Henderson, Paul, "Taste of Freedom." *Daily Mail*, July 18, 1990.

2. Murphy, Caryle, and David B. Ottaway, "Iraq Has Tested Satellite Rocket, U.S. Confirms." *Washington Post*, December 9, 1989.

Chapter Twenty-Three

1. White, David, and Victor Mallet, "Astra Confirms Unusual Request." *Financial Times*, April 19, 1990.

INDEX

C

James Adams
Secret Armies £4.99

The Full Story of the SAS, Delta Forces and Spetsnaz

Entebbe, Mogadishu, Grenada, the siege on the Iranian Embassy:
these are the flashpoints of recent history. Sporadic shots in an
incessant hail of warfare that has been waged across the world since
1945.

At times of political high tension, it is secret armies like the SAS,
Spetsnaz and Delta Force that form the cutting edge in today's
international conflicts. These are the special forces that have won –
and lost – the most spectacular military operations since the last
World War; and that are destined to be in the vanguard of the next.

But who recruits and trains these special forces? How effective are
they? And who is in control of their undercover operations, in war
time and in times of peace?

In this chilling and revelatory analysis, James Adams, Defence
Correspondent of *The Sunday Times* and co-author of *Ambush: The
War between the SAS and the IRA*, unravels the complex workings
of the deadly armies hidden from public scrutiny. Drawing on
previously unpublished material, it is a terrifying yet thrilling account
of irregular warfare: from 1945 . . . through to a future under the
ominous shadow of the ultimate confrontation.

'Blends solid research, military technology, lucid explanation and
clear narrative with a leavening of marvellous anecdotes, some zany,
others tragic' FREDERICK FORSYTH

James Adams, Anthony Bainbridge and
Robin Morgan
**Ambush: The War Between the SAS
and the IRA** £4.99

In the last twelve years, a new kind of war has been fought over
Northern Ireland across a battlefield that has grown to include
Europe. A war of attrition between the SAS and the IRA.

Now, in this the first detailed account of the truth behind the
headlines, the full extent of the SAS's role can be revealed.
Spearheading the British government's counter-terrorist attempts,
the SAS have prevented terrorist acts by countering ambush with
ambush, and meeting terrorism with their own brand of subterfuge.

Ambush: The War Between the SAS and the IRA contains
information never before made public. From the SAS's training and
planning methods, through the most recent attacks in Northern
Ireland and Europe, to the undeclared facts about the Gibraltar
incident, it provides a dispassionate assessment and overview of the
twelve-year-old secret war.

Max Hastings and Simon Jenkins
The Battle for the Falklands £4.99

This is the book on the Falklands war that serious readers have been
waiting for. Max Hastings' reports from the battlefront for the
Standard made him Journalist of the Year. Simon Jenkins,
Economist political editor, offers a cogent analysis of the war's
political and diplomatic background. At once a vivid chronicle of a
feat of arms and a thoughtful and informed analysis of an
astonishing historical chapter – the definitive account of the war.

'Few would deny Hastings whatever awards are going for the finest
war reporting for many years; and there can be few better analysts of
Westminster and Whitehall than Jenkins' SIMON WINCHESTER

Phillip Knightley
The First Casualty £7.99

From the Crimea to the Falklands: The War Correspondent as Hero,
Propagandist and Myth Maker

'The first casualty when war comes is truth.' These words of Hiram
Johnson to the US Senate are as true today as they were in 1917.

Laying bare the role of the war correspondent and the censor in
suppressing and creating facts, Phillip Knightley's classic study of
propaganda stabs many of our myths about war in the back. Here
are insights and anecdotes about fascinating personalities – Winston
Churchill, Hemingway, Evelyn Waugh as well as rare information
about the bloody conflicts themselves from the Crimea to
Afghanistan via the First World War and Vietnam . . .

The First Casualty changes our perception of governments, generals
and the press. It paints an alternative and shaming portrait of
received truth.

'Entertaining, lively . . . exasperating . . . it will be read with
admiration for his journalistic duty of revealing the truth'
THE TIMES LITERARY SUPPLEMENT

'Disturbing, even dismaying, yet also in its painful way, enormously
entertaining' THE NEW YORKER

All Pan Books are available at your local bookshop or newsagent, or can be ordered direct from the publisher. Indicate the number of copies required and fill in the form below.

Send to: Pan C. S. Dept
               Macmillan Distribution Ltd
               Houndmills Basingstoke RG21 2XS
or phone: 0256 29242, quoting title, author and Credit Card number.

Please enclose a remittance* to the value of the cover price plus £1.00 for the first book plus 50p per copy for each additional book ordered.

*Payment may be made in sterling by UK personal cheque, postal order, sterling draft or international money order, made payable to Pan Books Ltd.

Alternatively by Barclaycard/Access/Amex/Diners

Card No.

Expiry Date

_____
                        Signature

Applicable only in the UK and BFPO addresses.

While every effort is made to keep prices low, it is sometimes necessary to increase prices at short notice. Pan Books reserve the right to show on covers and charge new retail prices which may differ from those advertised in the text or elsewhere.

NAME AND ADDRESS IN BLOCK LETTERS PLEASE

....

Name _____

Address_____

_____

_____

_____
                                       3/87